PHOTOGRAPHIC HANDBOOK

WILDFOWL

OF THE WORLD

PHOTOGRAPHIC HANDBOOK

WILDFOWL

OF THE WORLD

MALCOLM OGILVIE AND STEVE YOUNG

NEW
HOLLAND

This paperback edition first published in 2002 by
New Holland Publishers (UK) Ltd
London • Cape Town • Sydney • Auckland

First published in 1998

Garfield House, 86-88 Edgware Road, London W2 2EA, United Kingdom
www.newhollandpublishers.com

80 McKenzie Street, Cape Town 8001, South Africa

Level 1/Unit 4, 14 Aquatic Drive, Frenchs Forest, NSW 2086, Australia

218 Lake Road, Northcote, Auckland, New Zealand

2 4 6 8 10 9 7 5 3

ISBN 1 84330 328 0

Publishing Manager: Jo Hemmings
Project Editor for this edition: Lorna Sharrock
Editorial Assistant: Michaella Standen
Copy-editor: David Christie
Designer: Alan Marshall
Cover design: Gulen Shevki
Production: Joan Woodroffe and Lucy Hulme
Topography: Richard Allen

Reproduction by Pica Colour Separation Overseas (Pte) Ltd, Singapore
Printed and bound in Malaysia by Times Offset (M) Sdn. Bhd.

Cover picture: Mute Swan
Spine picture: Pink-eared Duck
Back cover pictures (from left to right):
King Eider, Pochards, Eurasian Teal

TOPOGRAPHY (MALLARD)

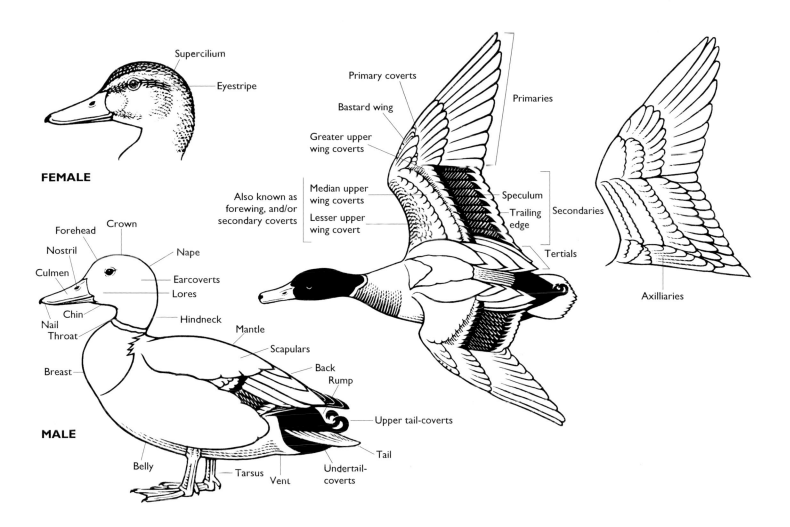

FEMALE

Supercilium

Eyestripe

MALE

Forehead
Crown
Nostril
Nape
Culmen
Earcoverts
Lores
Chin
Hindneck
Nail
Throat
Mantle
Breast
Scapulars
Back
Rump
Belly
Tarsus
Vent
Undertail-coverts
Tail
Upper tail-coverts

Primary coverts
Bastard wing
Primaries
Greater upper wing coverts
Also known as forewing, and/or secondary coverts
Median upper wing coverts
Lesser upper wing covert
Speculum
Trailing edge
Secondaries
Tertials
Axilliaries

ACKNOWLEDGEMENTS

AUTHOR'S ACKNOWLEDGEMENTS

The author is particularly grateful to Jane Dawson, for valuable discussions on seaducks.

PHOTOGRAPHIC EDITOR'S ACKNOWLEDGEMENTS

Collecting the photographs for this book proved to be a far more difficult task than I ever imagined. I fondly believed that wildfowl would be a relatively easy subject; that birds that have not been photographed in the wild could be photographed in captivity to complete the collection quickly. How wrong I was.

Not only did I find that many species and sub-species were not kept in collections, but also that wildfowl does not appear to be a popular subject with photographers actually in the 'wild', many preferring the easier option of visiting Wildfowl Trust centres. Eventually, however, most problems were overcome and all species covered, wherever possible using photographs of wild birds. In some cases it was necessary to include captive birds for completeness and the captions to these are in italics. For possible future editions I would be interested in photographs of the following sub-species: Madagascar White-backed Duck; Johansen's Bean Goose; Elgas' Greater White-fronted Goose; Vancouver Canada Goose; Colombian, Peruvian and Berlepsch's Torrent Duck; Andean and Merida Speckled Teal; Tropical and Borrero's Cinnamon Teal; Asiatic White-winged Scoter and Asiatic Goosander.

My thanks go to all of the photographers who have contributed their images to this book, but especially to David Tipling, David Hosking and Alan Tate, all of whom helped immensely; and to Colin Davies for his e-mail messages. Particular mention must go to Frank S. Todd and Jim Clements, for so much invaluable information and excellent photographs.

Many thanks also to Jo Hemmings, Richard Hammond and Michaella Standen at New Holland for their patience and assistance in sourcing some of the photographs.

Finally, special thanks to my family, Isobel, David, Nick and Holly: the "Duck Book" is finished at last!

PUBLISHERS' ACKNOWLEDGEMENTS

New Holland Publishers are particularly grateful for all the help and assistance given by Frank S. Todd and Jim Clements, author and publisher respectively of *Handbook of Waterfowl Identification* (Ibis 1997).

CONTENTS

CONTENTS

CONTENTS

INTRODUCTION

The term 'wildfowl' is generally used to indicate the birds comprising the family Anatidae, that is the swans, geese and ducks of the world. In North America, the word 'waterfowl' is sometimes used for this purpose, but this can embrace other groups of birds, such as grebes, herons and waders, which are associated with water.

There are 147 living species of wildfowl in the world, plus a further 87 or so subspecies. The precise number varies from time to time depending on the latest taxonomic thinking and also, sadly, on extinctions. Five species and at least three subspecies have become extinct since 1600, and others are very seriously threatened.

The family Anatidae is divided into a number of subsections or tribes. Current thinking suggests that there are twelve of these, four of which contain only a single species. The tribes do not, as it happens, follow the popular division into swans, geese and ducks, because the swans and the true geese are thought to be quite closely related and are therefore placed in the same tribe, while all the sheldgeese and ducks, with their great variety, are divided into the other eleven.

Wildfowl occur throughout the world wherever there is water, fresh or marine, from within a few hundred kilometres of the North Pole to the tropics. They have successfully colonized numerous small oceanic islands, including several in the sub-antarctic regions of the Atlantic and Indian Oceans. In many such cases, the populations on these islands have, over time, evolved into distinct subspecies, one or two even having become flightless, no longer requiring the powers of flight within a highly restricted range, and also saving the energy otherwise needed to grow full-length wing feathers.

There is enormous diversity within the wildfowl. The size range, for example, is huge, from the Trumpeter and Mute Swans, which are among the largest and heaviest flying birds of any kind, weighing in excess of 15 kilos and with a wingspan of nearly 2.5 metres, to the tiny pygmy-geese, which tip the scales at about 250 grams and have a wingspan of 50-60 centimetres. While all wildfowl are accomplished swimmers, some, such as the geese, feed extensively on land, walking and running with ease, while others, typified by the diving ducks, obtain all their food underwater and are quite clumsy on land. These differences relate to the success that wildfowl have had in exploiting the enormous range of ecological niches which wetland habitat provides.

Underlying the differences, though, are the many similarities which indicated to early taxonomists that, despite the diversity, the species were nevertheless closely related. The broad body possessed by all the wildfowl is a great aid to buoyancy, and all species apart from a handful of the more terrestrial geese have completely webbed feet to improve their progress through the water, whether on the surface or beneath it. The bill of all wildfowl is comparatively broad and often deep, and has numerous small comb-like projections along the edges of both mandibles. These vary in number and structure, acting as filters of plankton for some surface-feeding ducks and as aids to grasping prey in the case of fish-eaters.

All waterbirds need good insulation and waterproofing. The feathers of wildfowl are particularly thick and numerous - there are over 25,000 feathers on a swan - with an inner covering of down feathers which trap air in a very effective insulating layer. The preen gland of wildfowl is very well developed, and all species spend much time every day caring for their plumage and keeping it in top condition.

A feature of almost all wildfowl is that they become flightless for a period after the breeding season. All birds change their feathers in the course of a year, sometimes more than once. With the exception of wildfowl, some grebes and a handful of other species, however, when it comes to changing the main flight feathers on the wing, these are shed in sequence over a considerable period, so that the vital power of flight is retained throughout. Wildfowl, being able to find safety from predators on water, as well as all their food either in water or close by, shed all their main wing feathers simultaneously and cannot therefore fly again until they have grown a new set, a matter of weeks. Only the Magpie Goose does not become flightless during the wing moult. On the other hand, it is thought that all, or most, of the stiff-tailed ducks moult their wing feathers twice every year and so have two flightless periods.

The plumage of wildfowl is as varied as are their size and shape. Many species have brightly coloured males and much duller females, although in some, for example the swans and geese, the sexes have more or less identical plumage. Where the plumage differs between the sexes, this relates to the fact that only the females of most species of wildfowl incubate the eggs and need the camouflage provided by their dull plumage when sitting on the nest. The males, on the other hand, use their finery to attract the females at the start of the breeding season, as well as to indicate to other males that they are holding a territory.

Of particular note in nearly all the duck species, across four tribes, is the presence of a patch of iridescent colouring on the rear half of the secondary wing feathers. This is known as the speculum, and is often bordered in front and/or behind by a white stripe. Ducks in two other tribes have white on their wing, either as a panel, usually on the forewing, or as an elongated stripe running nearly the full length of the wing. The main function of such wing markings appears to be to act as a signal to other birds of the same species, especially when they are in flight, thus helping the birds in a group to stay together on migration or during feeding movements. In exactly the same way, all the goose species have a white base to the tail, which is highly visible to a following bird.

Other aspects of the behaviour and biology of wildfowl are dealt with in the following accounts of each of the twelve tribes.

Magpie Goose: Anseranatini

This is a remarkable kind of wildfowl, differing in many respects from all other species in the group and actually showing several similarities with the screamers (Anhimidae) of South America, including the very long legs, broad wings, only very slightly webbed feet and also the presence of a long hind toe, which is much reduced in all other wildfowl. The combination of little webbing between the toes and the long hind toe makes both rapid walking over the ground, where the Magpie Goose obtains most of its food, and perching on branches, which it does for safety at night, much easier. The sexes are almost identical.

Magpie Geese are restricted to northern Australia and parts of Indonesia. They are reasonably common, though they have suffered, as have so many wildfowl, from drainage of wetlands. There is some wandering in response to wet and dry seasons, but no regular migrations. These are sociable birds, often nesting in colonies, where polygamy (one male with two females) is relatively common. Both sexes incubate the eggs and rear the young. Uniquely among wildfowl, the parent birds feed their young directly, bill to bill, with small seeds and other vegetable matter. The young of all other wildfowl feed themselves, pecking instinctively at small particles and learning what is suitable food.

Whistling-ducks: *Dendrocygnini*

This tribe includes the eight species (plus three subspecies) of whistling-duck, together with the two White-backed Duck subspecies. Members of the tribe are found throughout the subtropical and tropical regions of the world. Some, such as the West Indian Whistling-duck, which is classed as 'rare' in world terms by the International Union for the Conservation of Nature (IUCN), are very restricted in range, while others, such as the Fulvous Whistling-duck, occur widely in the Americas, Africa and the Indian subcontinent. None of the species is truly migratory, although some wander some distance in response to local rainfall.

There are no sex differences in the plumage of any of the species in this tribe, though males tend to average a little larger than females. Once paired, the male and female tend to stay together for life. They are all very sociable birds, the whistling-ducks occurring in noisy flocks with almost constant calling, from which they get their name. Most species are colonial when breeding, but some become solitary at that time. Male and female incubate the eggs and care for the young.

Whistling-ducks are versatile birds, with broad wings allowing manoeuvrable flight, and long legs and large feet which enable them to perch with ease, and all are capable of diving very competently. Despite the ability to perch, their alternative name of tree-ducks is something of a misnomer, as they do not perch all that much and nesting in tree holes is uncommon. The closely related White-backed Duck is also an accomplished diver, but it rarely, if ever, perches.

Swans and true geese: *Anserini*

There are seven species (plus one subspecies) of swan and 15 species (with no fewer than a further 22 subspecies) of true geese, the latter so called to distinguish them from the sheldgeese (see below). The taxonomy of some of the geese, for example the Bean Goose and the Canada Goose, is complex and subject to discussion as to the precise number of both species and subspecies. All the species in the tribe are confined to the northern hemisphere, where many of them undertake long migrations between breeding and wintering grounds. The Lesser White-fronted Goose is classed by IUCN as 'rare', while the Hawaiian Goose is rated as 'vulnerable', though this is an improvement on its status 50 years ago, when it was close to extinction, being saved only by captive-breeding programmes.

Differences between the sexes of swans and geese are either very small, for example the size of the bill knob in the Mute Swan, or restricted to the male being slightly larger than the female. Although all species share in the upbringing of the young, only the female incubates the eggs. All species are highly gregarious outside the breeding season, occurring in flocks which can number many tens of thousands. Breeding can be highly colonial (Black Swan and Snow Goose) or equally territorial or solitary (Mute Swan and White-fronted Goose). The young stay with their parents throughout their first winter, and sometimes form 'super-families' in later years with their parents and with young of another season. Breeding maturity is usually attained after two or three years.

All the swans and geese have a long neck and strong bill adapted for grazing of both terrestrial and aquatic vegetation. Tooth-like lamellae along the sides of the mandibles help to grasp the vegetation, which is broken from the plant as the feeding bird jerks back its head. The swans include some of the heaviest flying birds in the world and are mostly clumsy on land, though contrastingly elegant on the water. The geese have proportionately longer legs and can walk, and run, with ease. They are very strong fliers, and apparently non-stop migration flights of 3000-4000 kilometres are regularly undertaken.

Cape Barren Goose: *Cereopsini*

A single species makes up this tribe. It has in the past been split into two subspecies, but these are no longer recognized. The Cape Barren Goose is confined to a few restricted areas of southern Australia and, while it may wander outside the breeding season, it does not undertake any regular migrations.

Cape Barren Geese are mostly terrestrial and, as a result, have lost most of the webbing between their toes. They walk and run without difficulty, as well as flying strongly, but they rarely enter the water, usually only when with very small young and when moulting their wing feathers, in both circumstances seeking the safety that water can offer from predators. They even copulate on land, which is otherwise known among the wildfowl only in the Hawaiian Goose, which is similarly terrestrial and with reduced webbing on the feet.

Breeding is generally solitary or in loose colonies. At this time, the male of a pair can become very aggressive towards other males and will strike them with opened wings, using bony spurs which protrude from the carpal joint. Only the female incubates, but the male helps rear the young.

Freckled Duck: *Stictonettini*

This is another single-species tribe, its one representative also living solely in Australia. The Freckled Duck has, in the past, been regarded as a somewhat aberrant dabbling duck, but the identical plumage of both sexes, apart from the red on the bill of the breeding male, and a complete lack of any contrasting pattern or speculum on the wings, as well as a number of skeletal differences, have led to its present taxonomic status in a tribe on its own. Its main range is restricted to south-west and south-east Australia, but individuals wander very widely outside the breeding season, mainly in response to the creation of temporary wetlands following rains.

It is rainfall that seems also to determine the breeding season, as this is unusually variable in timing. Nesting takes place at any time between June and December, apparently stimulated by suitable water levels giving the promise of adequate feeding for some weeks to come. Breeding may not occur at all in very dry years. Freckled Ducks are filter feeders in shallow water.

Sheldgeese and shelducks: *Tadornini*

Fourteen species, together with a further three subspecies, make up this somewhat disparate group. Six of the eight species of sheldgoose are confined to South

America, and the other two, the Blue-winged Goose and the Egyptian Goose, to South Africa. The six species of shelduck include the Ruddy and Common Shelducks, which are both widespread in much of Eurasia, while the other four species are confined to small areas of South Africa, Australia, Indonesia and New Zealand. None is particularly rare, even if some have declined through habitat loss. The most southerly breeding species in South America are true migrants, moving north to warmer climes after the breeding season. The others, however, are either sedentary or wander more randomly.

The sheldgeese show obvious superficial similarities with the true geese, being rather upright in stance on long, powerful legs, well adapted to mainly terrestrial feeding and to walking and running on land. The sexes are alike in some species, while others exhibit very strong sexual dimorphism. Indeed, the Kelp Goose of South America has perhaps the most conspicuously different male and female plumages within all the wildfowl, with the male pure white and the female heavily patterned chocolate-brown. Unlike the true geese, though, all the species have an iridescent speculum on their wings and all except the Blue-winged and Orinoco Geese have, additionally, a large white patch on their forewings.

Breeding is mostly in single pairs, although some species may form loose nesting groups. Both parents rear the young, but only the female incubates the eggs. Outside the nesting season, larger flocks are commonly formed, though the Orinoco Goose of northern South America is one of the least gregarious of the wildfowl, rarely seen in flocks of more than about 250.

The shelducks mostly show some sexual dimorphism, although it is relatively slight in some species and absent in the Radjah Shelduck. They are much more aquatic than the sheldgeese. Although they can walk and run well, and do much of their feeding by sifting mud and shallow water, they do not feed away from water and they also swim much more readily than sheldgeese. All the species nest in holes or sheltered hollows, including in mammal burrows and trees. The Egyptian Goose and the Orinoco Goose nest in similar locations.

Steamerducks: *Tachyerini*
There are just four species in this tribe, one of which, the White-headed Steamerduck, was not described as a separate species until as recently as 1981. All four are confined to southern South America, one being restricted to the Falkland Islands, and are either sedentary or make short movements after the breeding season. Despite their restricted ranges, none is thought to be threatened in terms of numbers of individual birds in the population, although all must be regarded as vulnerable to pollution, particularly from oil spills into their mainly marine habitat.

The name 'steamerduck' comes from their habit of threshing with wings and feet over the water when disturbed or chased. While this is a necessary preliminary to flight in the Flying Steamerduck, the other three species are completely flightless, with only short stubby wings, and this 'steaming' over the water is their only means of escape apart from diving.

The females of all the species are smaller than the males, and all show slight sexual plumage dimorphism, mainly involving head coloration. They are all solitary nesters, but immatures, in particular, may form larger flocks.

Feeding is largely in sheltered sea bays and along rocky coasts, where the birds dive for shellfish and aquatic invertebrates. The Flying Steamerduck is, perhaps obviously, the only species to venture inland and to feed on fresh waters, though never far from the coast.

Perching geese and ducks: *Cairini*
Thirteen different species of goose-like and duck-like wildfowl, together with another four subspecies, sit not altogether comfortably in this tribe, which taxonomists have used as a kind of 'catch-all' for what is a mixture of rather heterogenous species, some of which seem highly specialized, while others are more generalized in their structure and habits. They are found mainly in southern temperate, subtropical and tropical regions of the world. They are mostly sedentary, but the North American Wood Duck and the Mandarin Duck, which nest further north than any other species, are at least partial migrants, with northerly breeders moving south for the winter. The Comb Duck is particularly widespread, occurring in South America, South Africa and the Indian subcontinent, but the White-winged Wood Duck is classed by IUCN as 'vulnerable', having a total population in the wild of under 500, though there is probably a similar number in captivity.

There are two major groups, the first containing the Spur-winged Goose, Muscovy Duck, White-winged Wood Duck and Comb Duck. These four are rather generalized species, tending to large size and extensive areas of iridescent plumage, including a speculum, though lacking either much strong patterning or striking sexual dimorphism. Their pairing displays are generally not very elaborate and are accompanied by quite simple calls.

In contrast, the species in the second group, comprising Hartlaub's Duck, the pygmy-geese, Ringed Teal, North American Wood Duck, Mandarin Duck, Maned Duck and Brazilian Teal, are smaller and most of the males have bright, even elaborate, breeding plumage with only small amounts of iridescence, though also including a speculum, and correspondingly more complex displays and calls. The very bright males of North American Wood Duck and Mandarin Duck have duller 'eclipse' plumage adopted during the annual wing moult.

All the species breed in holes or tree hollows, some also nesting in thick cover on the ground. In most species, both parents care for the young, but only the female does so in the case of North American Wood Duck and Mandarin Duck.

Torrent ducks: *Merganettini*
The six subspecies of the Torrent Duck together form the single species in this tribe. Torrent Ducks are restricted to the fast-flowing rivers of the Andes mountains of South America, where, despite loss of habitat through silting, erosion and pollution, none of the subspecies is thought to be seriously threatened in terms of numbers. They are all sedentary, although they may move downstream short distances in cold weather.

The males differ from each other, but the females are broadly similar. These birds are highly adapted to life in fast-flowing water, in pattern for camouflage as well as in shape for streamlining. They feed on aquatic invertebrates obtained by diving and head-dipping. Both parents rear the young, although only the female is thought to incubate the eggs, which are laid in cavities in rocks or among thick vegetation close to the water.

Dabbling ducks: *Anatini*
This is much the largest tribe of wildfowl, with 40 species and a further 37 subspecies. These species also occur very

widely, having colonized all the major continents as well as many small oceanic islands. Many species are highly migratory, travelling thousands of kilometres between breeding and wintering grounds, but others, especially the island species, are entirely sedentary. The Mallard is the most widespread and numerous of all wildfowl, but one of its subspecies, the Laysan Duck, is confined to that island in the Pacific and numbers no more than 500 individuals, although it is regarded as safe at that level, having recovered from perhaps only one laying female 70 years ago. Several species are, however, listed by IUCN, including Baikal Teal, Madagascar Teal and Marbled Teal, which are categorized as 'vulnerable', and Brown Teal, which is treated as 'rare'.

A majority of dabbling ducks shows strong sexual dimorphism, with some of the males (eg Common Shoveler, Garganey, Blue-winged Teal) among the most colourful of all birds, not just wildfowl. In some species, the males are much more similar to the females, nearly all of which have overall brown plumage variably marked with paler feather edgings and spotting. All except the Pink-eared Duck and the Marbled Teal have an iridescent speculum. A dull eclipse plumage is adopted by all the brightly coloured males during the period of their post-breeding-season wing moult.

As their name implies, the dabbling ducks obtain their food by feeding in shallow water, sifting seeds and invertebrates from the surface or from shoreline debris. Most species also upend to reach the bottom, some, such as the pintails, having a longer neck to enable them to reach to greater depths.

Diving ducks: *Aythyini*
Fifteen species, and two subspecies, make up this tribe, occurring widely in North America and Eurasia, with single species in South America, Australia and New Zealand, and two in southern Africa. One of these last, the Madagascar Pochard, is rated as 'endangered' by IUCN and may, indeed, be now extinct. Baer's Pochard of eastern Asia is listed as 'vulnerable'. The majority of species are migratory, moving in winter to warmer areas, where their mainly freshwater habitat does not freeze up.

The diving ducks are bulky species, with a broad body and generally a short tail. Plumages tend to be subdued, but even so the males of most species are brighter than their females and adopt a duller eclipse plumage for the period of the wing moult. None of the species shows a speculum on the wing, though almost all have a white or whitish wing-bar running nearly the full length of the wing. Their legs are set further back than those of dabbling ducks, aiding their ability to dive, but making their progress on land much less agile. They are accomplished divers, obtaining vegetation and/or invertebrates from beneath the surface. Many spend their whole life on fresh water, although a few also occur on brackish lagoons and shallow sea bays, at least during the winter.

Seaducks: *Mergini*
A total of 18 species and 11 additional subspecies comprises the tribe of seaducks. With the exception of the Brazilian Merganser, all are restricted to the northern hemisphere, several occurring in both North America and Eurasia, with ranges extending into the high Arctic. The Brazilian Merganser is also the only species which does not occur in marine habitat during at least some part of the year. All the other species spend the winter on the sea, often in sheltered sea bays, but also in deeper water, while some breed far inland. Both sedentary and migratory species occur. The Scaly-sided Merganser is classified as 'rare' by IUCN, while the Common Eider is numbered in millions.

Seaducks fall into a number of groups. The eiders are mostly large-bodied birds with a heavy bill and strongly contrasting male and female plumages, the males showing much white plumage tinged with pastel shades. The scoters are similarly heavily built, but the males are predominantly black. The smaller goldeneyes, Long-tailed Duck and Harlequin Duck also have brightly patterned males and duller females. The final group is the sawbills, which, as their name implies, have an elongated bill with sharp tooth-like serrations along the sides of the mandibles to aid in the grasping of their principal diet of fish. The majority of the seaducks have white panels on their wings, while only some of them show any kind of iridescent speculum. The males of all species have an eclipse plumage adopted during the annual wing moult.

All the species of seaduck eat aquatic animals, from small invertebrates to quite large fish. The latter are obtained by diving, at which several species are expert; the Long-tailed Duck, for example, can dive to 50 metres, staying down for up to a minute.

Stiff-tails: *Oxyurini*
This final tribe of the wildfowl contains eight species, plus another two subspecies. Most occur only in the southern hemisphere, including South America, South Africa and Australia, only the White-headed Duck being confined to the northern hemisphere, in southern Eurasia, while one subspecies of the Ruddy Duck extends well into North America. The White-headed Duck is classed by IUCN as 'vulnerable'.

Stiff-tails are mostly short-bodied, even dumpy, birds with a relatively long tail comprised of stiff feathers and often held cocked up at an angle. The Musk Duck is considerably larger than the other species, especially the male, which is up to three times heavier than the female and has a remarkable wattle hanging below its bill. Males are generally brighter than the females and, in most species, have a conspicuous bright blue bill. Although most species have an eclipse plumage in the males, it is less distinctively different from the breeding plumage than in other ducks. Stiff-tails are distinct among wildfowl by virtue of the existence in most, if not all, species of a double wing moult: the wing feathers are shed both before and after the breeding season.

All the species are very aquatic in habits, spending little time on land. They are, however, accomplished divers, aided by the positioning of their legs well back on their bodies. The females carry out all of the incubation, though some males may help rear the young. One species, the Black-headed Duck, is parasitic, the female laying eggs in the nests of other wildfowl. The young forage for themselves soon after hatching and become independent, including from their foster parent, within a matter of days.

SYSTEMATIC LIST
OF SPECIES

WHISTLING-DUCKS

MAGPIE GOOSE

Anseranas semipalmata L 70-90 cm (28-35 in), WS 125-180 cm (49-71 in)
Monotypic. Very large, long-necked, black-and-white goose, unmistakable within Australasian range.

IDENTIFICATION Male breeding and non-breeding Head and neck black, extending onto upper breast. Flight feathers and all upperwing-coverts, except lesser, also black, as are rump, tail and feathers at extreme top of leg (thigh, though technically the upper tibia). Mantle, back and underparts white, together with lesser upperwing-coverts and all underwing-coverts. White areas can become stained orange-yellow. Prominent domed top to head (cranial knob). Bill long and straight, featherless back to eyes, flesh-coloured, tinged yellowish or, especially in breeding season, reddish, with grey nail and dusky grey-brown between nail and nostrils. Long legs and feet, with only very slight webbing between toes, dull yellow. Loud, goose-like honking given in flight or on ground; simultaneous calling by pair or group of birds frequent. Apart from bill and bare-skin colouring, no other change between breeding and non-breeding. In flight, rounded wings, with fingered primaries, and slow wingbeats recall heron or even vulture; black-and-white appearance striking from below and above. **Female** As male, but 10-15% smaller, with smaller cranial knob (as knob of male enlarges with age, size is not reliable guide to sex). Bill, legs and feet as male. Call similar to male, but higher-pitched. **Juvenile** Pattern of black and white as adult, but all black areas dull sooty-black, often mottled dark grey-brown, and white areas tinged paler grey-brown. No cranial knob. Bill dull grey-yellow; legs and feet flesh. Acquisition of adult plumage gradual over one to two years, though doubtfully distinguishable in field after 9-12 months. **Confusion risks** Unmistakable among wildfowl of region. Some similarity, especially in flight, to Spur-winged Goose of southern half of Africa, but that species has black body and upperparts.

DISTRIBUTION AND STATUS Breeds northern Australia and southern New Guinea (Irian Jaya, Indonesia, and Papua New Guinea), where found mainly close to coast in swamplands and floodplains of tropical rivers; reintroduced to Victoria, south-east Australia, where had become extinct. Wanders widely in Australia, especially during dry season, eg to Tasmania. No population census, but partial count, in Northern Territory, of c 380,000 in 1982, and concentrations of up to 10,000 birds reported from New Guinea. Latest population estimate 350,000 in 1992; thought to be stable.

SPOTTED WHISTLING-DUCK

Dendrocygna guttata L 43-50 cm (17-20 in), WS 85-95 cm (33-37 in)
Monotypic. Within range, only whistling-duck with spotted underparts and flanks.

IDENTIFICATION Male breeding and non-breeding Dark grey crown, rear of neck and eye patch, contrasting with pale grey supercilia, cheeks, throat and upper neck. Whitish patch at base of upper mandible, small white spot at base of lower mandible. Narrow dark grey collar separates pale neck from rufous-brown breast and flanks. Breast heavily spotted white, spots enlarging onto flanks, where prominently white with black borders, flank spotting continued on uppertail- and undertail-coverts; belly whitish. Upperparts and tail dark brown, with conspicuous rufous feather edgings on mantle and upperwing-coverts of closed wing. Bill dark grey but heavily marked with pink, especially towards base and along sides of upper mandible. Legs and feet dark grey, suffused pink-red on tarsus and toes. In flight, typical whistling-duck shape; rounded wings all dark above and below, except for rufous edgings to upperwing-coverts (barely visible on flying bird). Calls infrequently, at least compared with other whistling-ducks, typically *whee-ow* and *whe-a-whew-whew*, plus some other softer notes. In flight, wings make considerable whirring sound. **Female** As male, with no apparent plumage or soft-parts difference, and similar calls. **Juvenile** Similar in colouring and pattern to adults, but duller brown (not rufous-brown) on body. Spotting on breast reduced or absent; feathers of flanks white or whitish, edged black, forming irregular and ill-defined white or whitish streaks, not obvious rounded spots. Bill, legs and feet grey, lacking pink or pink-red of adult. **Confusion risks** Within range, only possible confusion with Wandering Whistling-duck, with which it often associates, but latter paler and more rufous and has a few whitish stripes on flanks, not bold black-bordered white spots. Outside range, Black-billed Whistling-duck of West Indies more similar, though larger, with black bill and black and white spotting on flanks.

DISTRIBUTION AND STATUS Resident Philippines (Mindanao), Indonesia (Sulawesi to New Guinea) and Papua New Guinea (including Bismarck Archipelago); appears to be sedentary. Locally common and widespread over most of range in wide variety of lowland freshwater wetlands, and total population thought, in absence of any census data, to be between 10,000 and 25,000. Not globally threatened.

PLUMED WHISTLING-DUCK

Dendrocygna eytoni L 40-45 cm (16-18 in), WS 75-90 cm (29-35 in)
Monotypic. Pale-headed and slim whistling-duck with elongated flank plumes, a combination not found in other whistling-ducks within or outside Australian range.

IDENTIFICATION Male breeding and non-breeding Light sandy-brown on crown, back of neck and breast, paler on cheeks and sides of neck. Upper flanks rufous with vertical narrow black bars; rear flank feathers greatly elongated and pointed, pale buff-yellow with

black edgings, overlapping closed wing; belly and undertail-coverts whitish or creamy-white. Upperparts dull olive-brown, paler on lower neck and darker on rump and tail, though tail-coverts pale buff with dark mottling. Bill flesh-pink with blackish blotches. Legs and feet flesh-pink. Iris yellow or flesh-coloured. In flight, wings dark above, but underwing-coverts paler brown than rest of wing. Noisy, with shrill calls, varying from loud *wa-chew* call to continuous twittering. Wings make loud whirring sound in flight. **Female** Similar to male, but elongated flank plumes not so long, though this distinguishable only when pair-members seen together. **Juvenile** Paler and duller brown than adults. Upper flanks less boldly barred black, while lower flank feathers much shorter and with wider black margins. **Confusion risks** Combination of overall pale colour and elongated flank plumes distinguishes this from other whistling-ducks, though at distance, when plumes inconspicuous, can be confused with Wandering Whistling-duck, only other member of genus within range. Slimmer than that species and swims more buoyantly; in flight, rump whiter.

DISTRIBUTION AND STATUS Confined to northern and eastern Australia; wanders widely outside normal range in response to wet and dry periods. Inhabits pools and swamps in grasslands and plains. No censuses, but population estimated at 30,000 and probably stable, with some recent expansion of breeding range, eg into south-east Australia.

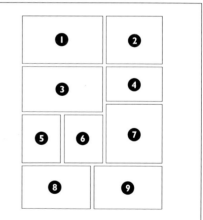

1 **Magpie Goose** (mud-stained adults, Northern Territory, Australia)
2 **Magpie Goose** (mud-stained adult, Northern Territory, Australia)
3 **Magpie Goose** (adults in flight, Kakadu, Australia)
4 *Spotted Whistling-duck (adult)*
5 *Spotted Whistling-duck (adult)*
6 *Spotted Whistling-duck (adult)*
7 **Plumed Whistling-duck** (adults, Kakadu, Australia)
8 **Plumed Whistling-duck** (adults, Kakadu, Australia)
9 **Plumed Whistling-duck** (adults, Kakadu, Australia)

WHISTLING-DUCKS

FULVOUS WHISTLING-DUCK

Dendrocygna bicolor L 45-53 cm (18-21 in), WS 88-95 cm (34-38 in)
Monotypic; may form superspecies with Wandering Whistling-duck, with which no overlap in range. Rufous-brown whistling-duck, very widespread, overlapping in southern Asia with similar but smaller Lesser Whistling-duck.
IDENTIFICATION Male breeding and non-breeding Crown and nape deep rufous-brown, darkening to blackish stripe down back of neck. Cheeks, neck, breast and belly cinnamon to warm rufous-buff; sides and front of upper neck paler whitish-buff, finely streaked dark brown. Flank feathers elongated, creamy-white, with blackish-brown outer webs, just overlapping closed wing and producing streaked appearance; lower belly to rear of legs and undertail-coverts creamy-white. Upperparts dark brown, with tawny feather edgings producing light barring across back and closed wings; uppertail-coverts creamy-white, tail black. Bill blackish. Legs and feet blue-grey. In flight, typical whistling-duck shape and behaviour, with broad wings, slow wingbeats and trailing legs; upperwings dark brown, with tawny edgings to wing-coverts, and underwings very dark brown, contrasting with rufous underparts. Loud whistling *wa-chew* calls often given in flight, when wings produce low whistling noise. **Female** Similar to male, though just a little smaller and duller. **Juvenile** Duller than adults, with darker edgings to feathers of upperparts, reduced tawny edgings on upperwing-coverts and brown margins to whitish uppertail-coverts. **Confusion risks** In Asia, overlaps with smaller Lesser Whistling-duck, which has darker cap to head but less obvious dark hindneck and therefore less contrast with rest of neck, which unstreaked buff rather than whitish-buff with darker streaks. Lesser has rufous, not whitish, uppertail-coverts, and more obviously chestnut on forewing rather than tawny feather edgings. No overlap in normal range with somewhat similar Wandering Whistling-duck, which has almost black crown down to eye.
DISTRIBUTION AND STATUS Widespread in mainly tropical latitudes of North and South America south to *c* 35°S, West Indies, Africa south to *c* 30°S, Madagascar and Indian subcontinent east to Burma; broadly sedentary, but has wandered north and south of main range. Marshes and swamps in flat terrain, where feeds extensively on rice-fields, Population estimates: Americas, over 1 million; Africa, *c* 500,000; Madagascar, up to 25,000; south Asia, 20,000. Thought to be declining over most of range, through pesticide poisoning and shooting to prevent crop damage on rice fields.

LESSER WHISTLING-DUCK

Dendrocygna javanica L 38-40 cm (15-16 in), WS 75-85 cm (29-33 in)
Monotypic. Smallest whistling-duck, similar to Fulvous Whistling-duck, but smaller than and lacking dark cap of Wandering Whistling-duck,

with which there is also a range overlap.
IDENTIFICATION Male breeding and non-breeding Grey-brown crown; rest of head, neck and upper breast unstreaked grey-buff, paler (almost whitish) on cheeks and throat, darker on sides and back of neck. Very narrow yellow eye-ring. Underparts and flanks unspotted chestnut-brown, with a few poorly defined creamy stripes along line of upper flanks; lower belly to rear of legs and undertail-coverts white or whitish. Upperparts dark brown, with bright chestnut feather edgings producing slight barring effect across back and closed wings (chestnut lesser coverts may show on closed wing); uppertail-coverts chestnut, tail dark brown. Bill dark grey, legs and feet dark blue-grey. In flight, upperwings dark brown but for chestnut on lesser coverts; underwings uniform dark blackish-brown. Flocks noisy, with constant *whi-wheee* calls in flight, when wings also make whistling sound. **Female** Similar to male. **Juvenile** Duller than adults. Feather margins of upperparts dingy chestnut instead of bright chestnut, and underparts paler and duller, less rufous; crown also paler grey-brown.
Confusion risks For comparison with Fulvous Whistling-duck, see latter. Small race of Wandering Whistling-duck darker on upperparts and with noticeable dark crown extending down to eye; also has more conspicuous buff markings on upper flanks and whitish, not chestnut, uppertail-coverts.
DISTRIBUTION AND STATUS Pakistan, India and Sri Lanka, east to China and Taiwan, and south through Indochina and Malay peninsula to Borneo, Sumatra and Java; mainly sedentary, but birds breeding in northern part of Chinese range move south in winter. Occurs in shallow marshy areas with small pools, and with trees for roosting. Population perhaps up to 1 million. Some shooting in rice-growing areas.

WHITE-FACED WHISTLING-DUCK

Dendrocygna viduata L 38-48 cm (15-19 in), WS 75-88 cm (29-35 in)
Monotypic. Whistling-duck of South America and South Africa, with boldly marked black-and-white head unlike any congeners. Often dives for food; perches less than most other whistling-ducks.
IDENTIFICATION Male breeding and non-breeding Pure white face and chin from bill to behind eye, also white throat separated from chin by more or less complete narrow black band; back half of head, and hindneck, black. Black band separates white throat from rich chestnut upper breast. Underparts, from central lower breast through belly to undertail-coverts, black; sides of lower breast and flanks finely barred black-brown and whitish-buff. Upperparts dark brown with broad pale brown feather edgings, so that effect of linear striping, not barring across back as on most other whistling-ducks; rump, uppertail-coverts and tail black. Bill black with grey subterminal band. Legs and feet dark blue-grey. Eye appears black against white face. In flight, dark brown above

except for dark chestnut lesser wing-coverts, sometimes inconspicuous, and some contrast between dark upperwings and paler back; underwings uniformly dark black-brown. Three-note call given frequently in flight, *tsri-ree-reeo*.
Female Similar to male. **Juvenile** Duller and less well marked than adults, with greyish face and grey-black rear of head; chestnut on breast duller and less extensive, while central dark area smaller and greyer. Becomes more adult-like during first winter. **Confusion risks** Adults can be distinguished from all other whistling-ducks by black-and-white head pattern. Juvenile perhaps confusable with young of Fulvous and Black-bellied Whistling-ducks, both of which occur within range: former has whitish or buff, not black, uppertail-coverts, while latter has considerable white in wing.
DISTRIBUTION AND STATUS Tropical America from Costa Rica south to northern Argentina and Uruguay, but avoiding west coast, and sub-Saharan Africa south to Cape, and including Madagascar and Comoro Islands; either resident or wandering short distances in response to water availability; vagrant north of range. Occupies wide diversity of freshwater wetlands. Population estimates: Americas, over 1 million; Africa, over 1 million; Madagascar, up to 25,000; stable or increasing throughout range. Up to 15,000 in some areas.

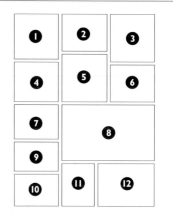

1 **Fulvous Whistling-duck** (adults, Cape Town, South Africa)
2 **Fulvous Whistling-duck** (adult, Loxahatchee, USA)
3 **Fulvous Whistling-duck** (adults, Loxahatchee, USA)
4 **Fulvous Whistling-duck** (adult, South Africa)
5 **Lesser Whistling-duck** (adults, India)
6 **Lesser Whistling-duck** (flight, India)
7 **Lesser Whistling-duck** (adults and immatures, Yala, Sri Lanka)
8 **Lesser Whistling-duck** (adults, Yala, Sri Lanka)
9 **White-faced Whistling-duck** (immature, The Gambia)
10 **White-faced Whistling-duck** (adults, The Gambia)
11 **White-faced Whistling-duck** (adults, The Gambia)
12 **White-faced Whistling-duck** (adults in flight, Okavango, Botswana)

WHISTLING-DUCKS

WANDERING WHISTLING-DUCK

Dendrocygna arcuata
Polytypic. Three subspecies: (1) East Indian Wandering Whistling-duck *D. a. arcuata*, in Philippines and Indonesia; (2) Australian Wandering Whistling-duck *D. a. australis*, in New Guinea and Australia; (3) Lesser Wandering Whistling-duck *D. a. pygmaea*, in New Britain and perhaps Fiji.

East Indian Wandering Whistling-duck

Dendrocygna arcuata arcuata L 40-45 cm (16-18 in), WS 80-90 cm (31-35 in)
Dark crown extending to eye distinguishes this from other whistling-ducks within range. Very aquatic, spending more time on water than most other whistling-ducks.
IDENTIFICATION Male breeding and non-breeding Medium-sized whistling-duck with blackish-brown crown extending down to top of upper mandible and to eye, and down nape and back of neck to base of neck (extent of dark crown variable, with some birds showing dark stripe through eye separated from crown by very slightly paler supercilium). Cheeks and sides of neck, also chin, throat and upper chest, pale tawny-buff, darkening on lower chest and becoming chestnut-brown on breast, flanks and belly. Lower neck and upper chest finely spotted and mottled with black centres to paler chestnut feathers; usually six to eight quite broad and elongated flank feathers, bright buffy-yellow with black and brown outer webs, overlapping edge of closed wing; belly, rearward from legs, and undertail-coverts buff or creamy-white. Upperparts dark brown, with chestnut or rufous edgings to feathers giving lightly scalloped appearance to back and closed wing; rump, central uppertail-coverts and tail black-brown, but outer uppertail-coverts buff or creamy-white. Bill black or dark grey-black. Legs and feet grey-black. In flight, upperwings dark brown, with chestnut or rufous edgings to scapulars and chestnut lesser and median coverts; underwings more uniformly blackish, but with pale stripe of flank feathers showing between dark of wing and chestnut of rest of flanks. Main call a five- to seven-note whistle, rapidly descending, often produced in flight as well as on the ground; the noise from a flock resembles a shrill twittering. The wings make a pronounced and distinctive whistling sound.
Female Similar to male, but sometimes with slightly less elongated flank plumes. **Juvenile** As adult, but duller and lacking the broad pale feather edgings on the back, so that mantle appears darker; underparts less chestnut and lacking some or all of black spotting on sides of lower neck and upper chest. Chestnut on lesser wing-coverts much reduced in extent and colour, and entirely absent from median wing-coverts. Bill, legs and feet paler greyish-black. **Confusion risks** Range of this race overlaps with that of Lesser Whistling-duck, which rather smaller. Latter species merely has dark centre to crown, compared with complete black crown down to eye of

Wandering; Lesser also lacks dark spotting and mottling of Wandering and has chestnut, not buff or creamy-white, uppertail-coverts.
DISTRIBUTION AND STATUS Resident in Philippines (apparently throughout) and parts of Indonesia, especially southern and eastern Borneo, Sulawesi, Java, Bali, Sumba, Rote, Timor, Lesser Sundas and Moluccas; local seasonal migrations and less regular dispersive movements may occur in response to availability of suitable fresh waters. Frequents larger waterbodies with emergent vegetation. No estimate of population, though reported as particularly numerous in Philippines, with flocks of many hundreds occurring widely, and as common in Indonesia. Also thought, however, to have declined in many areas.

Australian Wandering Whistling-duck

Dendrocygna arcuata australis L 43-48 cm (17-19 in), WS 85-95 cm (33-37)
Medium-sized to large whistling-duck with dark crown reaching to eye.
IDENTIFICATION Male breeding and non-breeding, female, juvenile Distinguishable from East Indian and Lesser Wandering Whistling-ducks only by size, and then considerable overlap. The birds in northern New Guinea are reported to be intermediate in size between East Indian and Australian races, and have not been assigned to one or other. **Confusion risks** Within Australian and New Guinea range, overlaps mainly with Plumed Whistling-duck. At a distance, Wandering is slightly dumpier, with shorter neck and legs; also spends far more time on water, when swims lower and does not hold head so erect. Wandering occupies larger waterbodies and dives freely for food, while Plumed less tied to water and forages on land for almost all its food. Dark crown of Wandering extending down to eye, and dark back of neck, contrast with paler cheeks, throat and sides of neck, whereas Plumed shows much more evenly pale head and neck, lacking any dark markings. Very elongated flank feathers of Plumed much more prominent than on Wandering, on which they show mainly as light stripe along upper flanks. Both species have chestnut or rufous underparts but, whereas on Wandering these are spotted and mottled black, on Plumed they are boldly marked with vertical black stripes. The fleshy-pink bill and legs of Plumed show pale at a distance, compared with the black or grey-black of Wandering. The five- to seven-note call of Wandering is distinct from the two-note call of Plumed.
DISTRIBUTION AND STATUS Occurs in southern New Guinea (Irian Jaya, Indonesia, and Papua New Guinea) and northern Australia, on a wide variety of larger, and preferably permanent, wetlands. In latter country, probably largely resident on permanent coastal wetlands, but elsewhere, and particularly inland and towards south of normal range, wanders widely in response to water conditions (hence its vernacular name)

and may become truly nomadic for extended periods. Population estimated in hundreds of thousands, perhaps over 1 million. Thought to be stable, but wetlands known to be at risk from agricultural and other developments, while some permanent waters in northern Australia deteriorating through salination and silting.

Lesser Wandering Whistling-duck

Dendrocygna arcuata pygmaea L 38-43 cm (15-17 in), WS 75-85 cm (29-33 in)
Smallest of three races, not overlapping in range with any other whistling-duck.
IDENTIFICATION Male breeding and non-breeding, female, juvenile Distinguishable from East Indian and Australian Wandering Whistling-ducks only by size, and then considerable overlap. **Confusion risks** For separation from possible vagrant Lesser or Plumed Whistling-ducks, see under East Indian and Australian races of Wandering.
DISTRIBUTION AND STATUS Isolated range in Fiji, where now almost certainly extinct, and New Britain (Papua New Guinea), where very small population thought to be just surviving.

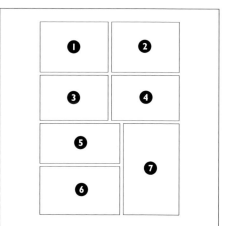

1 **East Indian Wandering Whistling-duck** (adults, Singapore)
2 **East Indian Wandering Whistling-duck** (flock in flight, Singapore)
3 **Australian Wandering Whistling-duck** (immatures and adults, Australia)
4 **Australian Wandering Whistling-duck** (adult, Cairns, Australia)
5 **Australian Wandering Whistling-duck** (immatures and adults, Cairns, Australia)
6 **Australian Wandering Whistling-duck** (adult, Australia)
7 **Australian Wandering Whistling-duck** (adult, Australia)

WHISTLING-DUCKS

WEST INDIAN WHISTLING-DUCK

Dendrocygna arborea L 48-58 cm (19-23 in), WS 90-100 cm (35-39 in)
Monotypic. Largest whistling-duck, having overall dark plumage with spotted flanks and underparts unlike that of any other within range.
IDENTIFICATION Male breeding and non-breeding Dark brown-black crown and nape. Upper half of cheeks and lower forehead rufous-brown; lower half of cheeks, sides of neck and throat whitish-buff, palest on throat, with a few fine black streaks on side of neck above variably white-streaked dark collar. Breast rufous-brown with black mottling, grading on flanks and belly into irregular pattern of black and white spots and stripes (largest markings towards rear of upper flanks); vent and undertail-coverts whitish, spotted black, especially towards rear. Upperparts brown-black with rufous edgings to feathers of mantle and wing-coverts, forming scalloped bars across back and closed wings; rump, uppertail-coverts and tail blackish-brown. Bill black. Legs and feet dark grey. In flight, grey greater, median and lesser upperwing-coverts show as area of pale extending almost full length of wing and contrasting with dark brown of primaries and secondaries; underwings uniformly dark. Five-note whistling call, though not so vocal as other whistling-ducks. **Female** As male, though can be seen to be very slightly smaller within a pair. **Juvenile** Duller and browner, less rufous, than adults, with much-reduced black and white spotting and streaking on underparts, where black may be completely absent at first. Little or no rufous on forehead and upper cheeks, and brown rather than black-brown crown and nape, making head appear less well marked. **Confusion risks** Fulvous and Black-bellied Whistling-ducks only congeners within range. Both smaller. Former also paler, with extensive warm rufous-buff plumage and without any spotting on flanks and underparts. Latter also lacks any spotting of underparts and additionally has prominent red bill and pink legs, and white, not grey, on upperwings in flight. Smaller Spotted Whistling-duck (extralimital) has much larger spots on flanks, pinkish colouring to bill and legs, and all-dark upperwings in flight.
DISTRIBUTION AND STATUS Confined to West Indies, where resident on Bahamas, Greater Antilles (Cuba, Jamaica, Haiti, Dominican Republic, Puerto Rico) and northern Lesser Antilles (Leeward Islands, Guadeloupe, Dominica, Martinique); only casual vagrancy has been recorded. Inhabits mangrove swamps and other marshy areas with abundant trees, on which this species is much more adept at perching than other whistling-ducks, and where it feeds on the fruits of the royal palm. Total population estimated at under 25,000 and currently declining. Isolated island populations vulnerable to illegal shooting and drainage of wetlands. May become extinct on one or more islands in near future.

BLACK-BELLIED WHISTLING-DUCK

Dendrocygna autumnalis
Polytypic. Two subspecies: (1) Northern Black-bellied Whistling-duck *D. a. autumnalis*, from Texas south to Panama; (2) Southern Black-bellied Whistling-duck *D. a. discolor*, from Panama south to Argentina. Intergrades occur in Panama.

Northern Black-bellied Whistling-duck

Dendrocygna autumnalis autumnalis L 45-53 cm (18-21 in), WS 85-95 cm (33-37 in)
Medium-sized whistling-duck with unique large white wing patch, waxy-red bill and legs, and black underparts.
IDENTIFICATION Male breeding and non-breeding Crown and back of neck rufous-brown; face, throat and sides of upper neck pale buff-grey, with conspicuous white ring around eye. Many birds exhibit slightly paler forehead. Lower neck and breast warm chestnut-brown, darker towards top; rest of underparts black, except for slight whitish mottling on vent and undertail-coverts. Upperparts dark chestnut-brown with indistinct paler feather edgings; rump, uppertail-coverts and tail black or blackish. Bill bright waxy reddish-pink with, on majority of birds, small yellowish area on top of upper mandible from nostrils towards, but not quite reaching, feathers at base; nail conspicuously white. Legs and feet bright flesh-pink. In flight, upperwing has small chestnut area on inner lesser coverts, whitish median coverts and white greater coverts, as well as white on bases of blackish flight feathers (shows broad white bar along length of wing, contrasting with dark flight feathers); underwings uniformly blackish. Very noisy, with frequent uttering in flight of loud five- to seven-note whistling call, *pee-chew-wee-wee-wee*. **Female** No apparent differences from male. **Juvenile** Duller and less well patterned than adults, with grey-white belly marked with ill-defined darker cross-barring; white of wing-coverts pale grey-white and so less obvious in flight. Bill, legs and feet mainly grey, tinged with pink or yellow. **Confusion risks** Little risk of confusion between flying bird and any other whistling-duck as no other has white wing-bar. Just West Indian Whistling-duck has pale grey on upperwing extending to leading edge. At rest, distinguished by combination of very pale head, bright pink bill, legs and feet, dark brown back and black underparts.
DISTRIBUTION AND STATUS Breeds from south-east of Texas, south through Mexico, Guatemala, Belize, El Salvador, Honduras, Nicaragua and Costa Rica to central Panama; at northern end of range birds migratory, moving south in winter, but over rest of range only local movements reported. Occupies variety of wetlands but rarely far from trees, as frequently perches; will forage on agricultural land, including rice-fields. Population thought to number *c* 500,000 and to be stable; only small numbers, low thousands, in USA, though increasing there. Several tens of thousands counted at single localities in, eg, Mexico and Costa Rica. Shot for sport and, in some areas, to prevent agricultural damage.

Southern Black-bellied Whistling-duck

Dendrocygna autumnalis discolor L 43-50 cm (17-20 in), WS 83-92 cm (32-36 in)
Medium-sized whistling-duck with unique large white wing patch, pinky-red bill and legs, and black underparts.
IDENTIFICATION Male breeding and non-breeding, female, juvenile Slightly smaller than Northern Black-bellied Whistling-duck. Plumage generally similar, but differs in having breast and lower neck grey-brown, not chestnut-brown, and back more grey-brown than chestnut-brown. **Confusion risks** As with Northern race, little risk of confusion with any other whistling-duck within range.
DISTRIBUTION AND STATUS Breeds from eastern Panama through northern South America, to Ecuador on west side and to northern Argentina on east side, also Trinidad and perhaps some of southern Lesser Antilles; mainly sedentary, but some short-distance seasonal movements. Similar habitats to Northern race. Population estimated at over 1 million; no information on trends. Concentrations of up to low tens of thousands reported. Some shooting for sport and for crop protection.

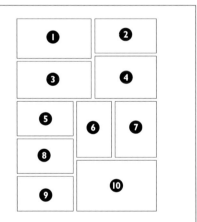

1 **West Indian Whistling-duck** (immatures, Bahamas)
2 *West Indian Whistling-duck (adult)*
3 *West Indian Whistling-duck (adults)*
4 *West Indian Whistling-duck (adult)*
5 **Northern Black-bellied Whistling-duck** (adult, Texas, USA)
6 **Northern Black-bellied Whistling-duck** (adult, Texas, USA)
7 **Northern Black-bellied Whistling-duck** (adult, Texas, USA)
8 **Northern Black-bellied Whistling-duck** (adults, Texas, USA)
9 *Southern Black-bellied Whistling-duck (family party)*
10 *Southern Black-bellied Whistling-duck (adult)*

DUCKS AND SWANS

WHITE-BACKED DUCK

Thalassornis leuconotus
Polytypic. Two subspecies: (1) African White-backed Duck *T. l. leuconotus*, West Africa (Senegal to Chad) and East and South Africa (Ethiopia to South Africa); (2) Madagascan White-backed Duck *T. l. insularis*, resident Madagascar.

African White-backed Duck

Thalassornis leuconotus leuconotus L 38-40 cm (15-16 in), WS 65-75 cm (26-29 in)
Short and thickset duck resembling thin-necked short-tailed stifftail, but white on face rules out Maccoa Duck, only stifftail within range. **IDENTIFICATION Male breeding and non-breeding** Crown, down to and including eye, and back of neck dark blackish-brown, speckled buff; cheeks paler, finely speckled black and buff. Oval white or whitish patch at base of bill, extending from level with top of upper mandible and eye to just below lower mandible. Neck, except at back, warm buff. Breast and upper belly tawny-brown, barred blackish (bars finer on breast, broader on flanks); lower belly, vent and undertail-coverts greyer-brown. Upperparts, apart from lower back and rump, dark tawny-brown, barred black; lower back white; rump and uppertail-coverts blackish-brown, barred white. Tail minute, blackish. Large bill blackish, with yellow sides blotched with black; yellowish underneath. Legs flesh-pink, darkening to blackish on feet. In flight, upperwing-coverts dark brown with buff and white spots and bars, flight feathers pale brown, with very narrow whitish tips to secondaries; underwings buff-brown. Two-note whistling call not dissimilar to that of whistling-ducks. **Female** Apparently similar to male. **Juvenile** Darker and duller than adults, with more black spotting on cheeks and upper neck; less distinctive barring below. **Confusion risks** Flies rarely, so that white of lower back, otherwise an excellent guide to identification, is not often visible. On water, superficial resemblance to stifftails, Maccoa Duck being only one within South African range; male Maccoa, however, has all-black head with prominent blue bill, while female lacks white face patch and has noticeable pale supercilium and dark eye-stripe below dark crown. **DISTRIBUTION AND STATUS** Mainly resident in two, apparently separate, areas of Africa: in western Africa in belt roughly between 10° and 20°N, from Senegal to Chad, and in eastern and southern Africa from Ethiopia south to South Africa and across to west coast in Angola and Namibia; probably mostly sedentary. Occupies wide variety of mainly shallow fresh waters, avoiding large open waters. West African population considered to be fewer than 10,000 birds and declining; now very scarce, and perhaps even extinct or nearly so. In eastern and southern Africa, population estimated at between 10,000 and 25,000 birds. Usually solitary or in very small groups, rarely in flocks of a few hundred, so censusing very difficult.

Madagascan White-backed Duck

Thalassornis leuconotus insularis L 36-38 cm (14-15 in), WS 60-70 cm (24-27 in)
Short and thickset duck resembling thin-necked short-tailed stifftail, but none within range. Slight resemblance to Little Grebe. **IDENTIFICATION Male breeding and non-breeding, female, juvenile** As African White-backed Duck, but slightly smaller. Markings, especially on head and body, stronger, thus giving overall darker appearance; crown darker black-brown, with heavier spots on cheeks. Underparts paler buff than African race but barring blacker and bolder, emphasizing barred effect. **Confusion risks** No stifftails live in Madagascar, and sole stifftail in southern Africa (Maccoa Duck) not reported to have wandered there. Only possible confusion, therefore, with grebes, either Little Grebe *Tachybaptus ruficollis* or Madagascar Grebe *T. pelzelnii*: both superficially similar in shape, with dumpy body and almost complete lack of tail, but head and bill small and dainty in comparison with those of White-backed Duck; at close range, plumage differences very apparent. **DISTRIBUTION AND STATUS** Confined to Madagascar, where occurs at up to about 800 m above sea-level; seasonal movements probable, in response to availability of water. Occupies variety of small wetlands, avoiding large open waters. Population estimated at fewer than 10,000 birds and declining; extinct at some former haunts, much less common than formerly at others. Shooting and trapping implicated in decline.

COSCOROBA SWAN

Coscoroba coscoroba L 90-115 cm (35-59 in), WS 140-160 cm (55-63 in)
Monotypic. Only all-white swan within range, further distinguished by red bill, legs and feet. **IDENTIFICATION Male breeding** All-white plumage but for black tips (approximately outer third) to outer six primaries, though these often barely visible on closed wing. Unlike other swans, area between base of bill and eye is feathered. Some brown or pale orange staining may be present on head and neck after extensive feeding in iron-rich water. Bill bright waxy-red with paler nail, more duck-shaped than typical swan or even goose. Legs and feet bright flesh-pink. Iris colour varies, perhaps seasonally or with age, from yellowish to reddish. In flight, black wing tips quite conspicuous. Loud three-note call, *cos-cor-ooo*, not unlike toy trumpet, with first note highest. **Male non-breeding** As male breeding, but, during flightless period of *c* four weeks, lacks black tips to wings. Timing of moult variable across range, from November to April. **Female** As male. Iris reported as dark brown, but this apparently not reliable as guide to sex. Call as male, but lower-pitched (wrongly reported as higher by some authorities), thus more goose-like than swan-like. **Juvenile** First

plumage white or whitish with extensive areas of brown or grey-brown, especially on head, upperparts and wing-coverts. Head markings form distinct dark crown down to eye and extending down nape and back of neck, contrasting with white lower cheeks; rest of neck and upperparts variably blotched brown or grey-brown, less apparent on underparts. Juvenile feathers gradually moulted to white over course of first winter, with some persisting, especially on upperwings, until second autumn and winter. Bill grey-blue, with paler nail and edges to mandibles, and legs and feet grey-blue; all become as adult in first summer and autumn. Iris dark brown, gradually turning yellowish to reddish, perhaps intensifying in colour with age. **Confusion risks** Unmistakable within range. Only other largely white waterbird within range is Black-necked Swan, which has all-black head and neck, as well as red knob at base of bluish bill. **DISTRIBUTION AND STATUS** Breeds South America from southern Chile and central Argentina south to Tierra del Fuego; relatively frequent visitor to Falklands (may have bred). Winters north to central Chile, northern Argentina, Uruguay and extreme south-east of Brazil; southernmost breeding areas vacated in winter. Main habitat large, well-vegetated swamps and lagoons. Population estimated at up to 100,000 birds and probably stable; only counts include over 12,000 wintering in Argentina. Little or no shooting occurs, but some risk from loss of wetland habitat.

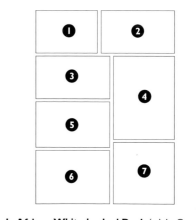

1 **African White-backed Duck** (adult, Cape Town, South Africa)
2 *African White-backed Duck (adult)*
3 *African White-backed Duck (adult)*
4 **African White-backed Duck** (adult)
5 *Coscoroba Swan* (flock in flight, Argentina)
6 *Coscoroba Swan (adult)*
7 *Coscoroba Swan (adult)*

SWANS

MUTE SWAN

Cygnus olor L 145-160 cm (57-63 in), WS 210-240 cm (83-94 in)
Monotypic. Large white waterbird, differing from other swans of northern hemisphere in reddish bill, curved neck and pointed tail.
IDENTIFICATION Male breeding All-white plumage, though may have brownish or orange staining on head and neck after feeding in iron-rich water. Bill orange-red; nail, cutting edge to mandibles, nostrils, knob at base of bill, and bare skin running back in V to eye black. Large, fleshy knob variable in size, enlarged in spring, then reducing after nesting season, though still conspicuous. Legs and feet dark grey-black. Uncommon 'Polish' colour morph has pink-grey legs and feet. In flight, broad wings produce far-carrying throbbing sound. Gives wide variety of hissing, grunting and snorting calls. **Male non-breeding** As male breeding, but knob reduces and bill colour fades after nesting. During flightless period of six to eight weeks (July to September), lack of wings produces marked change in silhouette of swimming bird, with pointed tail much more prominent. **Female** As male, but with smaller knob and less bright bill. **Juvenile** First feathered plumage largely grey-brown overall, darker on upperparts. White plumage acquired gradually, and variably, through first winter and into second year, with some grey-brown feathers retained, eg on wings and tail, until well into second winter. Bill and bare skin to eye dark grey, becoming pinkish-grey to pink during first winter, but not as adult until second winter, and then paler than breeding adult. Knob absent until second winter. Legs and feet grey or pinkish-grey, but flesh-pink on 'Polish' birds. Note, also, that 'Polish' juveniles are largely white in first feathered plumage. **Confusion risks** Best distinguished from all other northern-hemisphere swans at distance by curved neck and reddish bill, with black knob, held pointing downwards, arched wings curved over back, and pointed tail. Last character most visible on moulting bird, but also very obvious on upending feeding bird, even at great distances, and also in flight. Length of neck proportionately greater in relation to body length than all other swans. In flight, only all-white swan to produce sound from wingbeats.
DISTRIBUTION AND STATUS Resident or partial migrant through northern temperate Europe, from British Isles east to Baltic, then patchily from Black Sea to northern China. Introduced and locally established North America, South Africa, Australia, New Zealand and Japan. More northerly European breeders move south for winter. Inhabits wide variety of fresh and brackish waters, from small ponds to large lakes and estuaries. Population increasing in north-west Europe (c 250,000) and Black Sea-Caspian area (c 150,000+), but perhaps declining east Asia (low thousands). 4,000+ in North America, but only hundreds in introduced populations elsewhere. Threats from habitat loss and, locally, lead poisoning.

BLACK SWAN

Cygnus atratus L 110-140 cm (43-55 in), WS 160-200 cm (64-79 in)
Monotypic. Unique combination of black body and white outer half to wings.
IDENTIFICATION Male breeding All sooty-black body; feathers of, especially, upperparts fringed with grey. Greater wing-coverts and tertials broadened and curled to give peculiar ruffled appearance to top of closed wing. Primaries and outer secondaries, also alula, white, some inner secondaries tipped white; these white feathers largely concealed on swimming or standing bird, though may show as broad horizontal line above flanks. Bill orange-red to bright waxy-red, with whitish subterminal bar and nail, and bare red skin back to reddish or whitish eye. Legs and feet black. In flight, dramatic contrast between white flight feathers and black coverts, both above and below; neck longer in proportion to body than on any other swan. Rather weak, high-pitched, bugling call. **Male non-breeding** During period of annual moult, white wing feathers shed. **Female** As male, but smaller and less bright red on bill. **Juvenile** Grey-brown instead of black, with pale feather tips producing mottled appearance, and paler underparts; flight feathers white but with grey-brown tips. Bill grey, gradually becoming pink and then red. Moults into adult plumage during first year, though dull tips to flight feathers may be retained until third year. **Confusion risks** Unmistakable within or outside range.
DISTRIBUTION AND STATUS Australia and Tasmania, except for extreme north and in central deserts. Introduced and well established in New Zealand. Has occurred in southern New Guinea. Breeds mainly on large, permanent lakes and lagoons, both fresh and brackish, but occurs at other times on wide variety of waterbodies, including temporary floods. Sedentary on permanent waters, but wanders widely in response to droughts or rainy periods. Population unknown, but certainly hundreds of thousands, perhaps more, in Australia. Currently c 60,000 in New Zealand, where numbers deliberately controlled by egg-collecting. Some shooting for sport, but mainly in relation to crop damage.

BLACK-NECKED SWAN

Cygnus melanocoryphus L 100-125 cm (39-49 in), WS 135-155 cm (53-61 in)
Monotypic. Unique combination of black head and neck and white body distinguishes this from all other swans and large waterbirds.
IDENTIFICATION Male breeding Head and all of neck except base black, with irregular white stripe from base of knob through and around eye tapering to back of head (shows some individual variation in width, especially between eye and bill). Rest of body and all wings and tail pure white. Bill blue-grey with pinkish nail; large double-lobed fleshy knob and extensive area of facial skin from bill to eye bright scarlet-red.

Legs and feet pink. In flight, black head and neck and white body completely distinctive; not so long-necked or long-winged as most swans. Wings produce loud rustling or whistling sound. Only call a rather weak and wheezy whistle. **Male non-breeding** As male breeding, but knob reduced in size and slightly less bright red. **Female** As male, but noticeably smaller, especially when paired birds seen together. Knob smaller, but still brightly coloured. **Juvenile** As adult, but dark brown instead of black on head and neck, and with feathers of upperparts and flanks tinged brownish-grey; blackish tips to primaries. Adult body plumage acquired during first year, but primaries may still show dark tips through second and into third years. Bill grey, gradually turning reddish, and lacking knob until second year. **Confusion risks** Unmistakable within or outside range.
DISTRIBUTION AND STATUS Breeds southern South America (Paraguay, Uruguay, Argentina and Chile) and Falkland Islands. Some northward movement in winter, as far as south-east Brazil, with southernmost breeding areas vacated, but full extent of movements unknown. Occurs on freshwater and some brackish-water lagoons and swamps. Population up to 100,000 and thought to be stable, with c 50,000 in Argentina, 20,000 in both Chile and Uruguay, and up to 2,500 on Falkland Islands. Little or no shooting, but drainage of wetlands a threat in some areas.

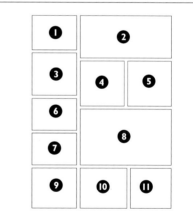

1 **Mute Swan** (family, Greater Manchester, England)
2 **Mute Swan** (adult in flight, Kent, England)
3 **Mute Swan** (pair, about to copulate, Seaforth, England)
4 **Mute Swan** (first winter/first summer, Seaforth, England)
5 **Black Swan** (adult, Perth, Australia)
6 **Black Swan** (juvenile, Perth, Australia)
7 **Black Swan** (adult, Perth, Australia)
8 **Black Swan** (flock in flight, New Zealand)
9 **Black-necked Swan** (adult, Falklands)
10 **Black-necked Swan** (family group, Falklands)
11 **Black-necked Swan** (adult in flight, Falklands)

SWANS

TRUMPETER SWAN

Cygnus buccinator 150-180 cm (60-71 in), WS 230-260 cm (91-102 in)

Monotypic. Very large all-white swan with black bill, distinguishable by size and proportions from Whistling Swan within range.

IDENTIFICATION Male breeding and non-breeding All white, though can have orange-brown staining on head and neck after feeding in iron-rich water. Very long black bill, showing straight line from feathers to tip, and with black facial skin extending back to dark brown or black eye; slight reddish line along sides of upper mandible. Legs and feet black. On ground and in flight, shows very long head and neck in proportion to body. Loud resonating, trumpeting calls, usually two-note *ko-hoo*. Duetting with female common within pair. **Female** As male, though within a pair female is always slightly smaller than male. **Juvenile** Grey-brown, darker on crown and back of neck, paler on underparts, gradually becoming whiter through first winter but retaining some grey-brown on head, neck and wings into second year. Bill flesh-pink, but nail and nostril black, and base of bill and facial skin variably blotched black. Legs and feet greyish. Bare parts become black by second year.

Confusion risks From extralimital Whooper Swan by all-black bill. From Whistling Swan, with which extensive range overlap, especially in winter in western states of USA, principally by considerably larger size and proportionally longer bill, head and neck, and by louder, deeper, trumpeting, rather than honking, calls. Most Whistling Swans have small yellow patch at base of bill, while profile of bill is slightly concave from base to tip.

DISTRIBUTION AND STATUS Breeds Alaska and western Canada, wintering through southern Alaska, British Columbia and north-west USA; also more or less resident in several scattered locations in north-west USA, mostly established by reintroductions. Nests in swamps and marshes; winter habitat similar, also estuaries and coastal bays. Population of Alaska c 13,000 and increasing, with further 2,000 in north-west USA. Has recovered from very low numbers, perhaps only hundreds, in early 20th century; increase largely attributable to protection from shooting, formerly excessive.

WHOOPER SWAN

Cygnus cygnus L 140-165 cm (55-65 in), WS 220-245 cm (86-98 in)

Monotypic. Very large all-white swan with black and yellow bill, distinguishable from smaller Bewick's Swan within range.

IDENTIFICATION Male breeding and non-breeding All white, though sometimes with orange-brown staining on head and neck from feeding in iron-rich water. Large black and bright lemon-yellow bill; yellow extends from base of bill to nostrils on top of upper mandible and to below and beyond nostrils on side, with remainder black, including cutting edges of upper mandible back to base. Bare skin, from base of bill to eye, yellow. Legs and feet black. On ground and in flight, very long-necked, large-bodied swan. Loud trumpeting and honking calls, with duetting between pair-members. **Female** As male, but slightly smaller, this most noticeable within pair. **Juvenile** Grey-brown, darker on head and neck, paler on underparts. Gradually becomes whiter during first year, though a few scattered grey-brown feathers, eg on head and rump, retained well into second year. Bill pink at base, brown towards tip, pink slowly changing to yellow during first year. **Confusion risks** Distinguished from smaller Bewick's Swan not just by size, but by head, neck and body proportions, which are all longer. Yellow on bill more extensive, always to below and beyond nostrils. Calls deeper and both more musical and more trumpet-like. In distance, from Mute Swan by long straight neck and head held horizontal; in flight or when upending, tail rounded, not pointed.

DISTRIBUTION AND STATUS Two separate populations: breeding Iceland, and wintering there (small numbers), Britain and Ireland; breeding north Europe from Scandinavia to north-east Siberia, and wintering from north-west Europe to Black and Caspian Sea areas, and east Asia (China, Korea, Japan). Nests beside pools, lakes and slow-flowing rivers; winters mainly on lowland fresh waters and estuaries, often feeding on agricultural land. Icelandic population c 16,000; north-west Europe (winter), 25,000; Black Sea (winter), 17,000; east Asia (winter), perhaps up to 100,000. European populations thought to be increasing. Main threat is drainage of winter wetland habitat.

TUNDRA SWAN

Cygnus columbianus
Polytypic. Two subspecies: (1) Whistling Swan *C. c. columbianus*, in North America; (2) Bewick's Swan *C. c. bewickii*, in Eurasia.

Whistling Swan

Cygnus columbianus columbianus L 120-150 cm (47-59 in), WS 190-220 cm (75-87 in)

All-white swan, distinguished by size and proportions from much larger Trumpeter Swan, which overlaps in range.

IDENTIFICATION Male breeding and non-breeding All white, though head and neck may be stained orange-brown from feeding in iron-rich water. Long black bill, slightly concave in profile from base to tip, with black facial skin extending back to eye (most have small yellow patch on facial skin, below and in front of eye, but can be very small or absent); very slight reddish line along sides of upper mandible, difficult to see except at close range. Legs and feet black. Typical long-necked swan shape on ground and in flight. Loud honking, goose-like calls, *kow-wow-wow*. **Female** As male, but averages slightly smaller, apparent within a pair.

Juvenile Grey-brown, darker on head, paler on underparts and wings. Becomes progressively whiter through first winter; may retain a few brownish feathers on head and rump into second winter. Bill pink, with blackish nail, cutting edges and nostrils, and paler towards base. Becomes as adult during second summer. **Confusion risks** For distinction from Trumpeter Swan, see that species. Conspecific Bewick's Swan always has much more yellow on bill and is smaller, with proportionally shorter head and neck.

DISTRIBUTION AND STATUS Breeds arctic North America from Alaska to Hudson Bay, wintering on western and eastern coasts of North America. Nests on tundra pools and streams; winters in coastal marshes, often feeding on agricultural land. Population regularly censused, with mid-1990s totals of c 64,000 in western North America and c 110,000 in eastern. Populations stable or increasing, and shooting legally permitted.

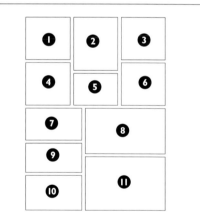

1 **Trumpeter Swan** (adult, Montana, USA)
2 **Trumpeter Swan** (pair, Yellowstone, USA)
3 **Trumpeter Swan** (adults in flight, Yellowstone, USA)
4 **Trumpeter Swan** *(juveniles)*
5 **Whooper Swan** (adults in flight, Hebrides, Scotland)
6 **Whooper Swan** (adult, Lancashire, England)
7 **Whooper Swan** (first winter birds, Lancashire, England)
8 **Whooper Swan** (first winter plus adult, Lancashire, England)
9 **Whistling Swan** (adult, Alaska, USA)
10 **Whistling Swan** (adults, Manitoba, Canada)
11 **Whistling Swan** (adult, Alaska, USA)

SWANS AND GEESE

Bewick's Swan

Cygnus columbianus bewickii L 115-135 cm (45-53 in), WS 180-210 cm (71-83 in)
All-white swan, distinguished by size and proportions from much larger Whooper, which overlaps in range; less extensive yellow on bill.
IDENTIFICATION Male breeding and non-breeding, female, juvenile As Whistling Swan, but bare facial skin of adult always yellow and with variable amounts of yellow on bill, though stopping short of nostrils. High-pitched, musical yelping and honking. **Confusion risks** From Whooper Swan by smaller size and, especially, shorter head and neck in proportion to body; by reduced amount of yellow on bill, never extending beyond nostrils; and by higher-pitched, more yelping calls.
DISTRIBUTION AND STATUS Breeds almost throughout arctic Siberia. Three main wintering areas: north-west Europe; Caspian Sea; and eastern China, Korea and Japan. Habitat similar to Whistling Swan. Populations (winter): north-west Europe, 17,000; Caspian Sea, 6,500; east Asia, 30,000. Illegal hunting, lead poisoning and habitat loss main threats.

SWAN GOOSE

Anser cygnoides L 81-94 cm (32-38 in), WS 165-185 cm (65-73 in)
Monotypic. Large, long-necked and very long-billed goose; bill plus unique head-and-neck pattern separate it from all other geese.
IDENTIFICATION Male breeding and non-breeding Dark chestnut-brown of crown extends to eye and down back of neck, with sharp demarcation from pale buff-brown cheeks and throat, and from front and sides of neck, which is pale buff to nearly pure white at base. White line around base of bill variable in thickness. Breast and belly warm brown, darker on flanks, and grading to white on vent and undertail-coverts; broad white border to upper flanks shows just below closed wing; buff-white edgings to flank feathers produce light barring effect. Upperparts ashy-brown, with buff edgings forming thin light-coloured parallel bars across closed wings; rump and uppertail-coverts white, tail grey-brown with whitish tip and sides. Very long bill black. Legs and feet reddish-orange. In flight, wings lack strong pattern, though upperwing-coverts grey-brown, paler on lesser and primary coverts, darker on median and greater, showing some difference from grey-black primaries and secondaries, but white rump shows clearly; underwings uniform dark grey. Goose-like honking and cackling calls, close to those of farmyard goose.
Female As male, but smaller, with slightly shorter and less deep bill and shorter neck. Differences best seen between members of a pair. **Juvenile** Like dull adult, lacking white at base of bill, and with browner, less white, edgings on upperparts and closed wings producing irregular, scaly effect, not barred as on adult. Bill and feet duller orange.
Confusion risks Distinctive head-and-neck

pattern unique among geese. At distance, long, thin neck and much longer head and bill than any other goose. Some domestic geese exhibit similar head-and-neck pattern, but always much heavier in body and with thicker neck; adult domestic geese have prominent black knob at base of bill.
DISTRIBUTION AND STATUS Breeds south-central Siberia, Mongolia and northern China, wintering eastern China. Formerly more widespread and also wintering Japan and Korea. Nests in marshy and grassy areas of steppes and forests; winters lowland grassland, marshes and agricultural land. Population estimated at 50,000. Has declined considerably in recent decades and thought to be still declining, with excessive winter shooting the main cause.

BEAN GOOSE

Anser fabalis
Polytypic. Five subspecies currently recognized within northern Eurasian range, though taxonomy under review and some may, in future, be considered separate species: (1) Western Bean Goose *A. f. fabalis*, breeds northern Scandinavia and north-west Russia, winters western Europe; (2) Johansen's Bean Goose *A. f. johanseni*, breeds central Siberia, winters western China; (3) Middendorff's Bean Goose *A. f. middendorffii*, breeds eastern Siberia, winters eastern China and Japan; (4) Russian Bean Goose *A. f. rossicus*, breeds northern and north-western Siberia, winters western Europe; (5) Thick-billed Bean Goose *A. f. serrirostris*, breeds north-eastern Siberia, winters China, Korea and Japan. Separation of subspecies in field possible in some cases, but relies more on geographical location in others. Intergrades also occur.

Western Bean Goose

Anser fabalis fabalis L 68-84 cm (27-33 in), WS 145-175 cm (56-70 in)
Large brown goose with long neck and comparatively long, thin bill. Black and orange bill, orange legs; darker on head than other grey geese within range.
IDENTIFICATION Male breeding and non-breeding Dark chocolate-brown head and neck, darkest on head, occasionally with very thin white band around base of bill; neck strongly furrowed. Chest and underparts light brown, flanks darker, and darkening towards rear and with whitish edges producing faint barring; white line at top of flanks showing below closed wing; vent and undertail-coverts white. Upperparts dark brown, with buff edgings forming thin, parallel barring across closed wing; rump dark brown, uppertail-coverts white; tail dark brown, edged white. Bill black, with bright orange-yellow band over upper mandible behind black nail, and variably along sides of upper mandible sometimes to base. Legs and feet bright orange-yellow. Very dark-winged in flight, above and below, with little contrast between very slightly paler, browner, upperwing-coverts and blackish-

brown flight feathers. Double *ungk-ungk* call, plus other cackling. **Female** As male, though slightly smaller within pair. **Juvenile** As adult, but with less even markings on back and wing-coverts, so barring on closed wing irregular and scaly. Never has white at base of bill. Orange-yellow of bill, legs and feet paler and duller. Adult characteristics acquired by second winter. **Confusion risks** For separation from other Bean Goose subspecies, see below and also measurements in *Birds of the Western Palearctic*, vol. 1, pp.396-7. Much darker and browner than other grey geese. Dark head and neck distinguishes from Greylag, as do black and orange bill and, in flight, lack of pale grey in wings. White-fronted Goose, especially juvenile of Greenland race, similar in brown tone and lack of contrast in wings, but head less dark in comparison with neck and little or no black on bill, apart from nail. Western Bean looks long-headed and long-necked when standing, and, in flight, long-necked with comparatively long wings.
DISTRIBUTION AND STATUS Breeds taiga zone from north Scandinavia east to Urals (Russia), wintering western Europe. Nests by lakes, pools and marshes; winters mainly on lowland marshes and agricultural land. Population (winter) estimated at 80,000, and increasing.

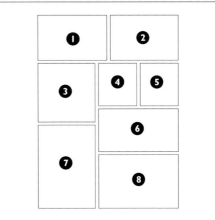

1 **Bewick's Swan** (adult, Lancashire, England)
2 **Bewick's Swan** (adults with first winter, Lancashire, England)
3 **Bewick's Swan** (adults in flight, Welney, England)
4 **Swan Goose** (adult in flight, Beidaihe, China)
5 **Swan Goose** (adult, Beidaihe, China)
6 **Western Bean Goose** (adult, Hortobagy, Hungary)
7 ***Western Bean Goose*** *(adult)*
8 **Western Bean Goose** (adults)

GEESE

Johansen's Bean Goose

Anser fabalis johanseni L 70-85 cm (28-33 in),
WS 150-180 cm (59-71 in)
Intermediate in size between *A. f. fabalis* and *A. f. middendorffii*; less orange on bill than former.
IDENTIFICATION Male breeding and non-breeding, female, juvenile As Western Bean Goose, but slightly larger. Orange-yellow on bill confined to band across upper mandible behind black nail, or, sometimes, with thin streak running back along sides of upper mandible to base, but rarely as much as on Western Bean. **Confusion risks** Separation from other subspecies of Bean Goose difficult, probably possible only by direct comparison and within known geographical range (see below). Reduced yellow on bill compared with very slightly smaller Western Bean, and slimmer, much less deep bill compared with rather larger Middendorff's Bean. Situation confused by probable intergrades between this subspecies and Western Bean in west of breeding range, and with Middendorff's in east (see below). In hand, bill length and, especially, depth critical (see measurements in *Birds of the Western Palearctic*, vol. 1, pp.396-7). Bill of Johansen's longer and proportionately slightly deeper than that of Western.
DISTRIBUTION AND STATUS Breeds taiga of west Siberia from Urals to Lake Baikal; winters western China and west to Kazakhstan, Kirghizstan, Turkestan and Iran, though some reported from central Europe. Apart from the last, no overlap in wintering grounds with other subspecies, but breeding grounds contiguous with those of Western Bean at western edge and of Middendorff's at eastern edge, producing zones of probable intergrading. Habitat as Western Bean Goose. No estimate of numbers.

Middendorff's Bean Goose

Anser fabalis middendorffii L 75-90 cm (30-35 in),
WS 155-190 cm (61-75 in)
Largest subspecies, with long and moderately deep black bill with restricted amount of orange.
IDENTIFICATION Male breeding and non-breeding, female, juvenile As Western Bean Goose, but considerably larger in all dimensions, and especially bill, which proportionately much longer, and also deeper at base. Orange-yellow on bill confined to band across upper mandible behind black nail; unlike Western and Johansen's Bean Geese, no yellow on sides of upper mandible. **Confusion risks** Lack of yellow on sides of bill shared by much smaller, short-billed Russian Bean Goose and by slightly smaller and very stout-billed Thick-billed Bean Goose. Some intergrading probable with Johansen's Bean Goose breeding to west (see above), but less certain whether intergrading also occurs with Thick-billed Bean Goose breeding to north, as has been reported. Bill appears large and stout, being longer than all other subspecies and deeper than all but Thick-billed (see measurements in

Birds of the Western Palearctic, vol. 1, pp.396-7). Appearance in distance and when flying is of very large-headed goose.
DISTRIBUTION AND STATUS Breeds taiga of eastern Siberia, mainly east, and north, of Lake Baikal, from Khatanga to the Kolyma region, and extending to Pacific coast of Russia as well as south to the Altai and northern Mongolia; winters eastern China and Japan, and perhaps also Korea. Habitat that of as Western Bean Goose, with more dependence on lakes and marshes, feeding on aquatic vegetation, and much less on agricultural land than all other subspecies. Population has declined rapidly in recent years; estimates of 25,000 in early 1990s now replaced by one of less than 10,000 and still declining in 1996. Habitat loss and excessive hunting main causes of decline.

Russian Bean Goose

Anser fabalis rossicus L 65-80 cm (26-31 in), WS 140-165 cm (55-65 in)
Smallest Bean Goose, with short, comparatively stout bill with orange confined to band over upper mandible.
IDENTIFICATION Male breeding and non-breeding, female, juvenile As Western Bean Goose, but smaller and with shorter neck, more rounded head and shorter bill; also shorter body and legs. Orange-yellow on bill confined to band across upper mandible behind black nail; unlike Western, no yellow on sides of upper mandible. **Confusion risks** Distinctly smaller and dumpier than all other Bean Geese. Closer in shape to Pink-footed Goose (which see), but still dark brown as other Bean Geese, especially on head, back and wings, where Pinkfoot greyer; latter also has pink band on bill, and pink legs. Probably intergrades with Western Bean Goose in west and with Thick-billed Bean Goose in east of breeding range, and perhaps with Johansen's Bean Goose to south. Bill noticeably shorter than in all other races (see measurements in *Birds of the Western Palearctic*, vol. 1, pp.396-7), and, for its length, quite stout.
DISTRIBUTION AND STATUS Breeds tundra of north-west Siberia; winters western and south-eastern Europe, perhaps also east to western China, though situation in latter region obscure. Nests beside tundra pools and rivers; winters on lowland farmland, roosting on lakes and estuaries. By far the commonest subspecies, with population (winter) estimated at 300,000, mainly in western Europe, where large increases recorded in last few decades.

Thick-billed Bean Goose

Anser fabalis serrirostris L 70-85 cm (28-33 in), WS 150-180 cm (59-71 in)
Similar in size to Johansen's Bean Goose, with very deep bill, and orange confined to band behind nail.
IDENTIFICATION Male breeding and non-breeding, female, juvenile As Western Bean Goose, but slightly larger and with extremely heavily built bill, very deep at base, and almost straight line from top of head to tip

of bill, lacking distinct forehead of other races. Orange-yellow on bill confined to band across upper mandible behind black nail; unlike Western, no yellow on sides of upper mandible. **Confusion risks** Bill size and shape, and also shape of head and bill together, most obvious characteristics separating this subspecies from all others. Bill length similar to Johansen's Bean Goose, but depth significantly greater than in all other subspecies (see measurements in *Birds of the Western Palearctic*, vol. 1, pp.396-7). Restricted orange-yellow on bill also rules out Western and Johansen's. Within wintering range, overlaps with Middendorff's Bean Goose, which has longer, less deep bill and shows distinct forehead instead of straight line from crown to bill tip.
DISTRIBUTION AND STATUS Breeds tundra of north-east Siberia, from Khatanga to the Anadyr; winters China, Korea and Japan, overlapping with, but generally to north of, winter range of Middendorff's Bean Goose, though precise winter ranges of these two subspecies not clearly defined. Breeding habitat similar to that of Russian Bean Goose. In winter, makes more use of marine wetlands than does Middendorff's Bean Goose and feeds extensively on agricultural land, especially harvested rice-fields. Population probably in range 25,000-50,000 and thought to be declining, probably through excessive hunting and habitat loss, as formerly in Japan, where now protected and wintering numbers have shown a slight increase to the present level of c 9,000.

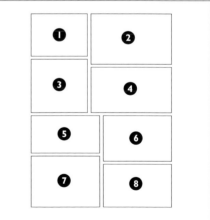

1 *Middendorf's Bean Goose* (adult)
2 *Middendorf's Bean Goose* (adult)
3 *Russian Bean Goose* (adult, Norfolk, England)
4 *Russian Bean Goose* (flock, Wieringermeer, Netherlands)
5 *Russian Bean Goose* (flock in flight, Kent, England)
6 *Russian Bean Goose* (juvenile)
7 *Thick-billed Bean Goose* (adult)
8 *Thick-billed Bean Goose* (adult)

GEESE

PINK-FOOTED GOOSE

Anser brachyrhynchus L 60-75 cm (24-30 in), WS 135-170 cm (53-67 in)
Monotypic. Medium-sized, rather short-necked, round-headed goose, distinguished by overall pinkish tinge to grey-brown colouring, and with pink legs and pink band over tip of bill.
IDENTIFICATION Male breeding and non-breeding Head and well-furrowed upper neck dark chocolate-brown, occasionally with very thin white line around base of bill, or just a few white feathers at base of upper mandible. Lower neck paler brown, shading to slightly darker on breast and belly, and to dark brown on flanks, especially to rear; flank feathers tipped buff, giving lightly barred appearance; white line along top of flanks, showing below closed wing; vent and undertail-coverts white. Back and upperwing-coverts brown, tinged pinkish-grey, with whitish edgings producing neat thin barring across closed wing; rump and tail dark grey, latter with white edgings; uppertail-coverts white. Bill black, with distinctive bright pink band behind black nail and variably pink (often lacking) along sides of upper mandible. Legs and feet bright pink. In flight, grey coverts contrast with blackish primaries and secondaries; underwings more uniformly dark. High-pitched two- or three-note call, *wink-wink-wink*, given constantly in flight and, with other, softer, calls, on ground.
Female As male, but very slightly smaller, observable within a pair. Pink of bill and, especially, legs a little less bright. **Juvenile** Duller and less pink-grey on back than adults, with irregular light brown edgings to coverts producing scaly effect instead of barring across closed wing. Pink of bare parts duller. May show light mottling effect on underparts. **Confusion risks** Compared with Bean Goose, smaller, more rounded head, shorter bill and pink (not orange) on bill and legs, though Russian Bean can look somewhat similar (but neck usually longer in proportion to body). Grey-pink tinge to upperparts gives overall paler appearance, compared with darker brown of Bean and Greater White-fronted, but not so pale grey as larger Greylag. Light grey area on upperwing of flying bird differs from much darker wings of Bean and Greater White-fronted, but not so pale as Greylag.
DISTRIBUTION AND STATUS Two discrete populations: breeding Iceland/east Greenland, wintering Scotland/England; breeding Svalbard, and wintering Denmark, Germany, Netherlands and Belgium. Nests in marshy tundra, on rock outcrops and on rocky sides to valleys and gorges; winters agricultural lowlands, roosting on estuaries, lakes and reservoirs.
Iceland/Greenland population 200,000-250,000; increased greatly in recent decades. Svalbard 30,000-35,000; also increased, but perhaps levelling out.

GREATER WHITE-FRONTED GOOSE

Anser albifrons
Polytypic. Five subspecies currently accepted within northern-hemisphere range, though some doubt about validity of Elgas's subspecies: (1) European Greater White-fronted Goose *A. a. albifrons*, breeds Siberia east to Kolyma River, winters Europe and south-west Asia; (2) Pacific Greater White-fronted Goose *A. a. frontalis*, breeds north-east Siberia, Alaska and arctic Canada, winters east Asia and western North America; (3) Tule Greater White-fronted Goose *A. a. gambelli*, breeds north-west Canada and Alaska, winters Mexico and south-west USA; (4) Elgas's Greater White-fronted Goose *A. a. elgasi*, breeds south-west Alaska, winters California; (5) Greenland Greater White-fronted Goose *A. a. flavirostris*, breeds west Greenland, winters Britain and Ireland.

European Greater White-fronted Goose

Anser albifrons albifrons L 65-75 cm (26-30 in), WS 130-155 cm (51-61 in)
Medium-sized grey-brown goose with white forehead and black belly bars.
IDENTIFICATION Male breeding and non-breeding Medium-brown head and neck, with conspicuous white forehead narrowly bordered at rear with darker brown; extent of white variable, rarely to above eye. Neck paler brown, furrowed on rear half; chest pale brown, darkening below and onto flanks, which more grey-brown. Belly irregularly blotched with black bars of varying thickness and length. Flank feathers have dark centres and pale edgings, showing as fine, pale barring; white line at top of flanks shows just below edge of closed wing. Vent and undertail-coverts white. Upperparts grey-brown, variable in tone, with narrow pale feather edgings producing fine parallel barring across closed wings; rump and tail dark grey-brown, latter edged whitish; uppertail-coverts white. Bill pale pink, though often with yellow tinge in centre of upper mandible, with white nail. Legs and feet orange-yellow. Up to 20% of birds have orange eye-ring. Upperwing-coverts grey-brown and, in flight, show slight contrast with blackish primaries and secondaries. Loud musical laughing calls, *kow-lyowk*. **Female** As male, but the slightly smaller bird within a pair. Apparently never has orange eye-ring. **Juvenile** As adult, but duller grey-brown and without fine barring on closed wing-coverts, having instead mottled appearance. Lacks white forehead until well into first winter; lacks black belly bars until first summer, underparts appearing slightly mottled. Bill and legs duller. **Confusion risks** For separation from other Greater Whitefront subspecies, see below. Adult's combination of white forehead and black belly bars separates it from all other grey geese. Juvenile close to Bean Goose, but has shorter bill, without obvious black areas, and generally has a shorter neck and body. In flight, lack of obvious contrast on upperwing recalls pattern of Bean but different from Pinkfoot and Greylag, which both show grey forewings.
DISTRIBUTION AND STATUS Breeds on Siberian tundra from north-west Russia east to Kolyma River; winters in western Europe, south-east Europe, Black Sea coasts and Caspian Sea area. Nests on arctic tundra pools and marshes, wintering in open farmland and steppes. Total population some 1.4 million in early 1990s, *c* 50% in western Europe; has roughly doubled in last 30 years.

Pacific Greater White-fronted Goose

Anser albifrons frontalis L 65-75 cm (26-30 in), WS 130-155 cm (51-61 in)
Similar in size to European subspecies, but with slightly longer bill.
IDENTIFICATION Male breeding and non-breeding, female, juvenile As European Greater White-fronted, with following minor differences: bill around 10% longer, though considerable overlap; generally darker brown, though wide individual variation; white forehead averaging slightly smaller. **Confusion risks** Separation from European subspecies probably impossible in the field. Zone of intergradation probably exists in eastern Siberia, where breeding ranges meet, if not actually overlap.
DISTRIBUTION AND STATUS Breeds north-east Siberia from Kolyma River east to Pacific coast, Alaska and St Lawrence Island, and arctic Canada east to Queen Maud Gulf; winters China, Korea, Japan, and western USA south to Mexico. Habitat as European subspecies. Populations (winter) around 50,000 east Asia, and censused at 240,000 and increasing western USA.

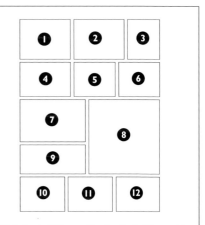

1 **Pink-footed Goose** (feeding flock, Merseyside, England)
2 **Pink-footed Goose** (feeding flock, Lancashire, England)
3 **Pink-footed Goose** (first winter, Lancashire, England)
4 **Pink-footed Goose** (flock in flight, Merseyside, England)
5 **European Greater White-fronted Goose** (flock in flight, Tymyr, Russia)
6 **European Greater White-fronted Goose** (adult, Norfolk, England)
7 **European Greater White-fronted Goose** (flock taking off, Netherlands)
8 **European Greater White-fronted Goose** (adult, Kent, England)
9 **European Greater White-fronted Goose** (adults and immature, Merseyside, England)
10 *Pacific Greater White-fronted Goose* (adult)
11 **Pacific Greater White-fronted Goose** (adult, North Alaska, USA)
12 **Pacific Greater White-fronted Goose** (adult, North Alaska, USA)

Tule Greater White-fronted Goose

Anser albifrons gambelli L 70-80 cm (28-31 in),
WS 140-165 cm (55-65 in)
Larger and darker Whitefront of North
America, closely similar to Elgas's subspecies.
Note possible confusion of English names, as
this subspecies sometimes called Gambell's
Greater Whitefront and Elgas's sometimes
called Tule Greater Whitefront.
**IDENTIFICATION Male breeding and non-
breeding, female, juvenile** As Pacific
subspecies, but larger and overall much darker,
both in brown colour of body and in amount of
black barring on underparts. Bill and legs both
relatively longer. **Confusion risks** Almost
indistinguishable from slightly larger Elgas's
Greater Whitefront, though apparently lacks
orange eye-ring of that subspecies. Reported to
fly more steadily and less buoyantly than Pacific
Greater Whitefront. Geographical location
important in assessing likelihood of
identification. Closer in size and colouring to
Greenland Greater Whitefront, but no overlap
in range and latter has orange, not pink, bill.
DISTRIBUTION AND STATUS Breeds taiga zone
of north-west Canada and adjacent Alaska,
wintering Mexico and neighbouring states of
USA (eg Texas). Nests beside pools and rivers;
winters on marshes and adjoining agricultural
land. Population in winter 1991/92 *c* 8,000, and
increasing; almost all of these along Gulf coast
of Mexico. Threatened by overhunting of very
small population on wintering grounds, as well
as by drainage and disturbance of winter
haunts, though recent protection has
contributed to increase in population.

Elgas's Greater White-fronted Goose

Anser albifrons elgasi L 70-80 cm (28-31 in), WS
140-165 cm (55-65 in)
Measurements shown are same as for Tule
Greater Whitefront, but has been reported to
be slightly larger and with longer bill. See Tule
Greater Whitefront (above) for possible
confusion of English names.
**IDENTIFICATION Male breeding and non-
breeding, female, juvenile** As Pacific
subspecies, but larger and overall much darker,
both in brown colour of body and in amount of
black barring on underparts. Bill and legs both
relatively longer. Apparently constant orange-
yellow eye-ring present on adults of both
sexes. **Confusion risks** Almost
indistinguishable from very slightly smaller and
shorter-billed Tule Greater Whitefront, except
for orange eye-ring. As Tule subspecies,
reported to fly more steadily and less buoyantly
than Pacific Greater Whitefront. Geographical
location important in assessing likelihood of
identification. Closer in size and colouring to
Greenland Greater Whitefront, but no overlap
in range and latter has orange, not pink, bill.
DISTRIBUTION AND STATUS This subspecies
named only in 1975, and difficulty of
identification, as well as some (continuing)
dispute about validity of subspecies, has made
determination of range and status problematic.

Breeding apparently restricted to south-west
Alaska, within taiga zone, and wintering
grounds thought to lie exclusively within
Sacramento Valley of California. Thus occupies
breeding and wintering ranges geographically
isolated from those of Tule Greater
Whitefront, this fact, among others, being used
as justification for separate subspecies status.
Habitat similar to that of Tule Greater
Whitefront. Population not properly known,
but perhaps 1,500 individuals. Uncertainty as to
exact range and status creates difficulty in
assessing threats, whether through shooting or
from habitat loss, especially as large numbers of
Pacific Greater Whitefronts winter in same
area, and impossible for shooters to distinguish
their quarry.

Greenland Greater White-fronted Goose

Anser albifrons flavirostris L 70-80 cm (28-31 in),
WS 140-165 cm (55-65 in)
Slightly larger, and obviously darker, than
European Greater Whitefront, only subspecies
with which it overlaps in wintering range.
**IDENTIFICATION Male breeding and non-
breeding** As European subspecies, but very
slightly larger and much darker, both in brown
colour of body and through greater amount of
black barring on underparts. Underparts
sometimes almost completely black, though
considerable individual variation. White of
forehead generally smaller, extending less far
towards crown, and more obviously bordered
blackish-brown. Whitish edgings to back and
wing feathers narrower, enhancing darker
effect, both on closed wing and on bird in flight,
when little or no contrast between coverts and
flight feathers. Noticeably longer bill orange-
yellow, tinged pink towards tip, which has
white nail. Legs and feet orange, as European
subspecies. **Female** Female sometimes stated
to be same size as male, but within a pair
always smaller, even if only very slightly so.
Juvenile As European subspecies, but overall
darker and more obviously mottled on
underparts, at least for first half of winter, with
belly feathers dark brown, edged white. White
of forehead similarly gained through first
winter, but often preceded by a few dark
brown or blackish feathers. Bill much duller
orange and sometimes with dusky patches on
sides; nail dark brown to start with, becoming
white during first winter. **Confusion risks**
Distinguished from European subspecies by
longer orange-yellow bill, as well as overall
darker colouring, smaller white forehead and,
when the two together, larger size. Note that
black barring on underparts, although generally
greater in Greenland subspecies, is variable in
both subspecies and so not, by itself, reliable.
Juvenile, early in first winter, could be confused
with Bean Goose, though not so dark-headed
in comparison with neck colour, and much less
black or dark colouring on bill.
DISTRIBUTION AND STATUS Breeds west
Greenland, wintering northern and western
Scotland, Ireland and Wales. Nests beside
tundra pools and winters on marshes and

adjoining agricultural land. Population 30,000 in
1995, having increased from under 15,000 in
1982 as result of protection on wintering
grounds. Habitat loss still important threat.
Many former sites, especially in Ireland, lost in
last 40 years through drainage, afforestation
and peat extraction.

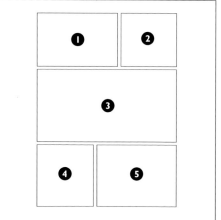

1 Tule Greater White-fronted Goose (adult)
**2 Greenland Greater White-fronted
Goose** (adults, Islay, Scotland)
**3 Greenland Greater White-fronted
Goose** (group, Wexford, Ireland)
**4 Greenland Greater White-fronted
Goose** (adult, Islay, Scotland)
5 Greenland Greater White-fronted Goose
(juvenile)

GEESE

LESSER WHITE-FRONTED GOOSE

Anser erythropus 53-66 cm (21-26 in), WS 120-135 cm (47-53 in)
Monotypic. Smallest grey goose, distinguished from Greater White-fronted by size, shape, and extent of white on forehead.
IDENTIFICATION Male breeding and non-breeding Dark brown-grey head and upper neck, slightly paler on foreneck. White forehead extends onto crown, coming to point above eye. Neck well furrowed. Upper breast paler brown, darkening below and onto belly and flanks, latter with dark feather centres and pale edgings producing fine, pale barring; white line along upper flanks showing below closed wing. Black markings on belly form irregular, and individually variable, bars and blotches. Vent and undertail-coverts white. Upperparts dark brown, pale feather edgings on mantle and wing-coverts forming neat, parallel whitish barring across closed wing; rump dark brown, uppertail-coverts white; tail blackish with white tips and outer edgings. Tips of closed wings project beyond tail of standing or swimming bird. Small, stubby bill bright pink all over, with white nail. Legs and feet orange-yellow. Eye-ring bright yellow to orange-yellow, slightly swollen and conspicuous. In flight, little or no pattern on wings, above or below, appearing dark, with forewing just a shade lighter than flight feathers. High-pitched, somewhat squeaky calls, *kyu-yu-yu*, with yelping quality. **Female** As male, but averaging very slightly smaller.
Juvenile Duller than adults, lacking white forehead until well into first winter and black belly bars until first summer, with underparts appearing lightly mottled. Bill, legs and feet duller. **Confusion risks** Although considerably smaller than very similar European Greater Whitefront, size difference not always obvious. Combination of larger extent of white on forehead, above noticeably short bill, presence of yellow or orange-yellow eye-ring and wing tips projecting beyond tail aids identification, though note that minority of European Greater Whitefronts have orange eye-ring. Also walks and feeds more rapidly than all other grey geese.
DISTRIBUTION AND STATUS Breeds northern Eurasia from extreme north of Scandinavia to Pacific coast, wintering south-east Europe, south-west Asia and China. Nests in scrub tundra and in montane areas close to water; winters steppes and agricultural lowlands. Population has declined greatly in recent decades; estimated 100,000 in 1965 probably not very reliable, but currently only 25,000-30,000 wintering in south-east Europe/south-west Asia and only 6,000 in China, and still declining in both regions. Habitat destruction and excessive shooting main causes.

GREYLAG GOOSE

Anser anser
Polytypic. Two subspecies: (1) Western Greylag Goose *A. a. anser*, breeds Iceland and north and central Europe, winters Europe within and to south of breeding range; (2) Eastern Greylag Goose *A. a. rubrirostris*, breeds Europe east to China, winters within breeding range and south to India and southern east Asia.

Western Greylag Goose

Anser anser anser L 75-85 cm (30-33 in), WS 147-175 cm (58-69 in)
Large, grey-brown goose with heavy orange-pink bill and conspicuous pale grey forewings.
IDENTIFICATION Male breeding and non-breeding Rather uniform grey-brown on head, neck, underparts and upperparts. Some birds have narrow white line around base of bill or, more usually, a few white feathers at base of upper mandible, but often none. Slightly paler on foreneck and breast, while sides and rear of neck strongly furrowed. Dark centres and pale edgings to flank feathers produce light barring effect; white line at top of flanks below edge of closed wing; vent and undertail-coverts white. Some show small black blotches on belly, but rarely forming more than very short bars. Mantle and upperwing-coverts have whitish edgings which form neat, parallel, transverse barring on closed wing; rump grey, uppertail-coverts white; tail dark grey-brown with white tips and edgings. Large, stout bill orange, with pinkish tinge behind nail and along mandible edges. Legs and feet pink or flesh-pink. In flight, upperwing-coverts pale grey or blue-grey with white tips to greater and median coverts, producing distinctive pale forewing contrasting with blackish flight feathers; underwing-coverts grey, slightly darker than on upperwing. Loud honking calls, similar to those of farmyard geese, *aahng-aang-aang*. **Female** As male, but averaging slightly smaller. **Juvenile** Similar to adults, but with more scaly, less barred, pattern on upperparts; no dark spots or blotches on belly. Bill, legs and feet duller. More adult-like by end of first winter, but any belly spots not acquired until second winter. **Confusion risks** Large and noticeably large-headed grey goose, with unique combination of stout orange bill and pink legs. In flight, pale grey forewing very conspicuous, while noisy calling also distinctive. Bulkier and proportionately larger-bodied and shorter-winged than eg Pink-footed and Bean Geese. For separation from Eastern Greylag Goose, see that subspecies.
DISTRIBUTION AND STATUS Several separate and overlapping populations: breeds Iceland, northern Britain, Scandinavia and central and south-east Europe, and winters both within this range and south into southern Europe and North Africa. Nests in marshes and beside variety of fresh waters, wintering on lowland farmland, steppes and marshes, including estuaries. Total population estimated at 350,000-400,000, with c 90,000 breeding in Iceland, 7,000 in Scotland, c 120,000 wintering in north-west Europe, 20,000 in central Europe, 25,000 in Black Sea area and 100,000 around Caspian Sea. Most populations either increasing or stable.

Eastern Greylag Goose

Anser anser rubrirostris L 78-90 cm (31-35 in), WS 155-180 cm (61-71 in)
Large, grey-brown goose with pink bill and legs and conspicuous pale grey forewings.
IDENTIFICATION Male breeding and non-breeding, female, juvenile Similar uniform grey-brown to Western Greylag, but overall paler, more grey tone, with whiter edgings to feathers which form more obvious white transverse barring on back and closed wing, while barring on flanks also stronger. Bill larger than Western Greylag's, and all pink. In flight, upperwing-coverts paler grey than Western, so contrast with blackish flight feathers more obvious. **Confusion risks** Larger and paler than Western, while pink bill distinctive. Intergrades between the two subspecies occur in eastern Europe and western Russia. Moreover, Eastern Greylags have been introduced into range of Western Greylag, eg in Belgium.
DISTRIBUTION AND STATUS Breeds from Eastern Europe and western Russia east to Mongolia, south-east Siberia and northern China; winters within southern part of central Asian breeding range, but most move south to Pakistan, India, Bangladesh, southern China and adjacent parts of south-east Asia. Habitat similar to that of Western Greylag. Population estimated at 15,000 wintering in Indian subcontinent and up to 100,000 in China and south-east Asia.

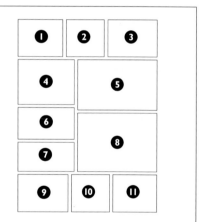

1 **Lesser White-fronted Goose** (flock, some from re-introduction scheme, Friesland, Netherlands)
2 **Lesser White-fronted Goose** (adult, Friesland, Netherlands)
3 *Lesser White-fronted Goose* (adult)
4 *Lesser White-fronted Goose* (juvenile)
5 **Western Greylag Goose** (adults, Merseyside, England)
6 **Western Greylag Goose** (flight, Kent, England)
7 **Western Greylag Goose** (adult plus two immatures, Flevoland, Netherlands)
8 **Western Greylag Goose** (adult, Lancashire, England)
9 **Eastern Greylag Goose** (flock, India)
10 **Eastern Greylag Goose** (adults in flight, Bharatpur, India)
11 **Eastern Greylag Goose** (group in flight, India)

GEESE

SNOW GOOSE

Anser caerulescens
Polytypic. Two subspecies: (1) Lesser Snow Goose *A. c. caerulescens*, breeds north-east Siberia, Alaska and arctic Canada, winters western and southern USA and Mexico; (2) Greater Snow Goose *A. c. atlanticus*, breeds eastern arctic Canada and Greenland, winters Atlantic coast of USA.

Lesser Snow Goose

Anser caerulescens caerulescens L 66-76 cm (26-30 in), WS 132-155 cm (52-61 in)
Medium-sized white, or grey-blue and white, goose with black outer wings, considerably larger than Ross's Goose.
IDENTIFICATION Male breeding and non-breeding Two colour phases, white and blue; also intermediates. *White phase:* All white except for wings, which have grey primary coverts and black primaries and so show striking contrast in flight, while black primaries show above white tail on standing or swimming bird. *Blue phase:* Head and upper neck white; lower neck very dark grey, with streaks reaching variably into upper neck, more frequently on hindneck. Underparts also very dark grey, though often becoming paler to whitish in centre of lower belly, while vent and undertail-coverts usually greyish to whitish, but sometimes dark grey. Upperparts as underparts, but paler grey on rump, and uppertail-coverts grey-white. Tail dark grey, edged white, but sometimes whitish all over. Inner secondaries and tertials strongly edged white and elongated, so droop from closed wing over rear flanks. In flight, upperwing-coverts dark blue-grey, producing some contrast with black primaries; underwing-coverts paler grey, with white axillaries. *Intermediates:* Presumed hybrids between white and blue phases show varying amounts of white on body, especially white underparts except for upper flanks and sides of chest. *Both phases:* White of head and upper neck can be stained orange from iron-rich water. Bill deep pink to crimson, with black cutting edges to mandibles which, with curvature of upper mandible edge, produce so-called grinning-patch. Legs and feet deep pink. Variety of loud cackling and honking calls. **Female** *Both phases:* As male, but slightly smaller. **Juvenile** *White phase:* Very pale grey above, darker on head and neck, and whitish below; upperwing-coverts tinged brownish and flight feathers dark brown. *Blue phase:* Duller grey-brown than adult, this colour including head and neck; tertials not elongated. *Both phases:* Bill, legs and feet grey. Plumage and bare parts gradually become adult-like in first winter. **Confusion risks** For separation of white phase from Greater Snow Goose and Ross's Goose, see those (below). Blue phase not unlike Emperor Goose, especially at distance, but latter has white restricted to head and back of neck, with black throat and foreneck, and overall colour grey, not grey-brown; also much dumpier in shape, with shorter bill and legs.
DISTRIBUTION AND STATUS Breeds Wrangel Island (north-east Siberia), Alaska, and arctic Canada east to Baffin Island and south to James Bay, wintering on west and Gulf coasts of USA and Mexico; formerly wintered (and small numbers probably still do so) in China and Japan. Nests on arctic tundra and marshes; winters on marshes and agricultural land, usually near coasts. Population greatly increased in recent decades, to just over 2 million, with principal breeding area around Hudson Bay. Numbers on Wrangel Island declined in recent years, through disturbance and predation.

Greater Snow Goose

Anser caerulescens atlanticus L 73-84 cm (29-33 in), WS 140-165 cm (55-65 in)
Large white goose with black wings.
IDENTIFICATION Male breeding and non-breeding, female, juvenile As white-phase Lesser Snow Goose, only differences being larger size and heavier bill, which has much more obvious grinning-patch. White of head and neck may similarly be stained orange from iron-rich water. Some hybridization between Lesser and Greater Snow Geese may occur, producing birds intermediate in size, and also giving rise to rare reports of blue-phase Greater Snow Geese, which not known to exist. **Confusion risks** Difficult to separate in the field from white phase of Lesser Snow Goose, though larger in all measurements and with noticeably larger head and deeper and longer bill. Grinning-patch of Greater Snow Goose much more obvious than on Lesser Snow Goose, on which often not particularly apparent.
DISTRIBUTION AND STATUS Breeds islands of north-east Canada and in north-west Greenland, wintering on Atlantic seaboard of USA. Habitat generally as Lesser Snow Goose. Population has increased enormously, from 42,000 in 1958 to present 350,000, achieved through protection at migration stop-overs and on wintering grounds coupled with adaptation to new foods on agricultural land.

ROSS'S GOOSE

Anser rossii L 54-66 cm (21-26 in), WS 120-135 cm (47-53 in)
Monotypic. Tiny all-white goose with black wing tips.
IDENTIFICATION Male breeding and non-breeding As white-phase Lesser Snow Goose in all plumage respects, but much smaller, shorter-necked, shorter-legged bird with more rounded body. Bill very short and stubby, deep pinky-red, usually with scarlet-orange area in centre of upper mandible, and with variable area of caruncles (warts) covering base on either side and, just, joined over top (extent of warts, which can be very slight or even absent, apparently increases with age); colour of warts usually bluish-grey or greenish, but sometimes purplish. Calls similar to those of Lesser Snow Goose, but higher-pitched. Very rare blue phase has been reported, but personal inspection of skins suggests likelihood that these are hybrids with blue-phase Lesser Snow Geese. **Female** As male, but smaller; sometimes (but not, as often reported, invariably) lacks warts at base of bill. **Juvenile** As white-phase Lesser Snow Goose, but paler, less obviously grey-brown. Bill, legs and feet grey-green. Gains adult-like features during first winter, but rarely any warts. **Confusion risks** Small size, especially of head and bill, but also short neck and rounder body, distinguish this from white-phase Lesser Snow Goose. Walks and feeds at faster rate than Lesser Snow and also more agile in flight, with faster wingbeats.
DISTRIBUTION AND STATUS Breeds mainly Perry River region of arctic Canada, but also around Hudson Bay; winters California south to northern Mexico, including Gulf coast. Habitat broadly as that of Lesser Snow Goose. Population probably never as low as few thousand reported in 1940s; better identification and censuses revealed 30,000 in mid-1960s, while increase to 77,000 in 1976 and to 160,000 by 1992.

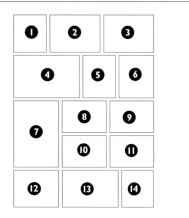

1 **Lesser Snow Goose** (adult in flight, New Mexico, USA)
2 **Lesser Snow Goose** ("blue phase", New Mexico, USA)
3 **Lesser Snow Goose** ("blue phase" in flight, New Mexico, USA)
4 **Lesser Snow Goose** (flock in flight, New Mexico, USA)
5 **Lesser Snow Goose** (adult, New Mexico, USA)
6 **Greater Snow Goose** (juvenile, New York State, USA)
7 **Greater Snow Goose** (adult, USA)
8 **Greater Snow Goose** (adult with Pink-footed Geese, Lancashire, England)
9 **Greater Snow Goose** (adults plus first winters, Quebec, Canada)
10 **Greater Snow Goose** (adults plus first winters, Quebec, Canada)
11 **Ross's Goose** (flock with Snow Geese, USA)
12 **Ross's Goose** (flight, Rottumeroog, Netherlands)
13 **Ross's Goose** (two adults, Rottumeroog, Netherlands)
14 **Ross's Goose** (adult with Greylag Goose, Lossiemouth, Scotland)

GEESE

BAR-HEADED GOOSE

Anser indicus L 71-76 cm (28-30 in), WS 140-155 cm (55-61 in)
Monotypic. Large, overall grey goose with striking black-and-white pattern on head and neck; no confusable species within or outside range, except perhaps in case of juveniles.
IDENTIFICATION Male breeding and non-breeding Head, throat and very top of neck white, with broad black stripe over top of head, running from eye to eye, and second, narrower, black stripe parallel and to rear of this. Foreneck dark grey, separated from blackish hindneck by white stripe running down sides of neck and slightly tapering towards bottom. Breast, belly and flanks pale grey, darker on rear flanks, with pale feather edgings producing lightly barred effect, most obvious on darker parts of flanks; vent and undertail-coverts white. Upperparts medium grey, with broad whitish feather edgings producing neat transverse barring across mantle and closed wings; uppertail-coverts white, tail dark grey with white edgings. Bill yellow-orange, tinged pink behind black nail. Legs and feet yellow-orange. In flight, upperwing-coverts pale grey to grey, showing some contrast with dark grey flight feathers; underwing similar. Nasal honking calls. **Female** As male, but slightly smaller. **Juvenile** As adult, but duller overall. Crown and hindneck grey-brown, with whitish forehead and brownish stripe from eye to base of bill; lacks black stripes over head. Bill, legs and feet duller yellow than adult. Becomes as adult during first winter. **Confusion risks** Patterned head of adult distinguishes it from all other geese. Juvenile not unlike juvenile Lesser or Greater Snow Goose, but has yellow or yellowish bill and legs and more uniform pale grey upperparts and underparts.
DISTRIBUTION AND STATUS Breeds central Asia, mainly Mongolia, western China and Kazakhstan, possibly also Uzbekistan and Kirghizstan, though breeding range much reduced from former extent and exact present limits uncertain; winters mainly northern India, and also north-east Pakistan, Bangladesh, Nepal and northern Burma, though some may remain in south-west China. Nests beside high montane lakes and other wetlands; winters in lowland marshes and by lakes and rivers. Population estimated at 50,000; has probably diminished considerably this century, but now thought to be increasing. Habitat destruction and excessive shooting probably mainly responsible for earlier range contraction and decline.

EMPEROR GOOSE

Anser canagicus L 64-71 cm (25-28 in), WS 122-145 cm (48-57 in)
Monotypic. White-headed, mainly silvery-grey goose of northern Pacific regions, where unmistakable.
IDENTIFICATION Male breeding and non-breeding White head and back of neck, though very often stained orange from iron-rich water. Chin, foreneck and sides of neck black. Rest of body, except for white tail, blue-grey to ash-grey, with all feathers having whitish tip and blackish subterminal band, producing striking scalloped or scaly effect all over. Scalloped pattern continues on ash-grey upperwing-coverts, which show moderate contrast with blackish-grey flight feathers; underwing more uniformly dark grey. Bill small, pink and with black nail, mandible edges and underside. Legs and feet bright orange-yellow. Calls a repeated *kla-ha* and *yang-yang*. **Female** As male, but very slightly smaller. **Juvenile** Sooty grey-brown all over, including head and neck, with much narrower, less obvious, scaling on feathers; tail buffish-white. Bill blackish; legs and feet dull brown to yellowish. Adult features acquired during first winter, with white on head and hindneck appearing first. **Confusion risks** With white head and overall blue-grey plumage, possibly confusable only with blue-phase Lesser Snow Goose, but that extremely rare within Emperor's range and is larger, longer-necked and longer-bodied and has pink legs. In flight, white tail to rear of evenly dark bird very distinctive, in comparison with darker tail and white uppertail-coverts of all other geese except Snow and Ross's Geese.
DISTRIBUTION AND STATUS Breeds arctic north-east Siberia, St Lawrence Island and west coast of arctic Alaska, wintering Alaska Peninsula, Aleutian Islands and Kamchatka. Nests in wet arctic tundra and winters along rocky coasts and in tidal lagoons. Population estimated at 165,000, of which perhaps 12,000 in Russia; undergoes major fluctuations, which poorly understood.

HAWAIIAN GOOSE

Branta sandvicensis L 56-71 cm (22-28 in), WS 120-140 cm (47-55 in)
Monotypic. Only goose within restricted range. Unique combination of black crown, buff cheeks and heavily furrowed neck.
IDENTIFICATION Male breeding and non-breeding Crown, hindneck, cheeks between bill and eye, and chin blackish-brown; rear cheeks tawny-buff. Neck, except to rear, pale buff, but deep furrowing shows darker bases to feathers to produce diagonal striped effect. Thin blackish line at base of neck separates it from pale brown breast, grading to darker grey-brown of belly and flanks, the latter with striped appearance from darker brown centres to feathers and paler edges; vent and undertail-coverts white. Upperparts dark brown with broad pale edgings, these forming parallel barring across mantle and coverts of closed wing; rump and tail black; uppertail-coverts white. Bill, legs and feet black; toes only partly webbed. Apart from pale edgings to upperwing-coverts, entire wing dark brown above and below and showing almost no pattern in flight. **Female** As male, but slightly smaller. **Juvenile** As adults, but duller brown and with less demarcation between colours of head and neck. Less obvious feather edgings to body so that striped and barred effect much reduced, especially on closed wing, where irregular scaly pattern. Bill, legs and feet as adult. **Confusion risks** Within restricted range in Hawaii, the only goose apart from very occasional vagrants, and therefore unmistakable. Widespread in captivity, but (presumed ancestral) Canada Goose, only other largely dark brown goose, always has white chin-strap.
DISTRIBUTION AND STATUS Confined as resident to Hawaiian Islands, where breeds on islands of Hawaii, Maui and Kauai; reintroduced on latter two. Occurs on upland lava slopes and, where available, grasslands; water not essential. Formerly abundant, but reduced by hunting and introduced predators to no more than 30 by 1952. Population increased by captive-breeding followed by reintroductions, though latter not very successful and, despite over 2,000 released since 1960, total population probably no more than 500 and thought to be declining.

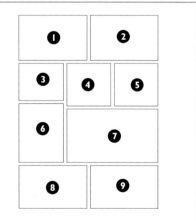

1 **Bar-headed Goose** (group, Bharatpur, India)
2 **Bar-headed Goose** (flock in flight, Bharatpur, India)
3 **Bar-headed Goose** (adults, Bharatpur, India)
4 *Emperor Goose* (adult)
5 *Emperor Goose* (juvenile)
6 *Emperor Goose* (adult, head close-up)
7 **Hawaiian Goose** (adults plus juvenile, Maui, Hawaiian Islands)
8 **Hawaiian Goose** (adult, Maui, Hawaiian Islands)
9 **Hawaiian Goose** (adults, Maui, Hawaiian Islands)

GEESE

CANADA GOOSE

Branta canadensis
Polytypic. Total of 11 subspecies recognized here, though taxonomy under review and identification made harder by considerable intergrading: (1) Atlantic Canada Goose *B. c. canadensis*, breeds eastern North America, winters eastern USA, also introduced Europe and New Zealand; (2) Giant Canada Goose *B. c. maxima*, breeds eastern USA, wintering within range and to south; (3) Central (or Todd's) Canada Goose *B. c. interior*, breeds eastern Canada, winters eastern and south-eastern USA; (4) Taverner's Canada Goose *B. c. taverneri*, breeds Alaska and north-west Canada, winters north-west USA; (5) Vancouver (or Western) Canada Goose *B. c. fulva*, breeds southern Alaska and British Columbia, wintering within and to south of breeding range; (6) Dusky Canada Goose *B. c. occidentalis*, breeds coastal Alaska, wintering south to British Columbia and Oregon; (7) Aleutian Canada Goose *B. c. leucopareia*, breeds Aleutian Islands, winters California; (8) Cackling Canada Goose *B. c. minima*, breeds western Alaska, winters California; (9) Richardson's Canada Goose *B. c. hutchinsii*, breeds arctic Canada and west Greenland, winters Louisiana and Gulf coast of Mexico; (10) Great Basin (or Moffitt's) Canada Goose *B. c. moffitti*, breeds western Great Plains of USA and southern prairies of western Canada, wintering south to southern and south-western USA; (11) Lesser Canada Goose *B. c. parvipes*, breeds central Alaska and east Canada, winters Oregon, California, New Mexico, northern Mexico and southern Mississippi River.

Atlantic Canada Goose

Branta canadensis canadensis L 90-100 cm (35-39 in), WS 160-175 cm (63-69 in)
Large brown goose with black neck and white patch on cheeks running under chin.
IDENTIFICATION Male breeding and non-breeding Head and whole of long neck black, with very broad white band extending from cheek, behind eye, across chin to other cheek. Breast close to base of black neck very pale buff, darkening to buff-brown on belly and flanks, latter with paler feather edgings producing very faint barring; vent and undertail-coverts white. Upperparts darker brown than underparts, with pale buff to whitish feather edgings forming very faint, even, transverse barring across mantle and wing-coverts of closed wing; centre of back and rump very dark brown; uppertail-coverts white; tail black. Bill, legs and feet black. Pale-edged wing-coverts differ only slightly from blackish-brown flight feathers, and both upperwings and underwings appear fairly uniform dark brown on flying bird. Loud honking calls, with rolling *ronk-ronk* notes. **Female** As male, but slightly smaller. **Juvenile** As adults, but slightly duller and with less contrast between head and neck, which brownish-black, and face patch, which tinged pale brown. Pale feather edgings on upperparts

less clear and forming irregular scales rather than transverse lines. Becomes as adult early in first winter. **Confusion risks** For separation from other subspecies (where possible), see those (below). Only possible confusion with Barnacle Goose, but this much smaller than present subspecies, overall black, grey and white, not black, brown and white, and with white face to base of bill, not restricted white chin-strap.
DISTRIBUTION AND STATUS Breeds south-eastern Canada, principally Newfoundland and Labrador, and north-eastern USA, and winters Atlantic coast of USA. Also introduced and well established in Britain, Sweden and New Zealand (where mixed with Giant Canada Goose and Taverner's Canada Goose), though see below under Great Basin Canada Goose. Nests in marshes, and by lakes and rivers, wintering on lowland agricultural land. North American population over 650,000 in 1992; British population over 60,000; New Zealand population over 40,000.

Giant Canada Goose

Branta canadensis maxima L 90-110 cm (35-43 in), WS 170-185 cm (67-73 in)
Very large Canada Goose, often with more white on head than other races.
IDENTIFICATION Male breeding and non-breeding, female, juvenile As Atlantic Canada Goose, but larger overall, with proportionately longer neck. Some birds show small rearward-pointing extensions at top of white on cheeks. White spotting on forehead comparatively common and, at extreme development, may form broken band across face. **Confusion risks** Typical Giant Canada Goose is the largest subspecies, with noticeably long, thin neck, though overlap in size with, especially, Atlantic Canada, which is also of similar colour, generally pale on underparts. The rearward-pointing extension to the white face patch is probably diagnostic on a particularly large bird, but cannot be wholly relied upon. Considerable intergrading with Great Basin Canada Goose, especially in western part of breeding range.
DISTRIBUTION AND STATUS Breeds mainly in eastern Great Plains area of USA, though exact distribution imprecise because of confusion with other races, especially Great Basin Canada Goose; mainly resident in southern part of breeding range, and also winters to south, reaching Gulf coast. Nests beside wide variety of fresh waters and has, additionally, penetrated into urban areas and colonized parks and river banks in many towns and cities. Population thought to be in excess of 500,000. Birds of this subspecies introduced into New Zealand in 19th century and subsequently, and also, very probably, into Britain (in addition to Atlantic Canada Geese and, possibly, Great Basin Canada Geese).

Central (or Todd's) Canada Goose

Branta canadensis interior L 80-95 cm (31-38 in), WS 155-175 cm (61-69 in)

Medium-sized to large Canada Goose, rather darker than either Atlantic or Giant subspecies.
IDENTIFICATION Male breeding and non-breeding, female, juvenile As Atlantic Canada Goose, but slightly smaller, and overall darker on both upperparts and underparts (darker tone arises from narrower pale feather edgings, as well as from darker feathers themselves). Pale on breast at base of black collar restricted or absent. Bill a little narrower and shorter. **Confusion risks** In eastern North America, this subspecies slightly smaller and darker than other common ones, *eg* Atlantic and Giant Canada Geese.
DISTRIBUTION AND STATUS Breeds northern Manitoba, Ontario and Quebec north to coasts of Hudson Bay, and winters mainly in Mississippi basin. Nests on tundra marshes and by lakes and pools, wintering mainly on lowland marshes and agricultural land. Population in excess of 750,000.

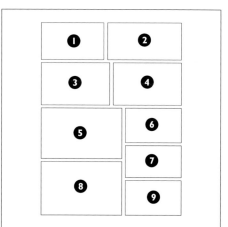

1 **Atlantic Canada Goose** (adult, Merseyside, England)
2 **Atlantic Canada Goose** (flock in flight, Midlands, England)
3 **Atlantic Canada Goose** (adult mating with "blue phase" Snow Goose, Merseyside, England)
4 **Atlantic Canada Goose** (flock in flight, Lancashire, England)
5 *Giant Canada Goose* *(adult)*
6 **Central (or Todd's) Canada Goose** (adults, Long Point, Canada)
7 **Central (or Todd's) Canada Goose** (adults and young, Long Point, Canada)
8 **Central (or Todd's) Canada Goose** (adult and young, Manitoba, Canada)
9 **Central (or Todd's) Canada Goose** (adult, Long Point, Canada)

GEESE

Taverner's Canada Goose

Branta canadensis taverneri L 75-85 cm (30-33 in), WS 155-170 cm (61-67 in)
Medium-sized, relatively dark Canada Goose of western North America.

IDENTIFICATION Male breeding and non-breeding, female, juvenile Smaller and darker overall than Atlantic Canada Goose and slightly smaller than Central Canada Goose, with dusky brown underparts with, on some birds, a narrow or incomplete white ring at base of black neck. Reported to be quite variable, some birds showing much paler underparts. These latter may be a result of intergrading with Lesser Canada Goose.
Confusion risks Difficult to distinguish from some Lesser Canada Geese, though that subspecies averages overall paler. Within western USA range, however, distinct from much larger dark-toned subspecies, Dusky Canada Goose and Vancouver Canada Goose, and also larger itself than very small and dark Cackling Canada Goose.
DISTRIBUTION AND STATUS Breeds in interior of Alaska and into adjacent areas of north-western Canada, wintering mainly in Washington and Oregon in north-west USA. Nests on marshes and pools among scrub tundra and taiga. Population estimated at 70,000 birds and thought to be increasing.

Vancouver Canada Goose

Branta canadensis fulva L 90-100 cm (35-39 in), WS 160-175 cm (63-69 in)
Similar in size to Atlantic Canada Goose, but much darker overall. Slightly larger than equally dark Dusky Canada Goose, also of western North America, but see that subspecies for comment on taxonomic separation.

IDENTIFICATION Male breeding and non-breeding, female, juvenile Of similar size to Atlantic Canada Goose, but much darker in general colouring, being dark chocolate-brown in tone on both upperparts and underparts, tending to rufous-brown on the underparts and flanks, but still very lightly barred from the paler feather edgings. Sometimes paler at base of neck, but may show rather little differentiation between black neck and dark breast. **Confusion risks** Very similar to Dusky Canada Goose, but rather larger and rarely, if ever, has white at base of black neck.
DISTRIBUTION AND STATUS Breeds southern Alaska north to about Glacier Bay, and south throughout coastal region and islands of British Columbia; birds from south of breeding range largely sedentary, but more northerly breeders move south into British Columbia and may go on through Washington and Oregon into northern California. Largely coastal throughout breeding range, and often on or close to saltwater habitat in winter, too, using coastal marshes and adjoining agricultural land. Population *c* 80,000 and increasing.

Dusky (or Western) Canada Goose

Branta canadensis occidentalis L 75-85 cm (30-33 in), WS 155-170 cm (61-67 in)
Medium-large and very dark Canada Goose. Sometimes regarded as forming single subspecies with Vancouver Canada Goose, which breeds to south.

IDENTIFICATION Male breeding and non-breeding, female, juvenile Very similar in colouring to Vancouver Canada Goose, but slightly smaller, though some authorities consider that there is a cline of increasing size from south to north and that these two subspecies should be considered as one. Some birds have narrow white ring, or some white feathers, at base of neck; this suggested as not being found on Vancouver Canada Goose.
Confusion risks Very similar to Vancouver Canada Goose, but slightly smaller and sometimes with white at base of black neck.
DISTRIBUTION AND STATUS Breeds coastal Alaska from Glacier Bay northwards to Cook Inlet and short distances inland; winters south into British Columbia, Washington and Oregon, thus overlapping with Vancouver Canada Goose. Habitat similar to that of Vancouver Canada Goose, though more northerly breeders nest in scrub and taiga zone. Population only 17,000, having more than halved in last 15-20 years, though now increasing. Formerly shot heavily on wintering grounds when mixing with other, more abundant, subspecies, but now controlled.

Aleutian Canada Goose

Branta canadensis leucopareia L 60-68 cm (24-27 in), WS 122-130 cm (48-51 in)
Very small, fairly dark Canada Goose, most with obvious white ring at base of black neck.

IDENTIFICATION Male breeding and non-breeding, female, juvenile Similar in general pattern to other subspecies, but very small (only smaller race is Cackling Canada Goose, see below), and usually distinguished by presence of white ring at base of neck which is normally broader in front than behind and occasionally incomplete behind. Majority of birds have white neck ring, but this can be absent. The white under the throat is often interrupted by a stripe, complete or partial, along middle of chin. The bill is quite short and steeply angled. Overall body plumage is quite dark, though not so uniformly dark as Cackling Canada Goose. Underparts slightly lighter than upperparts, but upper breast darkens towards base of neck. Although obviously small in size, appears quite long-legged. **Confusion risks** Distinguished from Cackling Canada Goose only with difficulty. Latter smaller and darker, and less often with neck collar. Forehead of Aleutian Canada Goose appears steeper, and bill usually straighter and with longer nail.
DISTRIBUTION AND STATUS Formerly bred most islands of Aleutian chain, from Kodiak Island in the east, and extending also to central Kuriles in the west; winters Sacramento Valley, California. Nests on marine islands, wintering on lowland agricultural land. Introduction of foxes for fur trade reduced population to 200-300 birds, solely on Buldir Island. Since then, captive-breeding and reintroduction programmes have brought about recovery to present population of *c* 8,000 birds.

Cackling Canada Goose

Branta canadensis minima L 56-63 cm (23-25 in), WS 115-123 cm (45-48 in)
Smallest Canada Goose, also one of the darkest.

IDENTIFICATION Male breeding and non-breeding, female, juvenile Similar in pattern to other subspecies, but smallest and also generally very dark in overall tone, though shows some variability. Bill very short and stubby and, in profile, either straight or convex from base to tip. Rather long-legged and also quite long-winged for size. Variability extends to face pattern, where white may be divided under chin by black line, which sometimes broad enough to show at side, when white cheeks may also have odd black feathers intermingled. Sometimes shows scattered white feathers in black neck. White ring at base of neck sometimes present and quite broad, at other times incomplete, or absent. Colour of underparts rich chocolate-brown, closest to Vancouver and Dusky Canada Geese, but sometimes more cinnamon or buffish-brown.
Confusion risks Difficult to distinguish from Aleutian Canada Goose. Latter very slightly larger and not quite so dark, and also more frequently has white neck collar.
DISTRIBUTION AND STATUS Breeds along western coast of Alaska and winters mainly in Sacramento Valley, California. Nests on arctic tundra and winters in agricultural lowlands. Population over 100,000.

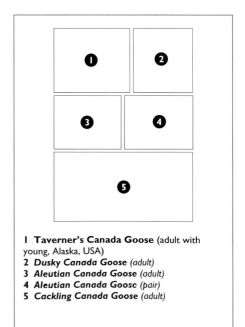

1 **Taverner's Canada Goose** (adult with young, Alaska, USA)
2 *Dusky Canada Goose* (adult)
3 *Aleutian Canada Goose* (adult)
4 *Aleutian Canada Goose* (pair)
5 *Cackling Canada Goose* (adult)

Richardson's Canada Goose

Branta canadensis hutchinsii L 60-68 cm (24-27 in), WS 122-130 cm (48-51 in)
Very small, mainly pale Canada Goose of Canadian arctic and central USA flyways.
IDENTIFICATION Male breeding and non-breeding, female, juvenile Similar in overall pattern to other subspecies, but small in size, pale in plumage, especially on breast, and with small, stubby bill. Rarely, if ever, white collar, at most a few white flecks. **Confusion risks** Some intergrading with larger Lesser Canada Goose may take place, especially around north-west Hudson Bay. Otherwise, separated from that subspecies by size and short bill. Much paler than slightly smaller Cackling Canada Goose.
DISTRIBUTION AND STATUS Breeds arctic Canadian islands and coast east to Baffin Island and, perhaps regularly, in west Greenland; winters principally Louisiana, USA, and Gulf coast of Mexico. Nests on arctic tundra, wintering on coastal marshes and agricultural land. Population over 250,000.

Great Basin (or Moffitt's) Canada Goose

Branta canadensis moffitti L 90-100 cm (35-39 in), WS 160-175 cm (63-69 in)
Large, generally pale Canada Goose, some with white collar at base of neck.
IDENTIFICATION Male breeding and non-breeding, female, juvenile Very similar to both Atlantic and Giant Canada Geese, and sometimes includes latter subspecies. Large and with overall pale plumage, tending almost to whitish on breast and sometimes with white collar at base of black neck, which may be quite broad, but usually incomplete at rear. Occasionally some white feathering on forehead. **Confusion risks** Difficult to distinguish from Atlantic Canada Goose, except that ranges do not overlap, and from Giant, with which thought to intergrade in east of range. May also intergrade with Lesser Canada Goose to north.
DISTRIBUTION AND STATUS Breeds mainly western Great Plains of USA and into southern prairie region of western Canada; winters within southern part of breeding range and south to southern and south-western USA. Habitat similar to that of Giant Canada Goose. Population between 300,000 and 400,000.

Lesser Canada Goose

Branta canadensis parvipes L 75-85 cm (30-33 in), WS 150-170 cm (59-67 in)
Medium-small Canada Goose, mostly pale, and breeding in both tundra and taiga zones.
IDENTIFICATION Male breeding and non-breeding, female, juvenile Smaller version of Central Canada Goose with mainly pale underparts, but can be more dusky brown towards west of range, though never as dark as similar-sized Taverner's Canada Goose. Bill quite short, but not particularly deep and therefore not stubby. An incomplete and usually narrow white ring present at base of

neck on a small proportion of birds.
Confusion risks Intergrades with most subspecies with which its breeding range adjoins or overlaps: with smaller Richardson's Canada Goose in extreme east of range and possibly with Taverner's Canada Goose in extreme west, and with Great Basin Canada Goose in south-west and Giant Canada Goose in south-east. Typical individuals told by medium-small size and overall pale colouring.
DISTRIBUTION AND STATUS Breeds from central Alaska east through northern Canada to north-west Hudson Bay, and south through Canadian prairie provinces; winters in Oregon and California, New Mexico, northern Mexico and along southern stretches of Mississippi River. Nests in tundra and taiga habitats, and winters principally on agricultural land and marshes. Population *c* 600,000.

BARNACLE GOOSE

Branta leucopsis L 58-70 cm (23-28 in), WS 132-145 cm (52-57 in)
Monotypic. Small black, grey and white goose, unique in range; only possible confusion with extralimital small subspecies of Canada Goose.
IDENTIFICATION Male breeding and non-breeding White or creamy-white face, forehead, chin and throat, with black crown, nape, neck and chest. Small and variable amount of black from eye to base of bill, occasionally extending back to join black of crown and sometimes with black forehead. Belly silver-grey, becoming greyer on flanks, where feathers have darker grey centres producing light barring effect; vent and undertail-coverts white. Upperparts blackish, or very dark grey, mantle and wing-coverts having broad black subterminal bars and fine white tips, though latter sometimes very small or even absent. Thus closed wing normally has fine white and broad black transverse barring, but sometimes just black. Rump and tail black, but uppertail-coverts white. Bill, legs and feet black. In flight, grey upperwing-coverts only slightly differentiated from blackish flight feathers; underwing paler grey on coverts. High-pitched barking and yelping notes uttered more or less continuously in flight and on ground. **Female** As male, but very slightly smaller. **Juvenile** As adults, but duller and browner, especially on underparts, with chest dull black, not glossy, and belly sometimes mottled; upperwing-covert borders narrow black and brown, and lacking any obvious barring effect. Becomes as adult in first winter, though a few juvenile wing-coverts retained until first summer. **Confusion risks** Small size and black, grey and white pattern rule out all other geese within north-west European range except vagrant small subspecies of Canada Goose, which, however, are black, brown and white.
DISTRIBUTION AND STATUS Three discrete populations: (1) breeding east Greenland, wintering northern and western Scotland and western Ireland; (2) breeding Svalbard,

wintering Solway Firth between Scotland and England; (3) breeding north-west Siberia, with offshoot on Baltic islands off Sweden, and wintering Netherlands. Nests on tundra, small islands in lakes or sea, and on cliff ledges; winters on agricultural land and small offshore islands. Numbers of all three populations have increased greatly in recent decades. East Greenland population *c* 45,000, compared with 14,000 in 1960s; Svalbard population 19,000, against 400 in 1945; Russian-Swedish population 230,000, yet only 25,000 in 1960s. Increases brought about through protection and through birds' adaptation to feeding on improved pastures, where they can, however, cause agricultural damage. Moreover, Russian-Swedish population received enormous boost from establishment, in early 1970s, of breeding colonies on islands in the Baltic. These Baltic-island birds able to breed earlier and much more successfully than those in arctic Russia, and have contributed disproportionately to total population increase.

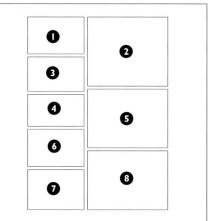

1 *Richardson's Canada Goose* (adult)
2 **Lesser Canada Goose** (adult, Lancashire, England)
3 *Great Basin (or Moffitt's) Canada Goose* (adult)
4 **Lesser Canada Goose** (adult, Lancashire, England)
5 **Barnacle Goose** (feeding flock, Caerlaverock, Scotland)
6 **Barnacle Goose** (flock in flight, Caerlaverock, Scotland)
7 **Barnacle Goose** (two in flight, Caerlaverock, Scotland)
8 **Barnacle Goose** (group, adults plus juveniles, Caerlaverock, Scotland)

GEESE

BRENT GOOSE

Branta bernicla
Polytypic. Three subspecies recognized here (birds breeding north-east Siberia sometimes separated as fourth subspecies, *B. b. orientalis*, but included here within *B. b. nigricans*): (1) Dark-bellied Brent Goose *B. b. bernicla*, breeds north-central Siberia, winters western Europe; (2) Light-bellied Brent Goose *B. b. hrota*, breeds north-east Canada, Greenland, Svalbard and Franz Josef Land, winters east coast of USA and western Europe; (3) Black Brant *B. b. nigricans*, breeds north-east Siberia and arctic North America, winters east Asia and western USA and Mexico. Some intergradation between *bernicla* and *nigricans*, and *nigricans* and *hrota*.

Dark-bellied Brent Goose

Branta bernicla bernicla L 56-61 cm (20-24 in), WS 110-120 cm (43-47 in)
Very small, very dark goose, mainly black and dark brown with some white. Distinct from all other geese, though confusion possible with other subspecies.
IDENTIFICATION Male breeding and non-breeding Head, neck and breast black, except for a small, somewhat variable and irregular, white or whitish patch on side of neck, near top. Underparts and flanks very dark slate-grey to very dark grey-brown, with limited differentiation from black of breast; lower belly and flanks with variable paler edgings producing light barring, especially towards rear; vent and undertail-coverts white. All upperparts very dark grey-brown, with very small and ill-defined paler edgings. Unlike adults of all other goose species, no pale parallel barring on mantle and closed wing. Uppertail-coverts white; very short tail black. Very small bill, legs and feet black. In flight, both upperwings and underwings appear all black. Calls not very loud, but uttered frequently in flight and on ground, mainly rolling *rrott-rrott* or *rronk-rronk*.
Female As male, but very slightly smaller.
Juvenile As adults, but duller and browner on black and dark grey areas. Flanks lack pale barring of adult and more uniformly dark brownish-black. White neck patch absent, but feathers of upperparts with whitish edgings producing light transverse barring on mantle and closed wing (of type normally seen on adults of other goose species). White neck patch acquired during first winter, while pale edgings to upperparts retained until first summer. **Confusion risks** Apart from overall very dark colour, its very small size, proportionately very small head and bill, short neck and short legs distinguish this from other geese. Also very fast, agile flier, often in dense packs undertaking aerial manoeuvres. In winter, rarely far from coastal habitats. Told from Light-bellied Brent Goose by much darker underparts, and from Black Brant by absence of whitish upper flanks and by restricted white neck patches which do not meet at front. Underpart colour and amount of barring on flanks quite variable, however, and some paler

individuals close to Light-bellied Brent. Also, intergrades with Black Brant occur in east of breeding range and these may cause difficulty.
DISTRIBUTION AND STATUS Breeds arctic north-central Siberia, principally Taymyr Peninsula, but west to Yamal; winters western Europe from Denmark to France and including southern England and Wales. Nests in wet areas of arctic tundra, in marshes and among pools; winters on coasts, feeding on adjacent agricultural land. Population has increased greatly in last 50 years, from c 20,000 in early 1960s to 250,000-300,000 in early 1990s.

Light-bellied Brent Goose

Branta bernicla hrota L 56-61 cm (20-24 in), WS 110-120 cm (43-47 in)
Very small goose with very dark upperparts and breast and much paler greyish underparts.
IDENTIFICATION Male breeding and non-breeding, female Essentially as Dark-bellied Brent in size and shape, with head, neck and breast black and with similar white neck patches. Underparts much paler grey-brown than Dark-bellied Brent, tending to silvery-grey in centre of belly; obvious demarcation between black breast and paler upper belly. Darker grey-brown barring apparent on belly and flanks, becoming more obvious to rear, but reduced in fresh plumage and showing considerable individual variation. Upperparts usually appearing browner, less grey, though still very dark. **Juvenile** As Dark-bellied Brent, with similar lack of neck patches until well into first winter, and presence of pale barring on mantle and wing-coverts. Underparts fairly uniform pale grey-brown. **Confusion risks** From other geese, as for Dark-bellied Brent; from latter, see above. From Black Brant by all-whitish flanks and underparts, instead of whitish restricted to flanks, and by neck patches not joining at front. Note that intergrades with Black Brant are relatively frequent and have varyingly larger amounts of whitish on flanks, sometimes extending to belly, while neck patches may become quite large and even join at front.
DISTRIBUTION AND STATUS Three separate populations: (1) breeds arctic Canada, winters Atlantic coast of USA; (2) breeds eastern arctic Canada, east of about Perry River, and northern Greenland, wintering Ireland; (3) breeds Svalbard, winters Denmark and north-east England. Habitat as Dark-bellied Brent, though with less use of agricultural land. Population wintering Atlantic coast of USA currently 110,000. Breeding failures, winter weather and heavy shooting all adverse factors. Population wintering Ireland has increased from c 8,000 in mid-1960s to 20,000 in early 1990s, mainly due to protection from shooting. Svalbard-breeding population declined from 4,000-5,000 in 1950s to 2,500 in 1970s, but recovered to current 5,000-6,000.

Black Brant

Branta bernicla nigricans L 56-61 cm (20-24 in), WS 110-120 cm (43-47 in)
Very small, very dark goose, with contrasting

whitish on lower flanks, and whitish neck patches joined at front.
IDENTIFICATION Male breeding and non-breeding, female, juvenile As Dark-bellied Brent Goose, though tendency to be browner above and below. White patches on neck deeper than either Dark-bellied or Light-bellied, though variable, and almost always join at front, where normally deepest. Underparts very dark but with contrasting white or whitish flanks, with some blackish barring, especially towards rear. Adults in worn plumage, mainly in spring, often show many brownish feathers on underparts, appearing paler but also somewhat mottled. **Confusion risks** For other geese, see under Dark-bellied Brent; for Dark-bellied and Light-bellied Brent, see those. Note that intergrades occur with both other subspecies.
DISTRIBUTION AND STATUS Two apparently separate populations: (1) breeds north and north-east Siberia from eastern Taymyr Peninsula eastwards to about Anadyr basin, winters Kamchatka, Japan, north-east China and perhaps Korea; (2) breeds north-east Siberia from approximately Anadyr basin east to Bering Strait and in arctic North America from Alaska to about Perry River region, wintering western USA and Mexico. Habitat as Dark-bellied Brent, though with less use of agricultural land. Population wintering in east Asia 5,000-7,000; that wintering USA and Mexico c 185,000, and stable or increasing.

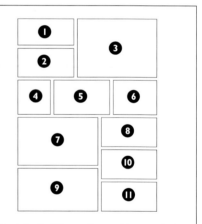

1 **Dark-bellied Brent Goose** (first year birds in flight, Kent, England)
2 **Dark-bellied Brent Goose** (flock of adults, Hampshire, England)
3 **Dark-bellied Brent Goose** (first year, Kent, England)
4 **Dark-bellied Brent Goose** (adult in flight, Sweden)
5 **Light-bellied Brent Goose** (flock of adults, Dublin, Ireland)
6 **Light-bellied Brent Goose** (adult, New York, USA)
7 **Light-bellied Brent Goose** (first year birds, Forsythe Refuge, USA)
8 **Light-bellied Brent Goose** (flight, Forsythe Refuge, USA)
9 **Black Brant** (adult, with dark-bellied adults, Terschelling, Netherlands)
10 **Black Brant** (adult with goslings, Canada)
11 **Black Brant** (adults, Canada)

49

GEESE

RED-BREASTED GOOSE

Branta ruficollis L 53-56 cm (21-22 in), WS 116-135 cm (46-53 in)

Monotypic. Very small, short-necked goose, boldly patterned in black, white and chestnut-red, unlike any other goose.

IDENTIFICATION Male breeding and non-breeding Forehead, crown, back of neck, forecheeks and throat black. Roundish white patch in front of eye; much larger chestnut-red patch on sides of head, with variable white border, wider towards top. Lower foreneck and breast deep chestnut-red, bordered behind by thin white line tapering towards base of neck, with further narrow white line down sides of breast and across front, separating breast from black belly. Very broad white band along line of upper flanks curving down to join white vent and undertail-coverts, broken on rear flanks by a few irregular black bars. Upperparts all black but for white uppertail-coverts, and two narrow white bars across closed wing formed by white edgings to greater and median wing-coverts. Very small, stubby bill black. Legs and feet black. In flight, wings all black above and below apart from two very narrow white wing-bars on upper surface. Two-note, staccato *kik-wik* calls. **Female** As male, but very slightly smaller. **Juvenile** As adults, but duller, brown-black instead of black, paler chestnut, and borders between black, white and chestnut of head and breast diffuse instead of clearly demarcated. Additional white tips to wing-coverts produce several very narrow wing-bars, none as bold as on adult. Tail tipped white. **Confusion risks** Small size, rounded head on thick neck, but tiny bill distinguish from other geese. Bold patterning less obvious at long range. Broad white flank band shows strongly on ground and in flight; this band narrower but longer and whiter than whitish flanks of Black Brant, and black tail extends further beyond white uppertail-coverts.

DISTRIBUTION AND STATUS Breeds western and central arctic Siberia, majority in Taymyr Peninsula, and winters around Black, Caspian and Aral Seas (principally first-named, in Bulgaria and Romania), with small numbers Greece and Turkey. Nests on tundra, including sides of river valleys, where usually in small colonies close to nest of eg Snowy Owl *Nyctea scandiaca*, Rough-legged Buzzard *Buteo lagopus* or Peregrine Falcon *Falco peregrinus*; winters on lowland agricultural land. Population believed to number 50,000 in 1950s and to have declined rapidly to 25,000 by 1963. Fluctuating and confusing figures reported over next 25 years, however, apparently now resolved by more co-ordinated winter censuses, resulting in counts of 65,000-75,000 in early 1990s.

CAPE BARREN GOOSE

Cereopsis novaehollandiae L 75-100 cm (30-39 in), WS 150-175 cm (59-69 in)

Monotypic; birds on Recherche Islands, Western Australia, described as separate subspecies on size and amount of white on crown, but not recognized here. Very large, nearly all-grey goose with yellow and black bill, only goose-like bird within southern Australian range.

IDENTIFICATION Male breeding and non-breeding Entire body pale ash-grey or dove-grey. Becomes a little paler, sometimes almost whitish, on centre of crown. Some feathers of breast, belly, mantle and lesser upperwing-coverts variably washed very pale brown with buff tips; most lesser and median upperwing-coverts and some scapulars have brownish rounded or heart-shaped subterminal spot. Tail black. Bill black but showing only at tip, nostrils and cutting edges, as remainder obscured by bulging pale greenish-yellow cere. Most of legs pale pink to carmine-red, but lower part and feet blackish; toes only partly webbed. In flight, outer half or so of primaries and most of secondaries black, contrasting with paler grey inner half and spotted coverts; inner secondaries (tertials) all grey; greater primary coverts unspotted and same paler grey as primaries; underwing, apart from primaries and secondaries, uniform pale grey. Main calls are loud trumpeting honks. **Female** As male, but calls different: a low, pig-like grunt. **Juvenile** Paler than adults, but with heavier spotting on upperwing-coverts. **Confusion risks** Unmistakable within or outside range. Appears very large and bulky, with rounded back, and wings drooping and nearly obscuring black tail. In flight, typically goose-shaped, but with broader wings.

DISTRIBUTION AND STATUS Breeds islands off south coast of Australia, from Recherche Archipelago in south-west to Furneaux group, between Tasmania and Victoria, in east; non-breeding flocks occur on adjacent Australian mainland. Nests in scrub and grass-tussock areas on islands; otherwise found in open grassy areas, usually close to the coast and wetland margins, sometimes causing agricultural damage. Population currently c 20,000, compared with c 5,000 thirty years ago, with recent counts and estimates of c 1,000 on Recherche Archipelago, 10,000 in South Australia, 9,000 on Furneaux group, and up to 500 in Victoria. Population increasing overall.

FRECKLED DUCK

Stictonetta naevosa L 50-55 cm (20-22 in), WS 75-82 cm (30-32 in)

Monotypic. Very dark duck, with unusual head shape distinguishing it from other Australian waterfowl.

IDENTIFICATION Male breeding Entire body uniform dark grey-brown, minutely freckled all over with pale buff or whitish markings on every feather. Freckles smallest on head and neck, which therefore appear darker, and largest on underparts, which thus appear paler, especially on lower belly, flanks and undertail-coverts, where the freckles merge into vermiculations. Head proportionately large and with slight crest, giving distinct small peak to rear crown and presenting an almost triangular profile. Deep, broad bill, flattened towards tip, slate-grey with basal third a bright orange-red. Legs and feet dark grey. In flight, upperwing-coverts freckled, but underwing-coverts whitish, blotched and edged dull brown; flight feathers dark brown above, pale brown below. Commonest call a soft fluting, also snorts and grunts, none audible from any distance. **Male non-breeding** Red on bill fades to dull red or may even disappear altogether. **Female** As male, but slightly smaller, and also paler overall, with rather larger freckles. Lacks red on bill. **Juvenile** Resemble female, but lighter brown and with deep buff freckles. **Confusion risks** No other Australian waterfowl is uniformly dark with distinctive crest. Australian Black Duck appears to have all-dark body at distance, but has dark crown-, eye- and chin-stripes on pale buff head.

DISTRIBUTION AND STATUS Confined to two restricted areas of southern Australia: in extreme south-west Western Australia, and in Murray-Darling Basin of south-east Australia; although mainly resident, responds to irregular rainfall by wandering extensively, turning up at temporary wetlands and sometimes breeding before these dry out, and it moves on. Favoured habitat well-vegetated fresh waters, eg swamps, lagoons and floodlands. Total population probably around 19,000, though subject to considerable variation depending on floods. Very vulnerable to shooting, despite protection, also to habitat loss.

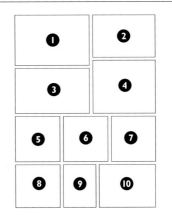

1 **Red-breasted Goose** (adults, Taymyr, Russia)
2 **Red-breasted Goose** (adults in flight, Taymyr, Russia)
3 **Red-breasted Goose** (adult with Dark-bellied Brent Geese, Kent, England)
4 **Red-breasted Goose** (adult with Barnacle Geese, Caerlaverock, Scotland)
5 **Cape Barren Goose** (adults with young, Tasmania, Australia)
6 **Cape Barren Goose** (adults with young, Tasmania, Australia)
7 **Cape Barren Goose** (adult, Tasmania, Australia)
8 **Freckled Duck** (female with young, Australia)
9 **Freckled Duck** (female)
10 **Freckled Duck** (male)

SHELDGEESE

ANDEAN GOOSE

Chloephaga melanoptera L 70-80 cm (28-31 in), WS 160-180 cm (63-71 in)
Monotypic. Unmistakable, mainly white sheldgoose with dark wings and tail, red bill and orange legs.
IDENTIFICATION Male breeding and non-breeding Pure white head, neck, underparts and upperparts. Upperwing boldly patterned black, white and purplish, with primaries and greater primary coverts, as well as tertials, black, secondaries and outer few greater secondary coverts, as well as all median and lesser coverts, white, but remaining greater secondary coverts with dark purplish iridescence forming dark bar along wing. Underwing as upperwing, but all greater coverts white, so no bar along wing. Tail black. Short and deep bill coral-red with black tip, and occasional and variable brownish mottling on upper mandible. Legs and feet orange to orange-red. **Female** As male, but noticeably smaller. **Juvenile** As adults, but greyish tinge to white plumage, especially on head and neck, and black on wings duller, tending to dark grey. Bill initially black, but soon becoming pink. Adult plumage fully attained in first summer. **Confusion risks** Unmistakable within range, where only goose-like bird. Superficially like Upland Goose, but has red bill and orange legs, not black as on that species.
DISTRIBUTION AND STATUS Resident in Andes above *c* 3300 m, from central Peru and western Bolivia south to central Chile and central Argentina; descends to lower altitudes during winter. Occupies high-ground lakes and marshes in grassland areas. Population thought to lie in range 25,000-100,000, but limited data. Inaccessibility limits opportunities for hunting, and habitat apparently not threatened.

UPLAND (or MAGELLAN) GOOSE

Chloephaga picta
Polytypic. Two subspecies: (1) Lesser Upland (or Lesser Magellan) Goose *C. p. picta*, breeds southern South America, winters there and to north; (2) Falkland Upland (or Greater Upland, or Greater Magellan) Goose *C. p. leucoptera*, resident Falkland Islands.

Lesser Upland (or Lesser Magellan) Goose

Chloephaga picta picta L 59-65 cm (23-26 in), WS 145-164 cm (57-65 in)
Large sheldgoose, male white-headed, female cinnamon-headed, with conspicuous black and white barring on flanks; male very distinctive, female more similar to *eg* Ruddy-headed Goose.
IDENTIFICATION Male breeding and non-breeding Two colour phases, white and barred. *White phase:* Head, neck, breast, belly and flanks white, with conspicuous black barring on rear flanks; vent and undertail-coverts white. Upperparts medium grey, with black and white barring on mantle and scapulars; rump and uppertail-coverts white; tail black, but can be edged and tipped white. *Barred phase:* As white phase, but with all underparts, from lower neck

to vent, closely barred black, bars broader towards rear. *Both phases:* Wings boldly patterned black, white, and metallic greenish: lesser and median upperwing-coverts white, greater coverts black, but shining with glossy iridescent green, forming broad dark bar along inner wing; primaries and primary coverts white and secondaries black; underwing all white, contrasting with black primaries. Bill, legs and feet blackish-grey. Main call a repeated whistling note. **Female** Shows variation in colour, but authorities disagree on whether these represent colour phases. Head and neck variable, from pale cinnamon-brown to deep brown and, sometimes, grey-brown, becoming more reddish-cinnamon on breast, anterior flanks and mantle, which all barred black as on barred-phase male, with rear flanks similarly barred black and white. Vent and undertail-coverts dark grey. Upperparts cinnamon-brown with greyish tinge. Wings, tail and bill as male, but legs and feet yellow. Reported to become duller, less reddish-cinnamon, outside breeding season, but no obvious non-breeding plumage; apparent changes may be result of feather wear or could be referable to normal colour variation, as above. Main call a low grating cackle. **Juvenile** Similar to adults, showing sex difference from first feathering, with males always as barred phase. Both sexes lack greenish speculum, while head and neck of male dusky grey-brown, and rump and lower back barred. Full adult plumage attained in third calendar-year, with phase of male becoming apparent in second. **Confusion risks** Male largely unmistakable within range; immature male Kelp Goose can be white-headed with barred plumage, but has yellow legs. Female not unlike Ruddy-headed Goose, which, though smaller and daintier, has much more finely barred cinnamon-buff underparts, including vent and undertail-coverts, and also a quite noticeable white eye-ring. Differences from Falkland subspecies, with which no overlap, mostly small, latter being larger, with male having white phase only, and with females brighter-coloured with more rufous and less black in barring of underparts.
DISTRIBUTION AND STATUS Breeds southern Chile and southern Argentina south to Tierra del Fuego: barred phase occupies extreme south of range in southernmost Patagonia and Tierra del Fuego, while white phase occurs over remainder; northern breeders apparently resident, but those from south of range migrate north to winter north of breeding range into central Chile and central Argentina. Mainly terrestrial bird of open grassy plains, though often breeds beside rivers and streams. Still numerous, with population estimated to number hundreds of thousands, though no longer occurs in former very large flocks. Habitat destruction, shooting and human persecution arising from conflicts with agriculture main causes of decline.

Falkland (or Greater) Upland (or Greater Magellan) Goose

Chloephaga picta leucoptera L 63-72 cm (25-28 in), WS 155-175 cm (61-69 in)

As Lesser Upland Goose, but restricted to Falkland Islands.
IDENTIFICATION Male breeding and non-breeding White phase only, no barred phase. As white-phase Lesser Upland, but with narrower black barring on rear flanks. **Female** As female Lesser Upland, but head and neck bright reddish-cinnamon without apparent variation, and underparts having wider cinnamon bars and narrower black bars. Also, vent and undertail-coverts pale, not dark grey. **Juvenile** As juvenile Lesser Upland, males similarly with well-barred underparts, bars being lost during second summer. **Confusion risks** For differences from Lesser Upland, Ruddy and Kelp, see above under Lesser Upland Goose.
DISTRIBUTION AND STATUS Resident Falkland Islands. Found in open and tussock grasslands, as well as sheep-grazed pastures, usually near the sea. Population *c* 200,000. Regarded as pest by sheep-farmers (though damage often exaggerated), but, despite massive destruction of eggs and birds, many thousands annually over most of the last 100 years, population has remained fairly static.

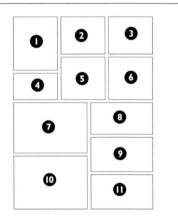

1 *Andean Goose* (adult)
2 **Andean Goose** (pair, Chile)
3 **Lesser Upland (or Lesser Magellan) Goose** (pair, male barred phase, Tierra del Fuego)
4 **Lesser Upland (or Lesser Magellan) Goose** (flight, Tierra del Fuego)
5 **Lesser Upland (or Lesser Magellan) Goose** (male, barred phase, with Ashy-headed Goose, Tierra del Fuego)
6 **Lesser Upland (or Lesser Magellan) Goose** (male, barred phase, Tierra del Fuego)
7 **Falkland (or Greater) Upland (or Greater Magellan) Goose** (family group, Falklands)
8 **Falkland (or Greater) Upland (or Greater Magellan) Goose** (male and two females, flight, Falklands)
9 **Falkland (or Greater) Upland (or Greater Magellan) Goose** (group - male, female and immature, Falklands)
10 **Falkland (or Greater) Upland (or Greater Magellan) Goose** (group - male, female and immature male, Falklands)
11 **Falkland Upland (or Greater Magellan) Goose** (flock in flight, Falklands)

SHELDGEESE

BLUE-WINGED GOOSE

Cyanochen cyanopterus L 60-75 cm (24-30 in), WS 120-142 cm (47-56 in)
Monotypic. Unmistakable grey-brown sheldgoose of Ethiopia, unlike any other goose-like bird within range.
IDENTIFICATION Male breeding and non-breeding Head and neck grey-brown, paler on forehead and throat and sometimes down onto upper foreneck. Breast, belly and flanks more brownish-grey, with pale centres to feathers producing lightly mottled effect; vent whitish, grading to white on undertail-coverts. Upperparts darker grey, with pale centres to feathers of mantle and scapulars, becoming browner-grey on lower back and then paler brown on rump and uppertail-coverts; tail black. Bill, legs and feet black. In flight, primaries and primary coverts black; secondaries black, but with glossy green iridescence, and coverts pale powder-blue (which can show on closed wing); underwing-coverts white, contrasting with black flight feathers. Rapidly repeated high-pitched whistling calls. **Female** As male, but noticeably smaller. Calls similar, but harsher and more wheezy in tone. **Juvenile** As adults, but duller in overall colour, more brown than grey, and lacking green gloss on secondaries. **Confusion risks** Unmistakable within or outside range.
DISTRIBUTION AND STATUS Resident in restricted area of highlands of Ethiopia, mainly above *c* 1800 m, and up to *c* 4200 m. Lives in grassy meadows and pastures on upland plateaux, usually close to running or standing water. Population unknown, but thought to be locally common within range and total almost certainly exceeds 5,000 birds and quite possibly 10,000; not regarded as threatened, as habitat exploitation minimal and local religion forbids its being eaten and so protects it from hunting.

KELP GOOSE

Chloephaga hybrida
Polytypic. Two subspecies recognized here, though some doubt has been expressed recently regarding validity of separation: (1) Lesser (or Patagonian) Kelp Goose *C. h. hybrida*, breeds southern Chile to Tierra del Fuego and extreme south of Argentina, wintering within range and to north; (2) Greater (or Falkland) Kelp Goose *C. h. malvinarum*, resident Falkland Islands.

Lesser (or Patagonian) Kelp Goose

Chloephaga hybrida hybrida L 52-62 cm (20-24 in), WS 127-145 cm (50-57 in)
Male all white and unmistakable; female, chocolate-brown with striped underparts, also unlike any other species.
IDENTIFICATION Male breeding and non-breeding All-white plumage, including wings and tail. Short and deep bill black, with crimson spot close to base of upper mandible (culmen), though this sometimes pinkish or yellowish, colour perhaps related to age or breeding

condition. Call a repeated whistle. **Female** Dark chocolate-brown head and neck, slightly paler on crown, and with thin, but conspicuous, white eye-ring. Breast, upper belly and flanks blacker-brown, less chocolate-brown, heavily marked with short white bars formed by broad white tips to feathers; centre of lower belly, vent and undertail-coverts white. Mantle, upper back and scapulars black-brown, unmarked; lower back, rump, uppertail-coverts and tail white. Upperwing shows similar pattern to other sheldgeese, not all-white of male: primaries and primary coverts blackish, secondaries white, while greater secondary coverts blackish, glossed with iridescent green, but all lesser and median coverts white; tertials black; underwing white, apart from blackish primaries. Bill flesh-pink, legs and feet deep orange-yellow. Call a harsh growl. **Juvenile** As adult female, but without green gloss on secondary coverts, and overall duller above and below, with diffuse, whitish barring on underparts (bars thinner and much less well defined than on adult female). Males acquire some whitish feathering on head, neck and upperparts early in first winter, becoming almost all white in second year, though may retain brownish tips to primaries into second winter. Females have greyish uppertail-coverts in first year. Bill brownish at first, but showing colour of sex within first winter. Legs and feet initially greenish-yellow. **Confusion risks** Adult male and female unmistakable within range, although at a distance, when size and, especially, shape not so apparent, confusion perhaps possible between male and Snowy Sheathbill *Chionis alba*. Juvenile and immature male could, in some intermediate plumages, be confused with male Upland Goose, which, however, is slimmer in build and has longer and blackish, not yellow, legs. Males cannot be told in the field from Greater Kelp Goose, while female less strongly barred on underparts (see below), but neither subspecies known to wander into the other's range.
DISTRIBUTION AND STATUS Breeds southern Chile and extreme south of Argentina, south throughout Tierra del Fuego; some resident, but most southerly breeders move north in winter, penetrating beyond breeding range. Always found on or very close to coasts, especially rocky and shingle shores, nesting beside freshwater coastal lagoons. Reported as common or even abundant in parts of Chilean range, though much scarcer in Argentina, and population estimated to lie in range 25,000-100,000 and probably stable. Only threats would appear to come from oil spillage washing ashore.

Greater (or Falkland) Kelp Goose

Chloephaga hybrida malvinarum L 55-65 cm (22-26 in), WS 135-155 cm (53-61 in)
As Lesser Kelp Goose, but confined to Falkland Islands.
IDENTIFICATION Male breeding and non-breeding As Lesser Kelp Goose, though slightly larger, especially wings, bill and legs.

Female As Lesser Kelp Goose, but white feather edgings to black-brown underparts broader, producing bolder and therefore much more prominent barring. **Juvenile** As Lesser Kelp Goose. **Confusion risks** For (unlikely) confusion with other species, see Lesser Kelp Goose, as also for potential for separation of the two subspecies.
DISTRIBUTION AND STATUS Resident Falkland Islands. Occupies same habitat as Lesser Kelp Goose. Population estimated at *c* 100,000 individuals and probably stable. Does not conflict with man or his agricultural activities, and only potential threat comes from oil spillage in adjacent seas.

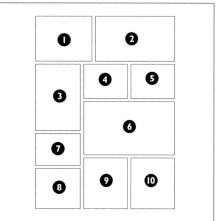

1 *Blue-winged Goose* (adult)
2 **Blue-winged Goose** (pair, Shewa, Ethiopia)
3 *Blue-winged Goose* (adult in threat display)
4 **Lesser (or Patagonian) Kelp Goose** (male, Tierra del Fuego)
5 **Lesser (or Patagonian) Kelp Goose** (female, Tierra del Fuego)
6 **Greater (or Falkland) Kelp Goose** (male, female, and young, Falklands)
7 **Lesser (or Patagonian) Kelp Goose** (immature male, Tierra del Fuego)
8 **Greater (or Falkland) Kelp Goose** (male, Falklands)
9 **Greater (or Falkland) Kelp Goose** (male with Turkey Vulture, Falklands)
10 **Greater (or Falkland) Kelp Goose** (female and young, Falklands)

SHELDGEESE

ASHY-HEADED GOOSE

Chloephaga poliocephala L 50-60 cm (20-24 in), WS 127-144 cm (50-57 in)
Monotypic. Medium-sized sheldgoose; sexes similar, and only species with grey head and chestnut neck and breast.

IDENTIFICATION Male breeding and non-breeding Head and upper neck ash-grey, paler, almost whitish, on crown and around base of upper mandible. Narrow whitish eye-ring. Lower neck chestnut, becoming brighter chestnut on breast and upper mantle; breast sometimes with fine black barring formed by blackish tips to feathers, but can be completely absent (seems unrelated to age or season). Sharp demarcation between breast and pure white belly, while flanks white with narrow black bars, often broken as they reach belly and sometimes extending onto legs either side of legs; vent buff, becoming pale chestnut on undertail-coverts. Lower mantle and scapulars brown, tinged grey, feathers edged rufous with narrow black subterminal band; back, rump, uppertail-coverts and tail blackish. Typical sheldgoose wing, with black primaries and primary coverts, white secondaries and lesser and median coverts, and green-glossed blackish secondary coverts forming dark bar along middle of wing; tertials blackish; underwing white, with blackish primaries. Bill black, sometimes with flesh-coloured areas along sides of upper mandible. Legs orange-yellow with variable black stripe down front, feet mainly black with variable orange-yellow markings. Call a soft, repeated whistle. **Female** Smaller than male and less brightly chestnut on breast and upper mantle. Fine black barring on breast more frequent, but can be absent and does not seem reliable for sexing. Harsh, grating cackle. **Juvenile** As adults, but with brownish tinge to grey head and to white of flanks, while chestnut breast duller and always with fine black bars. Secondary coverts unglossed brownish-black. Legs and feet dull yellow. Acquires adult plumage in second year. **Confusion risks** Only sheldgoose with combination of grey head, chestnut breast and white belly, together with black-striped white flanks. Females of Ruddy-headed Goose and Upland Goose both have chestnut head and coloured belly.

DISTRIBUTION AND STATUS Breeds southern Chile and southern Argentina south to Tierra del Fuego; birds from southernmost breeding areas winter further north in southern Argentina. Has wandered to Falkland Islands. In breeding season frequents swampy clearings in forests, both in mountainous regions and on larger islands; winters in more open habitats, such as grasslands and agricultural land. Population unknown, but thought to be relatively common, especially in Chilean mountain areas, and rough estimate of several hundred thousands seems reasonable. Has suffered persecution owing to its association in winter with other sheldgeese, eg Lesser Upland Goose, on farmland.

RUDDY-HEADED GOOSE

Chloephaga rubidiceps L 45-53 cm (18-22 in), WS 118-133 cm (46-52 in)
Monotypic. Smallest sheldgoose; sexes alike, with distinctive rufous body, lacking white except on wings.

IDENTIFICATION Male breeding and non-breeding Head and upper neck cinnamon-brown with white eye-ring. Lower neck pale grey, merging into buff on breast, but becoming paler grey-buff on flanks, all very finely barred black; belly, vent and undertail-coverts warm chestnut-buff. Mantle and upper back warm brown, feathers of back and scapulars edged rufous with narrow black subterminal band; lower back, rump, uppertail-coverts and tail black. Upperwing as other sheldgeese, with black primaries and primary coverts, white secondaries and median and lesser coverts, and blackish secondary coverts glossed green and forming dark bar on wing; underwing white, except for black primaries. Bill black. Legs and feet orange, variably blotched black on front, webs and toes. Shrill, repeated whistling notes. **Female** As male, but noticeably smaller. Call a harsh quack. **Juvenile** As adult, but duller, less cinnamon and chestnut, and lacking green iridescence on secondary coverts. **Confusion risks** Only possibility of confusion is with much larger female Upland Goose, which, especially at distance, is similarly cinnamon-brown on head and upper neck, but much brighter on breast and whiter on flanks, both with markedly heavier black barring (especially on Falkland subspecies), and also white, not chestnut, in ventral region. White underparts and on flanks also help to separate from Ashy-headed in flight, when wing patterns are closely similar.

DISTRIBUTION AND STATUS Breeds Tierra del Fuego (formerly also southern Chile and southern Argentina), wintering southern Argentina, and resident Falkland Islands. Inhabits coastal grasslands, with mainland wintering birds also on agricultural land. Falkland population estimated at 40,000 birds and stable. Numbers breeding Tierra del Fuego have declined severely in last 30 years and thought to be no more than 300 in 1993 and still declining, so almost certainly heading for extinction; main reason seems to be massive persecution, especially on wintering grounds, where accused of causing agricultural damage.

ORINOCO GOOSE

Neochen jubata L 61-66 cm (24-26 in), WS 114-127 cm (45-50 in)
Monotypic. Distinctive sheldgoose, with contrasting pale head, neck and breast and darker body and wings.

IDENTIFICATION Male breeding and non-breeding Head, neck and breast pale yellowish-brown, paler on forehead and throat and around eye, a little darker on cheeks. Nape and neck feathers noticeably elongated, also slightly furrowed rather as on grey geese, so that darker striations and mottlings appear;

erected during threat or display, making neck appear much thicker. Belly and flanks chestnut, shading to buff on upper flanks but to dark brown on vent, with contrasting white undertail-coverts. Upper mantle and scapulars chestnut, broadly edged buff, becoming blackish towards centre of back; rump, uppertail-coverts and tail all very glossy black with green sheen. Wings also iridescent, purplish on primaries and primary coverts, but greenish on secondaries except for white patch formed by basal part of outer vanes (may show on closed wing); underwing uniform blackish. Bill black, with red sides to upper mandible. Legs and feet bright salmon-pink. Call a strong, high-pitched whistle. **Female** As male, but smaller, with less elongated neck feathers. Call a harsh guttural honking. **Juvenile** As adults, but duller, especially on underparts and scapulars, and lacking green and purple gloss to back and wings. **Confusion risks** Unlike any other wildfowl in its contrasting pale upper body, chestnut lower body and almost completely black wings.

DISTRIBUTION AND STATUS Widespread resident of northern South America east of Andes, though distribution discontinuous: found in Orinoco basin (east Colombia, Venezuela), Guyanas, and Amazon basin (Brazil), south to Paraguay and extreme north of Argentina, and including extreme east of Peru and eastern Bolivia. Inhabits lowland tropical forested river banks, as well as wetlands within more open savanna. Population estimated at between 25,000 and 100,000 individuals and probably stable.

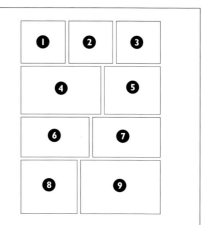

1 **Ashy-headed Goose** (adult, Tierra del Fuego)
2 **Ashy-headed Goose** (adult, Tierra del Fuego)
3 **Ashy-headed Goose** (male, Tierra del Fuego)
4 **Ruddy-headed Goose** (pair, Falklands)
5 **Ruddy-headed Goose** (adult, Falklands)
6 **Ruddy-headed Goose** (flock in flight, Falklands)
7 **Ruddy-headed Goose** (pair with young, Falklands)
8 *Orinoco Goose* (adult)
9 *Orinoco Goose* (pair in flight, Llanos, Venezuela)

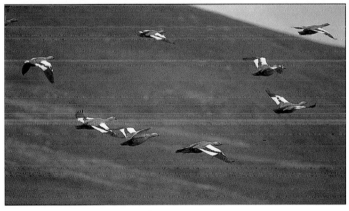

GEESE AND SHELDUCKS

EGYPTIAN GOOSE

Alopochen aegyptiacus L 63-73 cm (25-29 in),
WS 134-154 cm (53-60 in)
Monotypic. Large, long-necked and long-legged,
pale goose-like bird, with conspicuous dark eye
patch.

**IDENTIFICATION Male breeding and non-
breeding** Pale buff head and neck with
conspicuous dark chocolate-brown patch
around eye and another around base of bill, the
two usually (but not always) joined by narrow
line. Dark buff-brown mottling on crown, nape
and hindneck, sometimes appearing rufous;
narrow dark rufous-brown collar at base of
neck. Breast, upper belly and flanks buff, mostly
with grey tinge, becoming paler on flanks and
belly, with irregular-shaped and variable
(occasionally absent) chocolate-brown patch in
centre of lower breast; lower belly and vent
white, undertail-coverts pale yellow-buff.
Upperparts variable in colour, with mantle and
scapulars sometimes rufous-brown but more
usually grey-brown, though pale grey birds
occur; back, rump, uppertail-coverts and tail
black. Primaries and their coverts black,
secondaries black, strongly glossed with green,
forming duck-like speculum, this separated
from pure white forewings (often showing on
resting bird) by narrow black band, while
tertials rufous-brown; underwing black, with
contrasting white coverts. Bill quite long and
goose-like, pink with black nail, nostrils and
mandible edges; some dusky mottling around
base and nostrils. Legs and feet pink,
sometimes tinged purplish. Call a strong, but
laboured and husky breathing sound. **Female**
As male, but smaller. Often has darker
markings on upper mandible, at base and
around nostrils. Call a strident trumpeting
quacking. **Juvenile** As adult, but duller and
lacking dark patches around eye and on lower
breast, though with darker crown and neck.
Secondaries lack green gloss; white forewing
tinged grey. Bill, legs and feet yellow-grey.
Confusion risks Closer resemblance to large
shelduck than to goose or sheldgoose, but
larger and longer-necked than any shelduck,
while overall buff colouring, as well as
conspicuous eye and breast patches, rule out
any goose or sheldgoose. Juvenile, lacking dark
patches, closer to immature shelducks, but
much longer-legged and browner than eg
Common Shelduck.
DISTRIBUTION AND STATUS Widespread
almost throughout Africa south of Sahara, as
well as down Nile Valley into Upper Egypt;
mainly resident, but seasonal movements
reported, probably in response to rains.
Formerly more widespread, including, in 18th
century, eastern Europe and Mediterranean;
last bred Israel in early 1930s. Long-established
introduced population in eastern England.
Occupies almost every kind of fresh water
except in forests, from lowlands to at least
4000 m; feeds on agricultural land. No
population estimate; common in many areas
and abundant in some. British population

increasing steadily, 450 in 1984, 906 in 1991,
but range still restricted. Some shooting in
natural range for sport and to prevent damage
to crops, but not threatened.

RUDDY SHELDUCK

Tadorna ferruginea L 61-67 cm (24-26 in), WS
121-145 cm (48-57 in)
Monotypic. Only all rust-coloured shelduck in
northern hemisphere.
IDENTIFICATION Male breeding Buff head and
neck, more orange-buff on hindneck and
slightly paler around and below eye; some have
dusky patch on rear of crown. Narrow black
collar around base of neck. Underparts and
most of upperparts (not rump and uppertail-
coverts) rusty-orange, often tending to deep
chestnut in centre of breast and belly, and also
on vent and undertail-coverts; some paler
yellower tinges on flanks and scapulars, formed
from feather edgings, but also by bleaching and
wear prior to late-summer moult. Rump,
uppertail-coverts and tail black with green
gloss. Primaries and primary coverts black,
lightly glossed green, secondaries with stronger
green iridescence forming speculum behind
white forewing, feathers of which are washed
creamy-yellow when fresh (forewing and
speculum sometimes show on closed wing);
underwing with all-black primaries and
secondaries and all-white coverts. Bill, legs and
feet blackish. Trumpeting and honking calls,
choor and *aakh*, often repeated. **Male non-
breeding** As male breeding, but black neck
collar absent or very narrow and incomplete.
Such birds seen in autumn and early winter.
Female As male breeding, but with buff (less
orange-buff) head and neck, and distinct white
patch on forehead and upper cheeks, including
around eye. Calls deeper and harsher than
male's. **Juvenile** As female, but much duller
and paler, with grey-buff head, darker on
crown and hindneck; grey-buff tips to many
feathers on underparts and upperparts, while
black areas lack green gloss and white forewing
tinged grey. Becomes more like adult during
first autumn, though black areas remain dull
and unglossed until after first-summer moult.
Confusion risks Orange-buff plumage unlike
any other wildfowl in northern hemisphere.
Extralimital shelducks of similar body colour
have grey or grey and white head (South
African Shelduck) or white head (female
Paradise Shelduck).
DISTRIBUTION AND STATUS Breeds from
south-east Europe and Turkey east through
southern and central Asia to Mongolia and
western China; also separate populations in
north-west Africa and Ethiopia. Migrates south
for winter, with slight overlap with southerly
limit of breeding range, but mainly to
Afghanistan, Iran, Pakistan, India, Burma and
southern and eastern China; north-west
African birds disperse eastwards along coast,
while Ethiopian birds descend from highlands.
Occurs beside rivers and lakes, the latter often
brackish or salty. North-west African

population *c* 1,500, Ethiopian *c* 250-600;
population of rest of range estimated at
150,000-200,000, with *c* 20,000 in south-east
Europe. Has declined in west of range through
habitat loss, drainage for agriculture and
shooting.

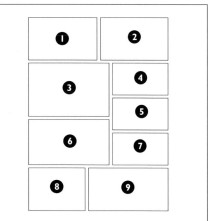

1 Egyptian Goose (two adults plus first
winter, Norfolk, England)
2 Egyptian Goose (pair, Norfolk, England)
3 Egyptian Goose (pair, Ngorongoro,
Tanzania)
4 Egyptian Goose (in flight, Norfolk, England)
5 Ruddy Shelduck (pair, India)
6 Ruddy Shelduck (male, Western India)
7 Ruddy Shelduck (female in flight, India)
8 Ruddy Shelduck (female in flight, Norfolk,
England)
9 Ruddy Shelduck (three immatures,
Cornwall, England)

SOUTH AFRICAN SHELDUCK

Tadorna cana L 61-66 cm (24-26 in), WS 121-145 cm (48-57 in)
Monotypic. Only shelduck of southern South Africa.

IDENTIFICATION Male breeding Uniform ashy-grey head and neck. Rusty-orange underparts, paler on breast and undertail-coverts, richer-toned on flanks and, especially, belly. Upperparts similar, paler on mantle; rump, uppertail-coverts and tail black. Wings almost exactly as Ruddy Shelduck (see above): contrasting white forewing, green speculum and black outer wing above, and white coverts and black flight feathers below. Bill, legs and feet blackish. Call as Ruddy Shelduck, but a little deeper. **Male non-breeding** As male breeding, but duller, more yellowish, on body and with very fine grey-black vermiculations on flanks and mantle. Lasts for a few months after post-breeding moult. **Female** Darker slate-grey head with very variable amount of white, which can be restricted to patch around eye or cover whole of front half of head, with extension behind eye, or, occasionally, virtually whole of head. Darker, richer-coloured on body than male, and less pale on breast. Occasional pink blotches on feet. Call as male, but harsher. **Juvenile** As adult male, but dull overall, with grey-brown tinge very apparent, including on forewing; no green on speculum. Moults into more adult plumage during first winter, with white appearing on head of female. **Confusion risks** Unmistakable within range, though much larger and long-legged Egyptian Goose has same wing pattern. No other shelducks with grey or grey and white head; even whitest-headed females still show some grey on nape and neck, absent on white-headed female Paradise Shelduck.

DISTRIBUTION AND STATUS Southern South Africa, including Cape Province, Orange Free State and Transvaal, north to central Namibia and southern Botswana; resident, except for moult movements within range. Nests by shallow fresh and brackish waters; moults on larger, deeper lakes. Population estimated at 42,000 in 1981, when thought to be stable, with few threats.

PARADISE SHELDUCK

Tadorna variegata L 61-67 cm (24-26 in), WS 122-145 cm (48-57 in)
Monotypic. Only shelduck within range, and only one with nearly all-black male and white-headed, chestnut-bodied female.

IDENTIFICATION Male breeding and non-breeding Head and neck black, glossed green. Nearly all underparts and upperparts sooty-black, breast, flanks and upper belly with fine grey vermiculations, mantle and scapulars finely vermiculated brown. Lower belly and undertail-coverts rich chestnut; rump, uppertail-coverts and tail black. Wings as Ruddy Shelduck, with black outer part, white forewing and, above, green iridescent speculum on black secondaries

(white of forewing often shows on resting bird, as do chestnut tertials). Bill, legs and feet dark grey. Guttural, rolling *horr*, plus *ha-hoo* in display. **Female breeding** Head and neck pure white. Almost all of body dark reddish-chestnut, with fine blackish vermiculations on mantle. Wings, tail and bare parts similar to male. Call a shrill honking. **Female non-breeding** As female breeding, but vermiculations over most of body produce overall grey-brown appearance. Lasts for few months post-breeding. **Juvenile male** As adult male, but much duller and browner, including on head; lacks green speculum, and feathers of white forewing washed dull rufous-brown. **Juvenile female** Initially as juvenile male, but whitish feathering quickly appears on head and gradually increases in amount, as does rufous feathering on body. Juveniles of both sexes gain near-adult plumage during first winter, though wings and tail not until after first-summer moult. **Confusion risks** Only shelduck of New Zealand. Both sexes differ from dark-headed, chestnut-breasted Australian Shelduck. Female has more extensive white head and neck than even whitest-headed female South African Shelduck.

DISTRIBUTION AND STATUS Resident North and South Islands of New Zealand, as well as Stewart Island, though absent from north of North Island; only movements apparently to moult gatherings. Widespread in variety of wetlands, both lowland and mountain fresh water, as well as coasts. Population thought to lie between 150,000 and 180,000, being most abundant in uplands of South Island.

AUSTRALIAN SHELDUCK

Tadorna tadornoides L 56-72 in (22-28 in), WS 116-149 cm (46-59 in)
Monotypic. One of two shelducks within Australian range, but combination of dark head, chestnut breast and dark body unlike Australian Radjah Shelduck.

IDENTIFICATION Male breeding and non-breeding Head and neck black, glossed green, quite often with small whitish area at base of upper mandible. White ring at base of neck. Breast and mantle reddish-cinnamon. Rest of underparts and upperparts sooty-black, very finely vermiculated brown on underparts, back and scapulars; rump, tail-coverts and tail black, tail with greenish tinge. Wings as Ruddy Shelduck, with black outer wing, white forewing, and green-glossed black secondaries forming speculum above, with tertials chestnut (show on resting bird, as does white forewing). Bill, legs and feet dark grey. Call a low honk, not unlike a goose. (A non-breeding plumage, duller than breeding, has been reported, but denied by other authors.) **Female breeding** As male, but smaller and very slightly duller on head and body, with well-defined white area at base of bill which is sometimes joined to conspicuous white eye-ring. White neck collar narrower, chestnut of breast brighter. Loud, honking and repeated *ong-gank*. **Female non-**

breeding Black areas duller and more grey-brown than breeding, and neck collar usually absent. Lasts for few months after breeding. **Juvenile** Much browner than adults, with whitish patches between bill and eye, but lacks white neck ring; breast and mantle pale brown. White forewing flecked grey-brown and some white tips to secondaries. Becomes as adult during first winter, but adult wings delayed until first summer. **Confusion risks** Only shelduck within range and unlike any other wildfowl, including all extralimital shelducks.

DISTRIBUTION AND STATUS Breeds in two widely separated areas: southern part of Western Australia; and in south-east from eastern South Australia, through Victoria to southern New South Wales, and Tasmania. No regular movements, but some moult gatherings, plus dispersal and wandering north to temporary floods after rains. Uses wide variety of fresh and brackish waters and coastal islands; feeds extensively on agricultural land, where may do considerable damage. Widespread and common, with population in range 100,000 to 1 million; has increased substantially in recent decades.

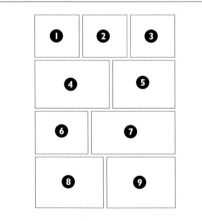

1 *South African Shelduck* (male)
2 **South African Shelduck** (male, South Africa)
3 **South African Shelduck** (female, South Africa)
4 **Paradise Shelduck** (pair with young, New Zealand)
5 **Paradise Shelduck** (male in flight, New Zealand)
6 **Paradise Shelduck** (female in flight, New Zealand)
7 **Australian Shelduck** (juvenile, Perth, Australia)
8 **Australian Shelduck** (pair, Perth, Australia)
9 **Australian Shelduck** (female, Perth, Australia)

SHELDUCKS

COMMON SHELDUCK

Tadorna tadorna L 58-67 cm (23-26 in), WS 110-133 cm (43-52 in)
Monotypic. Distinctive black-headed, white-bodied shelduck of northern hemisphere.
IDENTIFICATION Male breeding Black head and upper neck glossed green. Lower neck and upper breast white, separated from white sides of belly and flanks by broad chestnut band across lower breast, deeper in front than at sides, and extending across upper mantle; black stripe, varying in width individually, from centre of chest band (almost or completely dividing it into two) down to belly, where widens out on vent; undertail-coverts cinnamon, pale yellow at sides. Lower mantle, back, rump and uppertail-coverts white; tail white, narrowly tipped black. Scapulars black, show as broad band on closed wing. Wings with black primaries and white coverts as other shelducks, but speculum bronze-green; outer tertials deep chestnut on outer webs, white on inner webs, while inner tertials white. Bill, with prominent fleshy knob, bright carmine-red; nostrils and nail black. Legs and feet dark pink-flesh. Loud and melodious whistling calls. **Male non-breeding** As breeding, but loses green gloss to head, which becomes browner with whitish mottling on face. Knob shrinks and becomes duller red. White areas become tinged grey and cinnamon. **Female breeding** As male, but duller, with less green gloss on head and with variable whitish area around base of bill; black bar down belly narrower, and some blackish vermiculations on chestnut band over mantle. Lacks knob on bill, which duller red. Rapid, nasal *ag-ag-ag-ag*. **Female non-breeding** Duller all over than female breeding, with more white on head; chestnut breast band absent or shown only by few chestnut feathers at sides, while mantle grey-buff. **Juvenile** Top of head, hindneck and all upperparts dark grey-brown. Forehead, face, foreneck and underparts whitish, lacking breast band; flanks tinged grey. Scapulars dark brown. Wings as adults, but coverts greyish and secondaries tipped white. Attains adult plumage during first winter, but wings and tail retained until first-summer moult. **Confusion risks** Quite unmistakable. As juveniles so different from adults they can cause difficulty, though little to confuse them with except much larger juvenile Egyptian Goose.
DISTRIBUTION AND STATUS Widespread around coasts of north-west Europe, patchily in northern Mediterranean, and discontinuously from Black Sea east through central Asia to Mongolia and western and northern China. More northerly and inland breeders move south for winter, reaching eg North Africa, Iran, Iraq, India and southern China; others mainly sedentary, though major moult migration by otherwise resident British and coastal west European populations. Occupies both coastal estuarine habitats and large inland saline lakes. Population estimates: north-west Europe, 250,000; west Mediterranean, 15,000;

Black and Caspian Seas, 140,000; south and east Asia, 70,000. All but last thought to be increasing, and only likely threats are coastal pollution by, eg oil.

RADJAH SHELDUCK

Tadorna radjah
Polytypic. Two subspecies: (1) Moluccan (or Black-backed) Radjah Shelduck *T. r. radjah*, Moluccas (Indonesia) to Papua New Guinea; (2) Australian (or Red-backed) Radjah Shelduck *T. r. rufitergum*, coastal northern Australia.

Moluccan (or Black-backed) Radjah Shelduck

Tadorna radjah radjah L 51-61 cm (20-24 in), WS 94-113 cm (37-44 in)
Small white-headed shelduck, unique in range.
IDENTIFICATION Male breeding and non-breeding Pure white head, neck and upper breast, separated from pure white lower breast, belly, vent and undertail-coverts by prominent black band. Mantle to tail also black; scapulars mostly black but with rufous tinge, which shows on closed wing. Wing pattern similar to other shelducks, but more white on secondaries: above, primaries and their coverts black, while secondaries green-glossed black, forming speculum, but with broad white tips, and forewings white, separated from speculum by narrow black and white bands on greater coverts (white forewing, black and white band and green speculum can show on closed wing); tertials black; underwing much whiter than upperwing, as inner webs of secondaries whitish, so only black is on primaries. Bill pale pinkish-flesh, with obvious black spot at nostrils. Legs and feet usually slightly brighter pink. Eye very pale lemon-yellow. Call a wheezy whistle. **Female** As male, but slightly smaller. Call a harsh rattle. (Both sexes very vocal: call more or less continuously in flight, and very frequently at rest.) **Juvenile** As adults, but lacking green on speculum, which appears dull black, and black band in front of it rather wider; much of white areas washed pale brown. Bill, legs and feet very pale flesh. Acquires adult body plumage during first winter, adult wings in first summer. **Confusion risks** Only possible confusion with Australian subspecies, but not known to overlap; Australian has largely rufous in place of black on back and scapulars (see below). Birds of southern Irian Jaya and southern Papua New Guinea appear intermediate between the two subspecies. Only other wildfowl in area with somewhat similar pattern of white head, dark breast band, light underparts and dark back is male Green Pygmy-goose, but that barely half the size, with tiny bill, very short legs and dark crown.
DISTRIBUTION AND STATUS Resident in Indonesia, mainly Moluccas and Irian Jaya, and in Papua New Guinea, including some smaller islands, eg Fergusson Island. Coastal lagoons, mangrove swamps, mudflats and, occasionally, shallow fresh waters. Reported as widely distributed but local, and population estimated

as well in excess of 10,000 and perhaps two or three times as many. Although many reports of past declines, now regarded as stable, although some contraction of range has occurred in New Guinea. Vulnerable to hunting, as very confiding.

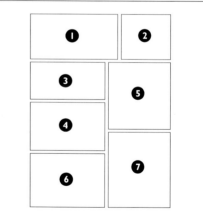

1 **Common Shelduck** (pair, Seaforth, England)
2 **Common Shelduck** (male in flight, Seaforth, England)
3 **Common Shelduck** (flock in flight, Norfolk, England)
4 **Common Shelduck** (eclipse, Lancashire, England)
5 **Common Shelduck** (immature, Kent, England)
6 *Moluccan (or Black-backed) Radjah Shelduck (adult)*
7 *Moluccan (or Black-backed) Radjah Shelduck (adult)*

Australian (or Red-backed) Radjah Shelduck

Tadorna radjah rufitergum L 51-61 cm (20-24 in), WS 94-113 cm (37-44 in)
Small white-headed shelduck, unique in range.
IDENTIFICATION Male and female breeding and non-breeding As Moluccan Radjah Shelduck, but breast band, mantle and scapulars rich chestnut instead of black. Brownish tinge to black of back and rump. **Juvenile** As Moluccan, but browner on breast band and upperparts. **Confusion risks** See Moluccan subspecies for separation from that and from Green Pygmy-goose.
DISTRIBUTION AND STATUS Mainly resident northern Australia, from Fitzroy River in Western Australia, through coastal Northern Territory into Queensland and south down coast as far as Cairns (formerly bred much further down, to northern New South Wales); disperses inland during rains, mainly following river valleys, returning to coast as any temporary wetlands dry out. Habitat as for Moluccan subspecies. Population at least 50,000 and perhaps as high as 100,000 or even more, with count of *c* 30,000 in one area of Northern Territory in 1990; believed stable. Excessive shooting probably caused withdrawal from New South Wales, but main threat nowadays habitat destruction, including conversion of coastal swamps to rice-fields.

STEAMERDUCKS

Tachyeres spp.
While steamerducks are easily distinguished from any other waterfowl by their very heavy build, large head and massive bill, identifying the individual steamerduck species presents considerable problems. All four are basically similar: slate-grey, more or less mottled brown, with white belly and white in wing. The most apparent differences are in the colour and pattern of head and neck, but there are as many similarities as differences, especially among immatures, many of which are likely to be impossible to identify. The situation is not helped by the occurrence of two or three plumages within the year, with associated moults. The full sequence of plumage changes and whether or not they are all complete are poorly understood. While the three flightless species (Magellanic, Falkland, White-headed) have discrete ranges and can be identified on basis of location, the fourth (Flying Steamerduck) overlaps in range with all of them and can be difficult, if not impossible in some plumages, to separate. Any steamerduck seen to fly strongly can be confidently named as a Flying Steamerduck; but note that latter is often disinclined to fly, and some, particularly large males, are probably unable to take off. In addition, individuals of all the flightless species can fly, but for only short distances and with little ability to manoeuvre. The following accounts concentrate on head and neck patterns as the principal means of distinguishing

each of the flightless species from Flying Steamerduck. The timing of plumages given is very approximate, as considerable individual variation exists.
It is worth noting that the White-headed Steamerduck was only described as a separate species in 1981 and consequently is not referred to in older works. Its separation, while helping to sort out earlier confusion between the flightless species, does not make field identification much easier

FLYING STEAMERDUCK

Tachyeres patachonicus L 66-71 cm (26-28 in), WS 100-110 cm (39-43 in)
Monotypic. Smaller and slimmer than other steamerducks, and capable of strong flight.
IDENTIFICATION Adults Three plumages and moults during year. Body plumage typical of all steamerducks, slate-grey above and on breast and flanks, all with quite broad darker edges producing noticeable mottled effect; feather edgings reddish-brown in this species. Belly, vent and undertail-coverts white. Tail dark grey and upturned at end. Dark grey forewing and primaries, with white secondaries. Tips of closed wings reach approximately to base of tail. **Adult male** *Head and neck* April to September: grey-brown, darker on crown, tinged cinnamon on throat, with short white stripe running back and down from behind eye. October to December: mainly very pale grey to whitish, darkest on lores, lacking stripe behind eye, still with cinnamon tinge on throat. January to March: much darker and very variable, can be (1) dark brown with white eye-ring and cinnamon throat, (2) dark grey on crown but brown on face, (3) dark greyish-purple with small whitish eye-stripe and cinnamon throat. Bill orange-yellow, paler and sometimes grey-tinged towards tip. Legs and feet orange-yellow with dusky webs. Calls a high-pitched whistle and lower grunts. **Adult female** *Head and neck* April to September: dark grey crown above dark brown face, becoming paler to rear and down neck, forming slight paler collar at base, but throat dark cinnamon; whitish stripe behind eye, as male. October to December: brown of face acquires rufous tinge, but eye-stripe and collar less obvious or absent. January to March: variable, some as in April-September but with whitish eye-ring and indistinct stripe to rear, others much paler on face and neck but with more obvious eye stripe. Bill slate-blue; legs and feet slightly paler than male. Low-pitched grunting calls. **Juvenile** *Head and neck* Dark, almost blackish-brown, slightly rufous on sides, with whitish eye-ring and thin stripe behind. Bill bluish-black, with slight orange at base; legs and feet yellow-brown. Acquires adult plumage during first year. **Confusion risks** For separation from other three steamerducks, see those. Only one to occur on inland fresh waters.
DISTRIBUTION AND STATUS Most widespread steamerduck, mainly resident southern Chile

and Argentina, including Tierra del Fuego, and Falklands; some dispersal to coasts and northward in winter. Though mainly coastal, also occurs on large inland lakes. No population estimates owing to difficulty of identification, but quite common on Argentine lakes, with 2,500 counted in one region. No known threats.

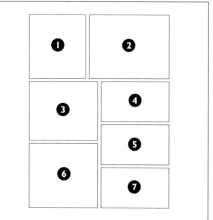

1 **Australian (or Red-backed) Radjah Shelduck** (adult, Australia)
2 **Australian (or Red-backed) Radjah Shelduck** (two adults plus young, Australia)
3 **Australian (or Red-backed) Radjah Shelduck** (adult, Australia)
4 **Flying Steamerduck** (pair, Tierra del Fuego)
5 **Flying Steamerduck** (juvenile, Tierra del Fuego)
6 **Flying Steamerduck** (male, Falklands)
7 **Flying Steamerduck** (flock flying, Tierra del Fuego)

STEAMERDUCKS

MAGELLANIC STEAMERDUCK

Tachyeres pteneres L 74-84 cm (29-33 in), WS 85-110 cm (33-43 in)
Monotypic. Largest flightless steamerduck, occurring southern Chile and Tierra del Fuego.
IDENTIFICATION Adults Two or, more probably, three plumages and moults per year. Body and wings as Flying Steamerduck but greyer, less brown, though female tinged slightly purplish-grey on back. Tips of closed wings do not reach base of tail, which only slightly upturned. **Male** *Head and neck* January to September: blue-grey, paler on forehead and crown (though not all individuals), and with noticeable white eye-ring, and rufous tinge to throat. October to December, possibly longer: uniformly paler grey, with forehead and crown no longer obviously darker, but retaining eye-ring and throat colour. Bill bright orange, darker towards base. Legs and feet bright yellow with brownish webs. Repeated, high-pitched whistling calls. **Female** Considerably smaller than male. *Head and neck* Darker grey on crown and neck, with brown face, white eye-ring plus white stripe curving back and to rear. Bill, legs and feet as male. Low croaking calls. **Juvenile** *Head and neck* Uniform dark grey, tinged brown; eye-ring present, but narrow, pale and inconspicuous. Bill, legs and feet brownish. **Confusion risks** From Flying Steamerduck by size, which obvious when the two seen together, including much more massive head and bill; longer gap between tips of wings and base of less upturned tail. Generally paler-headed than Flying Steamerduck, especially in breeding season, and body greyer, less brown, though this more obvious on males than females. Birds with obvious white rear eye-stripe probably always Flying Steamerducks, but not all have this and many have indistinct stripe as some Magellanic. Immatures probably not distinguishable on plumage. Magellanic never found on lakes well inland, but may visit fresh waters close to sea.
DISTRIBUTION AND STATUS Resident on coasts of southern Chile south to Tierra del Fuego. Purely coastal, mainly on rocky shores and among kelp beds. Quite common throughout range, and population estimated at several tens of thousands, with no real threats.

FALKLAND STEAMERDUCK

Tachyeres brachypterus L 61-74 cm (24-29 in), WS 84-94 cm (33-37 in)
Monotypic. Flightless steamerduck occurring solely in Falkland Islands.
IDENTIFICATION Adults Three plumages and moults during year, though poorly studied. Body and wings as Flying Steamerduck, with similar reddish-brown overall colouring. Tips of closed wings do not reach base of tail, which only slightly upturned. **Male** *Head and neck* January to September: pale grey, darker on sides of face; whitish eye-ring and backward- and downward-curving stripe; reddish-brown on throat and foreneck, becoming paler below,

but yellowish tinge at base. October to March: much paler grey, with darker patches on cheeks; whitish eye-ring and stripe become much less obvious. Bill bright orange, paler towards tip. Legs and feet yellow. Loud two-note whistle. **Female** Smaller than male. *Head and neck* Dark grey crown and hindneck, dark rufous-brown cheeks, sides and front of neck; noticeable white eye-ring with curving stripe to rear. Bill olive, yellow at base; legs and feet yellow. Grunting and creaking calls. **Juvenile** *Head and neck* Dull brown, with very pale eye-ring but no stripe. Bill grey; legs and feet yellow-brown. Acquires adult plumage during first year, though some second-year males still brown on cheeks. **Confusion risks** From Flying Steamerduck only with difficulty, unless latter flies strongly. When seen together, larger and with larger bill than Flying; also longer gap between tips of wings and base of less upturned tail. Presence of yellowish collar at base of neck indicates male Falkland, as does fully orange bill lacking any paler or greyer area towards tip shown by male Flying Steamerduck. Immatures probably indistinguishable on plumage. Never seen on inland fresh waters, though can walk up to 1 km to pools near coast.
DISTRIBUTION AND STATUS Confined to Falkland Islands, where resident. Found on rocky coasts, offshore islands and in sheltered inlets, visiting freshwater pools close to shore. Widespread and common, with 1982 estimate of 100,000 individuals. No known threats.

WHITE-HEADED STEAMERDUCK

Tachyeres leucocephalus L 61-74 cm (24-29 in), WS 84-94 cm (33-37 in)
Monotypic. Conspicuously pale-headed flightless steamerduck of small area of coastal Argentina.
IDENTIFICATION Adults Two plumages and moults per year known, but third probable. Body and wings as Flying Steamerduck, but lacking reddish-brown tinge to plumage. Tips of closed wings do not reach base of tail, which only slightly upturned. **Male** *Head and neck* March to September: whitish to very pale grey, especially on crown, with cheeks washed pale brown and centre of throat pale cinnamon. October to December: overall even whiter. January to February: darker grey-brown, with white eye-ring and obvious curving stripe behind. Bill orange, paler towards tip. Legs and feet yellow. Calls unknown, but presumed similar to Magellanic Steamerduck. **Female** *Head and neck* March to September: dark grey on crown, remainder of head and hindneck red-brown, becoming cinnamon on throat and upper foreneck; thin white stripes curve backwards from white eye-rings, then broaden and become more diffuse down sides of neck, before joining as narrow whitish collar near base. October to February: darker brown, tinged purplish; eye-stripe reduced, and stripe down sides of neck and collar sometimes, perhaps always, lacking. Bill yellowish-grey; legs and feet yellow. Calls presumed as Magellanic

Steamerduck. **Juvenile** *Head and neck* As female, though with reduced pale eye-ring and only short stripe, not curving down sides of neck. Bill grey; legs and feet brownish. Rate of progress to adult plumage uncertain, but probably mostly complete by end of first year.
Confusion risks Males always distinct from Flying Steamerduck in whiteness of head, as only dark-headed non-breeding birds of latter species occur within range of White-headed. White neck-stripe and collar of breeding females distinct, but non-breeding birds closer to Flying Steamerduck, though larger, with more massive head and bill and longer gap between tips of wings and base of less upturned tail. Immatures probably not distinguishable on plumage.
DISTRIBUTION AND STATUS Resident in small area of south coast of Chubut Province, southern Argentina, from where first named as separate species in 1981. Occupies similar habitat to Magellanic Steamerduck. Population reported as probably lying between 1,000 and 10,000 individuals and stable. Large flocks seen on some occasions, presumably of moulting or non-breeding birds. Species' very restricted coastal range must make it vulnerable to oil spillage.

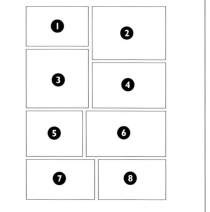

1 *Magellanic Steamerduck* (male)
2 *Magellanic Steamerduck* (female)
3 **Falkland Steamerduck** (female calling, Falklands)
4 **Falkland Steamerduck** (pair with young, Falklands)
5 **Falkland Steamerduck** (male, Falklands)
6 **Falkland Steamerduck** (pair, Falklands)
7 **White-headed Steamerduck** (pair, Chubut, Argentina)
8 **White-headed Steamerduck** (adult female and young females, Chubut, Argentina)

PERCHING GEESE AND DUCKS

SPUR-WINGED GOOSE

Plectropterus gambensis
Polytypic. Two subspecies: (1) Gambian Spur-winged Goose *P. g. gambensis*, breeds Africa south of Sahara south to about the Zambezi; (2) Black Spur-winged Goose *P. g. niger*, breeds South Africa north to about the Zambezi. Wide area of intergradation between the two.

Gambian Spur-winged Goose

Plectropterus gambensis gambensis L 85-100 cm (33-39 in), WS 165-200 cm (65-79 in)
Huge, long-legged, black-and-white goose, unlike any other wildfowl of region.
IDENTIFICATION Male breeding and non-breeding White on sides of head and chin; rest of head and neck black, glossed iridescent bronze and metallic-green. Bare area from in front of eye to base of bill bluish. Patch of white and deep flesh-coloured skin on side of upper neck, just below white of chin. Sides of breast and upper flanks glossy iridescent black, with irregular boundary with white centre of breast, lower flanks, belly, vent and undertail-coverts. Upperparts, including uppertail-coverts and tail, glossy, iridescent black. Upperwings also iridescent black, except for white on lesser coverts and around the carpal joint forming broad white leading edge to wing; all underwing-coverts white, contrasting with black flight feathers. Large bony spur on carpal joint. Bill reddish-flesh with pink nail, and enlarged reddish knob up forehead to above eye. Legs and feet reddish-flesh. Thin whistling call. **Female** As male, but considerably smaller. Bare skin in front of eye less than male, and knob reduced or even absent, as is bare patch on side of neck. Call a high-pitched squeaky twittering. **Juvenile** As adults, but black feathering duller and greyer, lacking all iridescence; white areas tinged brownish. Bare area on face feathered white, tinged brown. Bill, legs and feet as adult. Attains adult plumage and bare-skin areas by end of first year.
Confusion risks Cannot be confused with any other wildfowl except Black Spur-winged Goose (see below).
DISTRIBUTION AND STATUS Resident over large area of tropical Africa from south of Sahara south to Mozambique, Zambia and northern Namibia, approximately along line of Zambezi River, where considerable intergrading with Black Spur-winged Goose; some dispersal and seasonal movements related to rains, though poorly known. Uses wide variety of large freshwater wetlands in open areas. Reasonably common throughout range. Population not counted, but estimated to be in range 100,000 to 1 million and not subject to any major threats.

Black Spur-winged Goose

Plectropterus gambensis niger L 75-90 cm (30-35 in), WS 150-180 cm (59-71 in)
Huge, long-legged and mainly black goose, unlike any other wildfowl of region.
IDENTIFICATION Male breeding and non-

breeding Small amount of white around eye and on chin; rest of head, neck, sides of breast, flanks and upperparts black, strongly glossed with bronze and metallic green iridescence. Bare area between eye and base of bill reddish-flesh. Centre of breast and belly, together with vent and undertail-coverts, white, somewhat variable among individuals and often very reduced on breast and upper belly. Wings, above and below, as Gambian Spurwing. Bill, legs and feet as Gambian Spurwing, but knob smaller. **Female** As male, but with bare skin in front of eye reduced and knob smaller or absent. **Juvenile** As Gambian Spurwing.
Confusion risks Slightly smaller than Gambian Spurwing and with face patch reddish, not bluish, and males lacking bare patch on side of upper neck. Has less white on underparts, but this is variable, and, though extent of white rarely approaches that of Gambian subspecies and normally much less, the common presence of intergrades in area of range overlap means that this cannot be used as an identification character in that region.
DISTRIBUTION AND STATUS Resident South Africa, southern Namibia, Botswana, Zimbabwe and southern Mozambique approximately to Zambezi River. Habitat similar to that of Gambian subspecies. Population estimated at between 10,000 and 100,000, and with no known threats.

MUSCOVY DUCK

Cairina moschata L 66-84 cm (26-33 in), WS 114-150 cm (45-59 in)
Monotypic. Unmistakable, large duck, all black apart from white in wings.
IDENTIFICATION Male breeding and non-breeding Dark brownish-black to black head, neck and entire upperparts and underparts, strongly glossed with green and purple iridescence. Tufts of feathers on head produce domed crown and hanging crest on nape. Bare, swollen skin around eye and joining base of bill blackish, sometimes with reddish tinge. Primary feathers black, and secondaries glossed green, forming speculum behind white forewing (white shows on closed wing of resting bird); underwing-coverts white, flight feathers black. Bill black on nail, across middle of upper mandible and at base, where enlarged blackish knob extends along top of upper mandible to level with nostrils; rest of bill pale flesh-pink. Legs and feet dark grey. Only call a weak hissing sound. **Female** As male, but substantially smaller, with no overlap in measurements or weights. Lacks knob and bare area around eye. Has low quacking call.
Juvenile As adults, but lacking gloss to feathers and thus looking duller and browner, some appearing dark brown, mottled paler brown. White on wing-coverts acquired during first year, but continues to increase in extent during second year and perhaps subsequently.
Confusion risks Unmistakable, as no other all dark-bodied duck with or without white wing-coverts. Many domesticated variants, almost

always showing more white, as well as, especially, red on larger knob and more extensive bare skin on face.
DISTRIBUTION AND STATUS Largely resident in central America from Mexico southwards, and in South America east of the Andes as far south as Uruguay and northern Argentina; some dispersal and seasonal movements, but little information. Introduced in southern USA, though barely surviving, and (mainly domesticated forms) apparently naturalized in a few areas in Europe. Occupies wide variety of tropical wetlands, mainly in forested regions, also occurring on coastal marshes. Population estimated as between 100,000 and 1 million birds. Known to have declined in some areas through excessive hunting and habitat destruction.

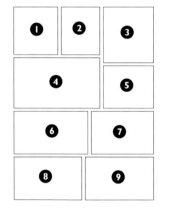

1 **Gambian Spur-winged Goose** (flock in flight, The Gambia)
2 **Gambian Spur-winged Goose** (adult male, The Gambia)
3 **Gambian Spur-winged Goose** (adult male, Tanzania)
4 **Gambian Spur-winged Goose** (immature, Tanzania)
5 **Black Spur-winged Goose** (adult, Botswana)
6 **Black Spur-winged Goose** (group, Botswana)
7 **Muscovy Duck** (domesticated form, Seychelles)
8 **Muscovy Duck** (male, Pantanal, Brazil)
9 *Muscovy Duck (immature female)*

PERCHING DUCKS

WHITE-WINGED WOOD DUCK

Cairina scutulata L 66-81 cm (26-32 in), WS 116-150 cm (46-59 in)
Monotypic. Large, very dark duck with black-speckled white head and neck, distinct within range.
IDENTIFICATION Male breeding and non-breeding Head and most of neck white, very variably freckled dark grey, from very heavily, appearing quite dark at a distance, to almost completely white and with white extending down onto breast and even upper belly. Majority of birds are well freckled, but still appear pale-headed. Lower neck, breast and upper belly dark brown to black; lower belly, flanks, vent and undertail-coverts dark chestnut-brown. Upperparts, including uppertail-coverts and tail, blackish-brown with glossy green iridescence. On upperwing, primaries and primary coverts dark brown-black, secondaries bluish-grey, forming speculum, with white forewing; tertials black, with white outer webs on outermost feathers; underwing with white coverts and black flight feathers. Bill yellow-orange, becoming redder in breeding season, when slightly swollen at base. Legs and feet yellow-orange. Harsh, honking call. **Female** As male, but rather smaller, measurements and weights barely overlapping. Plumage a little duller and head generally slightly more speckled, though also considerable variation. Call a squeaky honking. **Juvenile** Duller and browner than adults and head pale brown, though soon becomes white and freckled. Lacks green gloss in first year.
Confusion risks No other wildfowl is dark-bodied with freckled white head and neck, or pure white head, neck and breast as in extreme cases (most extreme white-headed birds found in south-east Asia but not apparently confined to that area). Old World Comb Duck, which overlaps in range, has slightly similar head and neck, but with dark crown and nape and extensive pale grey or white on underparts.
DISTRIBUTION AND STATUS Resident Arunachal Pradesh, Assam, Bangladesh, Burma, Thailand and Sumatra, and possibly Malaysia and Java, where may now be extinct. Inhabits pools and slow-flowing rivers in rainforest. Population in wild thought to number only 400-450 in 1995, with c 100 in India-Burma and c 150 each in south-east Asia and Indonesia, though censusing extremely difficult. Has declined severely, mainly through overhunting and habitat destruction. Protection, including network of reserves, being boosted by releases of captive-reared birds. Population in captivity several hundreds.

COMB DUCK

Sarkidiornis melanotos
Polytypic. Two subspecies: (1) Old World Comb Duck *S. m. melanotos*, resident Africa and Indian subcontinent; (2) South American Comb Duck *S. m. sylvicola*, resident northern and eastern South America.

Old World Comb Duck

Sarkidiornis melanotos melanotos L 60-76 cm (24-30 in), 122-145 (48-57 in)
Large, mainly black-and-white duck with substantial knob on bill of male.
IDENTIFICATION Male breeding Centre of crown, nape and back of neck black; rest of head white, speckled black, with variable yellow tinge on sides of head and neck. Lower neck, breast, centre of belly and vent white; flanks pale grey, marked at front and back by black lines extending down from black upperparts; undertail-coverts white, usually strongly tinged yellow. Upperparts black, strongly glossed with bronze, blue and metallic green; rump grey, tail black. Whole of upperwing black, strongly glossed bronzy-green, especially on secondaries and secondary coverts; underwing all black with little iridescence. Bill black, with greatly enlarged dark grey fleshy knob extending forwards along upper mandible almost to tip. Legs and feet dark grey. Very weak, churring call. **Male non-breeding** Knob considerably reduced in size. Lacks yellow tinge on head, neck and undertail-coverts. **Female** As male, but smaller and less glossy, often with brown tinge to underparts, while flanks are lightly barred grey-brown, and dark bars either side are ill-defined. Lacks any yellow tinge to head, neck or undertail-coverts. **Juvenile** Crown and upperparts dark brown; remainder of head and neck paler brown, but with darker stripe through eye. Underparts pale brown, shading to whitish on centre of belly, vent and undertail-coverts, with darker brown blotching to sides of belly and, especially, flanks. Moults into more adult-like plumage during first year, though still duller and darker on crown and back of neck. Attains adult plumage in second year. **Confusion risks** Adults unlike any other wildfowl of region, except perhaps White-winged Wood Duck (see above). Juveniles, if not accompanied by adult, sufficiently different to require care in identification.
DISTRIBUTION AND STATUS Extensive breeding range, throughout Africa south of Sahara, in Madagascar, and through tropical Asia from Pakistan to eastern China; partial migrant, mainly responding to dry and wet seasons. Inhabits lowland swamps and lakes in open or lightly wooded country. African population estimated at between 100,000 and 1 million, with some additional tens of thousands in Madagascar; scarce in south and south-east Asia, where no more than 6,000 and probably declining. Excessive shooting and habitat destruction main threats.

South American Comb Duck

Sarkidiornis melanotos sylvicola L 56-70 cm (22-28 in), 116-140 (46-55 in)
Large, mainly black-and-white duck with substantial knob on bill of male.
IDENTIFICATION Male breeding and non-breeding As Old World Comb Duck, but with black, glossed green and blue, on flanks, instead of grey, and with colour extending more onto underparts, leaving smaller amount of white on centre of belly. Knob on bill smaller, even in breeding season, extending perhaps halfway between nostrils and tip. **Female** As Old World Comb Duck, but flanks dark grey. **Juvenile** As Old World Comb Duck. **Confusion risks** No confusion likely with any other wildfowl within range. Smaller than Old World Comb Duck.
DISTRIBUTION AND STATUS Resident eastern Panama and Trinidad, and in South America from Colombia and Venezuela southwards, east of Andes, to northern Argentina. Habitat similar to that of Old World Comb Duck. Population cautiously estimated at between 20,000 and 200,000. Range has certainly contracted in recent decades, a result of habitat destruction, poisons used to combat foraging of wildfowl on rice-fields and excessive shooting.

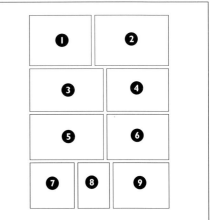

1 **White-winged Wood Duck** (adult)
2 **White-winged Wood Duck** (adult)
3 **White-winged Wood Duck** (adult)
4 **Old World Comb Duck** (breeding male, Tanzania)
5 **Old World Comb Duck** (female, Tanzania)
6 **Old World Comb Duck** (breeding male, Tanzania)
7 **Old World Comb Duck** (non-breeding male, Bharatpur, India)
8 **Old World Comb Duck** (female in flight, The Gambia)
9 **South American Comb Duck** (male)

PERCHING DUCKS

HARTLAUB'S DUCK

Pteronetta hartlaubi L 56-58 cm (22-23 in), WS 77-88 cm
Monotypic; former separation into two subspecies no longer recognized. Dark rich chestnut duck of African forests.

IDENTIFICATION Male breeding and non-breeding Black head and upper neck with variable amount of white, from small patch at base of bill to extensive area on forehead and crown, extending down around eye. Lower neck and entire underparts uniform rich chestnut-brown, sometimes appearing lighter on neck and breast in strong light. Upperparts similar, but darkening to olive-brown on lower back, rump, uppertail-coverts and tail. Primaries and primary coverts dark olive-brown, forewing pale grey-blue, secondaries edged grey-blue, and tertials edged black; underwing uniform dark olive-brown. Bill black, with pale pink to yellowish band behind tip and, though not invariably, small pale pink to yellowish mark below each nostril; bill becomes enlarged at base during breeding season. Legs and feet dusky brown. High-pitched wheezing call. **Female** As male, but smaller and rarely has any white on head. Chestnut colouring on body plumage a little duller. Loud, frequently uttered, quacking call. **Juvenile** As adult female, but duller still, pale straw-coloured edgings to feathers of breast, flanks and belly producing light mottling effect. Bill paler than adult. **Confusion risks** Unlike any other duck of region. Birds with most white on head found mainly in Zaïre, perhaps reflecting genetic tendency to partial albinism in population of the area.

DISTRIBUTION AND STATUS Resident equatorial West and Central Africa, from Guinea and Sierra Leone eastwards through Nigeria to extreme eastern Sudan, and southwards to Gabon, Congo and Zaïre. Inhabits tropical forest and more open woodlands with sheltered pools, swamps and small streams. Little information on numbers or abundance, but estimated to lie within range 10,000-100,000 and probably declining in areas of deforestation.

RINGED TEAL

Callonetta leucophrys L 35-38 cm (14-15 in), WS 58-64 cm (23-25 in)
Monotypic. Small duck of South American forests, distinct from other wildfowl within range.

IDENTIFICATION Male breeding and non-breeding Head and neck buff, with a few fine grey streaks. Black stripe on crown and down back of neck and then forward, forming half-ring at base. Breast buff-pink with small black spots, becoming buff and unspotted in front of grey flanks, which finely vermiculated with black; belly white, vent and undertail-coverts black but with large white patch on lower sides of rump. Mantle light olive-brown, more chestnut to the sides and on scapulars; lower

back, rump, uppertail-coverts and tail black. Primaries and their coverts black, secondaries iridescent green with white area on secondary coverts, lesser and median coverts black; underwing all dark. Bill blue-grey. Legs and feet pink. Soft *whee-ooo* call. Wings whistle in flight. **Female** Dark brown forehead, lores, crown and back of neck. Whitish supercilium and white cheeks and throat, with large 'fingerprint'-like smudge behind and below eye. Underparts dull brown, mottled darker on breast and barred pale buff-grey on belly and flanks; vent and undertail-coverts whitish, with small black bar on sides. Upperparts olive-brown, tail darker brown. Upperwings and underwings as male. Bill grey; legs and feet pink. Call a rising *hou-ii*. **Juvenile male** Overall colouring as adult female, but head pattern resembles dull adult male. **Juvenile female** Closely resembles adult female. **Confusion risks** Small size and distinctive pattern of both sexes, even though difficult to see in forest habitat, unlike any other wildfowl within range.

DISTRIBUTION AND STATUS Known to breed only in north-west Argentina and Paraguay, but also occurs, presumed as non-breeder, in eastern Bolivia, southern Brazil and Uruguay; extent of movements unclear, though some northward post-breeding. Inhabits wet areas within tropical forests and wooded lowlands, including marshes, pools and streams. Population unknown, but widespread and apparently quite common, leading to estimate of 25,000-100,000.

GREEN PYGMY-GOOSE

Nettapus pulchellus 30-36 cm (12-14 in), WS 48-60 cm (19-24 in)
Monotypic. Tiny duck with male distinctive, but female and juvenile show some similarity to Cotton Pygmy-goose.

IDENTIFICATION Male breeding Dark iridescent green crown, to below eye, and neck, finely barred dark brown on crown and nape, with white face patch on lower cheeks and chin. Upper breast, flanks and vent pale grey, with dark green and white scallop markings; lower breast and belly white; undertail-coverts dark grey. Mantle and scapulars dark iridescent green, becoming grey, with dark green barring, on lower back, rump and uppertail-coverts; tail black. Primaries and primary coverts blackish, secondaries white, and secondary coverts iridescent green. Bill dark grey, with pink nail and underside. Legs and feet dark grey. Shrill whistling call. **Male non-breeding** As male breeding, but duller, with less iridescence, and with grey freckles on white face and light mottling on foreneck. **Female** As male breeding, but slightly smaller and duller, with white on face greyer. Sides and front of neck lacking dark green and finely barred like upper breast. Whistling call, lower in tone than male's. **Juvenile** Similar to adult female, but face, chin and neck mottled dark brown. Green foreneck of male appears in first autumn, and both sexes as adults by end of first

winter. **Confusion risks** The dark head and neck and white cheeks distinguish this species from Cotton Pygmy-goose, which overlaps in range. Latter has dark stripe through eye and whitish supercilium, though this may not be obvious at long range, when confusion possible with female and juvenile Green Pygmy-goose.

DISTRIBUTION AND STATUS Breeds southern Papua New Guinea and northern Australia, including northern parts of Western Australia, Northern Territory and Queensland; resident, but disperses in rains. Occupies well-vegetated lowland lagoons and other permanent fresh waters. No estimates of population, though not uncommon throughout range, and no obvious threats.

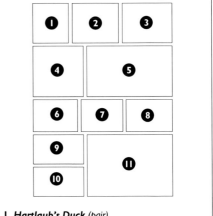

1 **Hartlaub's Duck** (pair)
2 **Hartlaub's Duck** (male)
3 **Hartlaub's Duck** (male)
4 **Hartlaub's Duck** ("white-headed" male)
5 **Ringed Teal** (female with young)
6 **Ringed Teal** (pair)
7 **Ringed Teal** (male)
8 **Green Pygmy Goose** (eclipse male)
9 **Green Pygmy Goose** (juvenile)
10 **Green Pygmy Goose** (pair, Kakadu NP, Australia)
11 **Green Pygmy Goose** (pair, Australia)

COTTON PYGMY-GOOSE

Nettapus coromandelianus
Polytypic. Two subspecies: (1) Indian Cotton Pygmy-goose *N. c. coromandelianus*, breeds southern and south-east Asia, wintering within and to south of range; (2) Australian Cotton Pygmy-goose *N. c. albipennis*, resident eastern Australia.

Indian Cotton Pygmy-goose

Nettapus coromandelianus coromandelianus L 33-38 cm (13-15 in), WS 52-62 cm (20-24 in)
Tiny duck of southern Asia, with no similar species within range.
IDENTIFICATION Male breeding Black forehead and crown and very narrow eye-ring; rest of head, neck and breast white, separated from white belly and grey-washed flanks by black breast band. Flanks very finely mottled grey towards rear; undertail-coverts blackish. Upperparts black, strongly glossed with green; uppertail-coverts whitish with black mottling; tail black. Broad white band across black primaries and white tips to black secondaries forming wing-bar above and below; upperwing-coverts black, glossed green; underwing-coverts blackish. Bill, legs and feet blackish. Staccato, cackling calls. **Male non-breeding** Resembles female, but whiter on head and neck and retains more extensive white on wing. This plumage adopted for at least half of year, timing dependent on breeding season, which varies across range. **Female** Dark greyish-brown crown, hindneck and eye-stripe, buffish-white face, foreneck and underparts, including undertail-coverts, and lacking any breast band. Breast and flanks with greyish-brown mottling and barring. Upperparts darker greyish-brown with slight green iridescence. Upperwings and underwings all dark greyish-brown except for white tips to secondaries. Bill, legs and feet blackish. Call a soft quack. **Juvenile** As female, but lacking any iridescence. Has broader eye-stripe and more prominent mottling on underparts. Male has more white on wing than female, and both as adult by end of first year.
Confusion risks White head of male prevents confusion with any other small ducks of range, and white wing-bar of male also very distinctive. Females and juveniles show some similarity to Green Pygmy-goose (see above).
DISTRIBUTION AND STATUS Widespread India, Bangladesh, Sri Lanka and Burma east to southern China, and south through south-east Asia to Malaysia; most resident, but some movement from China south and east into Indonesia as far as northern Irian Jaya and Papua New Guinea. Inhabits well-vegetated lakes and pools, also swamps and rivers. Estimated populations of up to 100,000 in Indian subcontinent, and of several hundred thousands in east and south-east Asia. No apparent threats.

Australian Cotton Pygmy-goose

Nettapus coromandelianus albipennis L 31-36 cm (12-14 in), WS 50-60 cm (20-24 in)
Tiny duck of eastern Australia, with possibility of confusion of females and immatures with Green Pygmy-goose.
IDENTIFICATION Male and female breeding and non-breeding, juvenile As Indian subspecies, but slightly smaller. Male non-breeding plumage adopted for much shorter period than in Indian subspecies, immediately following January-March breeding season, with reports that some have barely completed the moult into this plumage before moulting back into breeding plumage, so perhaps lasting little longer than three-week flightless period.
Confusion risks Range overlaps with Green Pygmy-goose and confusion possible, especially between females and juveniles of both at distance, when dark eye-stripe of this species less apparent.
DISTRIBUTION AND STATUS Breeds in restricted area of Queensland, where scattered very locally over about 1200 km of east coast from Cape Melville south to about Rockhampton; formerly also in northern New South Wales. Habitat similar to that of Indian subspecies, but never far from coast. Population very small, estimated at no more than 1,500 in 1960s, and currently no more than 2,500, but thought to be increasing, despite habitat loss through wetland drainage.

AFRICAN PYGMY-GOOSE

Nettapus auritus L 28-33 cm (11-13 in), WS 46-56 cm (18-22 in)
Monotypic. Tiny, brightly coloured duck, unmistakable within or outside African range.
IDENTIFICATION Male breeding White forehead, face, throat and foreneck, with iridescent greenish-black crown and stripe down hindneck. Large pale green patch on sides of upper neck, extending onto rear of cheeks, bordered with black. Lower part of foreneck, breast and flanks bright chestnut-orange, sometimes with fine black barring on breast and upper flanks; belly white, vent and undertail-coverts black. Entire upperparts black, strongly glossed green, especially on scapulars; tail black. Outer wing and inner wing-coverts black, glossed green, with large white patch on greater coverts and outer secondaries; underwing dark. Bill bright yellow with black nail. Legs and feet dark grey. High-pitched whistling calls. **Male non-breeding** Not fully documented and does not last long. Head pattern more as female, but bill remains bright yellow, and duller on upperparts, while underparts have greater amount of fine dark barring. **Female** Head and neck whitish, with ill-defined brownish-grey markings forming broken eye-stripe and patches on cheeks and upper neck; crown and back of neck blackish. Underparts similar to male, though chestnut-orange of breast and flanks slightly duller but lacking any black barring. Upperparts as male, but with reduced green iridescence. Wings as male, also with slightly less iridescence. Bill dull yellowish-grey; legs and feet dark grey. Call a weak quack. **Juvenile** As female, but with more obvious dark eye-stripe and less clear markings on cheeks and neck; breast and flanks paler, more buff in tone. Becomes as adult in first year. **Confusion risks** Both sexes unmistakable, as no other duck has orange-chestnut breast and flanks. White patch on wing conspicuous in flight.
DISTRIBUTION AND STATUS Widespread in Africa south of Sahara, and in Madagascar, though absent from Horn of Africa and from desert areas of south-west Africa. Inhabits wide variety of wetlands, both permanent and temporary, though preferring well-vegetated permanent waters. Scarce in West Africa, where population estimated at fewer than 10,000, but much commoner in eastern and southern Africa, with population estimated at several hundred thousands. Only a few thousand thought to occur in Madagascar, where hunting has reduced numbers.

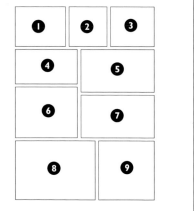

1 **Indian Cotton Pygmy-goose** (adult male, India)
2 **Indian Cotton Pygmy-goose** (pair, India)
3 **Indian Cotton Pygmy-goose** (immature female, Bharatpur, India)
4 **Indian Cotton Pygmy-goose** (immature female, Bharatpur, India)
5 **Australian Cotton Pygmy-goose** (male, breeding, Australia)
6 *African Pygmy-goose* (male, partial moult)
7 **African Pygmy-goose** (pair, Africa)
8 **African Pygmy-goose** (male, Tanzania)
9 **African Pygmy-goose** (male, flapping, Africa)

PERCHING DUCKS

NORTH AMERICAN WOOD DUCK

Aix sponsa L 43-51 cm (17-20 in), WS 68-75 cm (27-30 in)
Monotypic. Male unmistakable, but female and juvenile extremely similar to extralimital Mandarin Duck.
IDENTIFICATION Male breeding Mainly blackish head with long, shaggy, erectile crest, strongly glossed with green, blue and purple. Thin white lines from top of bill over eye and down crest, and from behind eye down sides of crest to tip. Chin and throat white, with broad extensions up into dark cheeks and around neck forming half-collar. Neck and breast purplish-maroon, with small triangular white spots. Broad white and black vertical stripes separate breast from finely vermiculated yellow-buff flanks, which bordered above and to rear by black and white crescents. Centre of lower breast and belly white; vent and undertail-coverts dusky brown. Feathers on sides of rump elongated, reddish-violet with bright orange stripes. Entire upperparts, including tail, blackish with bronze, green and purple iridescence. Upperwing blackish, glossed blue or greenish-blue, except for secondaries, which have stronger iridescence and are narrowly tipped white, and primaries, which have whitish outer webs; underwing dark brown, mottled black and white on coverts. Bill red with black tip, including nail, with white forward half of upper mandible and bright yellow line at base. Eye red, with orange-red eye-ring. Legs and feet orange-yellow with dusky patches on webs. Call a thin, squeaky whistle. **Male non-breeding** As female, but with smaller eye patch and whiter throat. Retains some gloss on upperparts. Bill with pink, not red, but retaining same pattern. From approximately June-July to September-October. **Female breeding** Dark grey head and neck with shaggy crest down nape, glossed greenish and purplish, especially on crown. Narrow white line around base of bill, and large oval white patch around eye with short rearward extension as thin line. Breast and flanks olive-brown, mottled with whitish spots and grading to white on centre of belly, vent and undertail-coverts, though some tail-coverts marked black. Upperparts, including tail, olive-brown to olive-grey with bronze and purplish sheens. Upperwing as male, but larger white tips to secondaries and reduced iridescence; underwing as male. Bill dark grey, with paler markings on upper mandible, and skin coming to a point at feathers. Legs and feet dull yellowish-grey. Narrow yellow eye-ring around brown eye. Variety of whistling notes. **Female non-breeding** As female breeding, but duller and browner, with reduced crest and less sheen on head, and eye patch reduced. Overall browner tone, with coarser spotting on breast. **Juvenile** As female, but duller, with less obvious eye patch, buff-streaked breast and flanks, and belly more streaked and mottled brown. Sex differences, especially on head, appear in first winter, with full adult plumage by end of first year. **Confusion risks** Male breeding unmistakable, through head pattern, shaggy crest, and conspicuous vertical white stripe at sides of breast. In flight, essentially dark, and dark-winged, with white belly, large-looking head and long, square-ended tail. Female and juvenile very similar to Mandarin Duck (see that species for separation).
DISTRIBUTION AND STATUS Breeds in two separated areas: in British Columbia, and Washington to California, and from Manitoba east to Nova Scotia and south to eastern Texas and Florida, also Cuba; winters within south of both ranges and also south to central Mexico. Occupies standing and slow-moving fresh waters in wooded country, though found in more open lowlands in winter. Population fell sharply in first part of 20th century through excessive shooting, but with strict protection, aided by nestbox schemes, recovered to over 1 million by 1970s and increased since then.

MANDARIN DUCK

Aix galericulata L 41-51 cm (16-20 in), WS 68-74 cm (27-29 in)
Monotypic. Male completely unmistakable, but female and juvenile extremely similar to extralimital North American Wood Duck.
IDENTIFICATION Male breeding Dark forehead, crown, and long crest drooping down neck, though erected in display, iridescent with green, bronze and purple. Broad buff-white band curves back from in front of and around eye, tapering into thin line down to tip of crest. Front of face and cheeks below eye warm buff, merging into chestnut of elongated feathers forming ruff around top of neck, shortest under chin, longest at rear, where adjoins crest. Breast rich maroon, bounded at rear by double white vertical stripes, bordered black; flanks warm cinnamon, finely vermiculated black, paler towards rear, bordered with narrow black and white bands along upper edge and at rear; centre of lower breast and belly, also vent and undertail-coverts, white. Upperparts, including tail, mainly olive-brown. Central tertial elongated to large 'sail', held upright on resting or swimming bird; sail mainly orange-gold with fine white tip, black edge to rear and iridescent purple-blue along base. Upperwing glossed blue-green on blackish coverts and flight feathers, especially secondaries, forming blue-green speculum; primaries have white outer webs, the secondaries white tips; underwing more uniformly dark grey-brown, with some whitish marks on coverts. Bill bright red with pink or whitish nail. Legs and feet yellow, with blackish markings on webs. Main call a nasal whistle. **Male non-breeding** As female, but retaining distinctive bill colour, and no white at base of bill and less white on face. Less spotted below. From about June to September. **Female breeding** Broadly as female North American Wood Duck (see that species). Main differences: overall paler and greyer; white at base of upper mandible rather than all around base of bill, and bill base square instead of coming to a point at feathers; smaller white eye patch, but with longer rearward extension as thin line; bill brown, with pink or yellow at base (occasionally more extensive) and whitish nail, instead of dark grey with blackish nail and paler subterminal area; much less gloss on upperwings. Sharp *kett* call in courtship. **Female non-breeding** As female breeding, but paler head with less well-defined white markings and shorter crest, and no white at base of upper mandible. Less distinct spots on breast. **Juvenile** As female, but duller, less clear face pattern and streaked rather than spotted underparts; white of belly spotted and streaked brown. Acquires adult plumage during first winter and spring. **Confusion risks** Male unmistakable. For separation from female North American Wood Duck, see above. Juveniles harder to separate, but have V-shaped junction between bill and feathers and soon acquire sufficient adult plumage to aid matters.
DISTRIBUTION AND STATUS Breeds south-east Russia, north-east China and Japan, wintering mainly Japan, Korea and east China. Introduced Britain. Uses variety of marshes, small pools and streams within forested areas. Population currently c 70,000, of which c 5,000 Korea, 15,000 China and 50,000 Japan. Thought to be declining in Korea and China, but better censusing has revealed population much larger than formerly believed, and c 7,000 in Britain no longer as important a component of world population as has been claimed. Habitat destruction and export of live birds continuing threats.

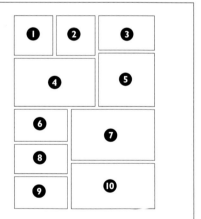

1 **North American Wood Duck** (*female moulting*)
2 **North American Wood Duck** (female, Ontario, Canada)
3 **North American Wood Duck** (*eclipse male*)
4 **North American Wood Duck** (breeding male, Ontario, Canada)
5 **North American Wood Duck** (pair, Holland)
6 **Mandarin Duck** (male, Norfolk, England)
7 **Mandarin Duck** (male eclipse, Lancashire, England)
8 **Mandarin Duck** (female in flight, China)
9 **Mandarin Duck** (first year female, Greater Manchester, England)
10 **Mandarin Duck** (pair, Norfolk, England)

PERCHING DUCKS

MANED DUCK

Chenonetta jubata L 44-56 cm (17-22 in), WS 78-90 cm (31-35 in)
Monotypic. Medium-small duck with small crest, superficially recalling goose in shape; dark-headed, with spotted underparts and green and white speculum, distinctive within Australian range.

IDENTIFICATION Male breeding and non-breeding Rounded, chocolate-brown head and upper neck, grading to blackish on nape, with slight erectile crest (or 'mane') running well down back of neck. Lower neck and breast pale buff, mottled with pale grey and whitish, with dark brown-black spots. Flanks, extending nearly to centre of belly, grey, very finely vermiculated black; centre of belly, vent and undertail-coverts black. Mantle and inner scapulars pale grey, outer scapulars black; lower back, rump, uppertail-coverts and tail black. In flight, upperwing shows pattern of black, grey, green and white, with primaries black, secondaries iridescent green with white towards tips, the white increasing outwards along wing, primary and secondary coverts pale grey, the latter with white tips and a black subterminal band bordering the green and white speculum, and tertials grey; inner half of underwing very pale grey, contrasting with black primaries and their coverts. Bill short and goose-like, dark grey. Legs and feet dark grey. Shrill, cat-like, *wee-ow* call. **Female** Medium-brown head and upper neck, with darker brown stripe through eye, from base of bill to nape, bordered by pale buff stripes above and below, the lower stripe reaching base of bill. Lower neck, breast, flanks and most of belly (except to rear) buffish-grey, heavily mottled with brown-black, grey and whitish spots, mottling becoming larger and bolder towards rear of flanks; centre of lower belly, vent and undertail-coverts white. Upperparts and tail as male, but darker, more brown-grey, on mantle and inner scapulars. Bill, legs and feet as male. Call a loud and hoarse *whroo*. **Juvenile** Resembles a pale female with less distinct eye-stripes. Males begin to acquire vermiculated flanks at about three months, and both as adult by end of first year. **Confusion risks** Very goose-like, with very short bill on rounded head and narrow neck, and comparatively upright stance on longish legs. No other small waterfowl within or outside range has these characters. In flight, wing pattern of white-bordered green speculum, black primaries and pale grey coverts also completely distinctive.
DISTRIBUTION AND STATUS Widespread in both western and eastern Australia, breeding south-west Western Australia, and from southern Australia and Tasmania north to Queensland; much dispersal, responding to irregular rains. Uses wide variety of inland fresh waters, often in open wooded country; rare on coasts. Population estimated at several tens of thousands. Hunted extensively in some areas to prevent agricultural damage, but this has not prevented continuing increase.

BRAZILIAN TEAL

Amazonetta brasiliensis
Polytypic. Two subspecies: (1) Lesser Brazilian Teal *A. b. brasiliensis*, resident northern South America, south to central-southern Brazil; (2) Greater Brazilian Teal *A. b. ipecutiri*, resident and partial migrant southern Brazil to northern Argentina.

Lesser Brazilian Teal

Amazonetta brasiliensis brasiliensis L 35-40 cm (14-16 in), WS 52-60 cm (20-24 in)
Small, rufous-brown dabbling duck, male with conspicuous red bill and female with distinctive black-and-white face pattern. No obvious confusion species within or outside range.
IDENTIFICATION Two colour phases recognized, but also some individual variation, especially in head colour and pattern. **Male breeding and non-breeding** *Dark phase:* Dark brown crown tending to blackish on nape, with very slight shaggy crest down hindneck. Cheeks from bill to just beyond eye and throat brown; rear cheeks and upper neck paler grey-brown. Lower neck, upper mantle, breast and upper anterior flanks rufous-brown with rusty-brown and blackish mottling and barring (larger rounded spots on anterior flanks), grading into paler buff-brown and unmarked posterior flanks, belly, vent and undertail-coverts. Upperparts darker brown, tending to blackish on rump, uppertail-coverts and tail. Upperwings blackish, glossed with green to purple, except for secondaries, which have iridescent green towards their bases and white on their outer halves separated by a narrow black bar, the white broadening towards inside of wing, while tertials dark brown; underwings with similar pattern, but less iridescence. *Pale phase:* As dark phase, except throat, rear cheeks and upper neck whitish, contrasting much more with dark crown, nape and hindneck; rest of body plumage lighter in tone. *Both phases:* Bill bright carmine-red with dusky nail. Legs and feet bright red. Call a strong, piercing, repeated whistle. **Female** *Dark phase:* As male on body and wings, but head pattern different: dark brown forehead, crown and upper neck, extending to include eye and base of bill; ill-defined buffish-white spot at base of bill and larger whitish patch from just above eye towards base of bill; lower cheeks, throat and foreneck buff, paler on throat. *Light phase:* Spots on head well defined and white, contrasting with dark forehead and crown. Throat almost white, lower cheeks and foreneck very pale buff. *Both phases:* Bill olive-grey; legs and feet dull reddish-orange. Call a deep quacking. **Juvenile** Closely similar to female, but duller, with poorly defined face spots and lacking most iridescence on wing.
Confusion risks The two phases are not separated geographically and include some individual variation. Despite this, no likelihood of confusion with other species. Separable from Greater Brazilian Teal only by size, but

measurements overlap.
DISTRIBUTION AND STATUS Resident in northern South America from eastern Colombia, Venezuela and Guyana south to central-southern Brazil. Inhabits small freshwater lakes and pools, mainly in heavily wooded areas. Population estimated at several hundreds of thousands, with no known threats.

Greater Brazilian Teal

Amazonetta brasiliensis ipecutiri L 39-45 cm (15-18 in), WS 58-66 cm (23-26 in)
Partially separable from Lesser Brazilian Teal on size.
IDENTIFICATION Two colour phases recognized; dark phase much commoner than light phase. Much less individual variation than in Lesser Brazilian Teal. **Male and female breeding and non-breeding, juvenile** *Both phases:* As Lesser Brazilian Teal. **Confusion risks** As with Lesser Brazilian Teal, colour phases not geographically separated. No information on intergrading between the two subspecies, though probably takes place as the two freely interbreed in captivity.
DISTRIBUTION AND STATUS Breeds eastern Bolivia, southern Brazil, Paraguay, northern Argentina and Uruguay; partial migrant, with more southerly breeders moving north well into range of Lesser Brazilian Teal, even reaching Colombia and Venezuela. Habitat as Lesser subspecies. Thought to be much less numerous than Lesser, with population estimated at several tens of thousands.

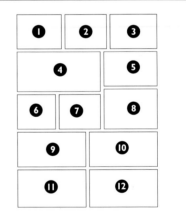

1 **Maned Duck** (pair and young, Perth, Australia)
2 **Maned Duck** (immature, Perth, Australia)
3 **Maned Duck** (male and young, Perth, Australia)
4 **Maned Duck** (female, Perth Australia)
5 **Maned Duck** (pair, Australia)
6 **Lesser Brazilian Teal** (pair, dark phase, Venezuela)
7 **Lesser Brazilian Teal** (pair in flight, probably pale phase, Llanos, Venezuela)
8 *Lesser Brazilian Teal* (female, pale phase)
9 *Lesser Brazilian Teal* (male, pale phase)
10 **Greater Brazilian Teal** (roosting group, Parque Elrey, Argentina)
11 *Greater Brazilian Teal* (male, pale phase)
12 *Greater Brazilian Teal* (female, pale phase)

TORRENT DUCKS

TORRENT DUCK

Merganetta armata
Polytypic. Six subspecies recognized here, though it has been suggested that Turner's, Garlepp's and Berlepsch's could be colour morphs of Peruvian: (1) Colombian Torrent Duck *M. a. colombiana*, Andes, from Venezuela to northern Ecuador; (2) Peruvian Torrent Duck *M. a. leucogenis*, Andes, from central Ecuador to central Peru; (3) Turner's Torrent Duck *M. a. turneri*, Andes, in southern Peru; (4) Garlepp's (or Bolivian) Torrent Duck *M. a. garleppi*, Andes, in Bolivia; (5) Berlepsch's (or Argentine) Torrent Duck *M. a. berlepschi*, Andes, in northern Chile and north-western Argentina; (6) Chilean Torrent Duck *M. a. armata*, Andes, in Chile and Argentina.

Colombian Torrent Duck

Merganetta armata colombiana L 43-46 cm (17-18 in), WS 58-69 cm (23-27 in)
Slim-bodied and long-tailed duck of northern Andean rivers, male with boldly marked head and female generally rufous below, dark above; completely unlike any other wildfowl.
IDENTIFICATION Male breeding and non-breeding Black stripe through centre of forehead over crown and down nape. Head and neck otherwise white, but with black stripe from just in front of eye running through eye and then curving back parallel with crown and nape band and then down sides of neck, before curving forwards again to end near base of white on neck; second stripe splits off from this stripe near top, and forms black 'V' on back of neck just below end of crown and nape stripe, then runs down neck to back. Usually small amount of black on chin. Breast, belly and flanks greyish-white, streaked with buff-brown and dark brown; vent and undertail-coverts dark grey. Mantle and scapulars elongated and pointed, with brown centres and pale buff edgings; lower back, rump and uppertail-coverts finely vermiculated grey and black. Long, stiff tail feathers dark grey-brown. On upperwing, primaries dark grey-brown, secondaries strongly iridescent green narrowly bordered in front and behind with white, and wing-coverts grey-blue; underwing fairly uniform brown. Sharp spur on carpal joint. Bill bright red. Legs and feet reddish with darker blotches, sometimes blackish over most of webs and toes. Call a sharp, clear whistle.
Female Forehead, crown down to eye, nape and hindneck grey (close to, this can be seen to be very finely vermiculated darker grey). Lower face, throat and all underparts and flanks pale rusty-orange. Upperparts grey, with elongated and pointed scapulars paler grey with blackish centres. Wings and tail as male. Bill, legs and feet as male. Call a sharp whistle, slightly lower in tone than male's. **Juvenile** Forehead, crown down to eye, nape and hindneck grey. Lower cheeks, throat and foreneck, as well as underparts, very pale grey to whitish, with darker grey barring on breast and, especially, on flanks. Wings and tail similar to adults, but

lacking green iridescence on blackish secondaries. Bill, legs and feet grey, tinged with red. **Confusion risks** Almost no other wildfowl inhabits the fast-flowing rivers of the Andes, while this duck's slender, long-tailed shape, as well as the very distinctive head pattern of the male and the grey and rusty-brown of the female, makes it completely unmistakable. Does not fly very often, but, when it does, usually stays close to the water on rapidly beating wings, which show pattern of dark outer wing, pale forewing and green speculum.
DISTRIBUTION AND STATUS Resident in Andes of Venezuela, Colombia and northern Ecuador. Inhabits mainly fast-flowing streams with clear water, mostly high up, but descending in winter to as low as 300 m. Population unknown, but estimated as at least 5,000 and probably decreasing. Several threats exist, including hydro-electric dams, deforestation causing increased run-off and consequent erosion and silting of streams, pollution from mining activities, and uncontrolled fishing and hunting.

Chilean Torrent Duck

Merganetta armata armata L 43-46 cm (17-18 in), WS 58-69 cm (23-27 in)
As Colombian Torrent Duck.
IDENTIFICATION Male breeding and non-breeding Head pattern differs from that of other torrent ducks in having additional black line running from eye to chin and then down centre of throat and foreneck to join blackish breast, while black of nape joins V-stripe running from eye and down hindneck. White of neck extends onto upper mantle. Breast, centre of belly and upper flanks blackish, while lower flanks and sides of belly rufous, streaked with blackish-brown. Elongated scapulars have black centres and whitish edgings. **Female** As Peruvian Torrent Duck. **Juvenile** As Peruvian Torrent Duck, but darker grey on upperparts. **Confusion risks** See Colombian Torrent Duck.
DISTRIBUTION AND STATUS Resident in Andes, from central Chile and neighbouring parts of Argentina south to Tierra del Fuego. Habitat as that of Colombian Torrent Duck. Population unknown, but perhaps 5,000. Faces most of same threats as Colombian Torrent Duck.

Turner's Torrent Duck

Merganetta armata turneri L 43-46 cm (17-18 in), WS 58-69 cm (23-27 in)
As Colombian Torrent Duck.
IDENTIFICATION Male breeding and non-breeding Similar to Peruvian Torrent Duck on head and neck, but underparts almost uniform brownish-black, lacking any streaks. Scapulars with black centres and dark brown edgings. **Female** As Peruvian Torrent Duck. **Juvenile** As Peruvian Torrent Duck, but dark grey on upperparts. **Confusion risks** See Colombian Torrent Duck.
DISTRIBUTION AND STATUS Resident in Andes of extreme southern Peru. Habitat as for Colombian Torrent Duck. Population unknown,

but probably only 1,000-2,000. Faces most of same threats as Colombian Torrent Duck.

Garlepp's (or Bolivian) Torrent Duck

Merganetta armata garleppi L 43-46 cm (17-18 in), WS 58-69 cm (23-27 in)
As Colombian Torrent Duck.
IDENTIFICATION Male breeding and non-breeding Similar to Peruvian Torrent Duck on head and neck, but underparts pale brown, with black and dark brown streaks. Scapulars with black centres and pale brown edgings. **Female** As Peruvian Torrent Duck. **Juvenile** As Peruvian Torrent Duck, but browner on upperparts. **Confusion risks** See Colombian Torrent Duck.
DISTRIBUTION AND STATUS Resident in Andes of Bolivia. Habitat as for Colombian Torrent Duck; has been found at up to at least 4500 m. Population unknown, but probably only 1,000-2,000. Faces most of same threats as Colombian Torrent Duck.

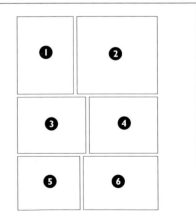

1 **Chilean Torrent Duck** (female, Chile)
2 **Chilean Torrent Duck** (pair, Chile)
3 *Chilean Torrent Duck (pair – male displaying to female)*
4 **Turner's Torrent Duck** (pair, Andes, Peru)
5 **Turner's Torrent Duck** (male, Andes, Peru)
6 **Garlepp's (or Bolivian) Torrent Duck** (male, Andes, Bolivia)

TORRENT DUCKS

Berlepsch's (or Argentine) Torrent Duck

Merganetta armata berlepschi L 43-46 cm (17-18 in), WS 58-69 cm (23-27 in)
As Colombian Torrent Duck.

IDENTIFICATION Male breeding and non-breeding Similar to Peruvian Torrent Duck on head and neck, but underparts medium grey-brown, with darker streaks not always very visible. Scapulars with black centres and grey-brown edgings. **Female** As Peruvian Torrent Duck. **Juvenile** As Peruvian Torrent Duck, but darker grey on upperparts. **Confusion risks** See Colombian Torrent Duck.

DISTRIBUTION AND STATUS Resident in Andes of northern Chile and north-west Argentina. Habitat as for Colombian Torrent Duck. Population unknown, but probably only 1,000-2,000. Faces most of same threats as Colombian Torrent Duck.

Peruvian Torrent Duck

Merganetta armata leucogenis L 43-46 cm (17-18 in), WS 58-69 cm (23-27 in)
As Colombian Torrent Duck.

IDENTIFICATION Male breeding and non-breeding Similar to Colombian Torrent Duck on head and neck, but underparts darker grey, with dark brown and black streaks. Scapulars with dark brown centres and pale brown edgings. **Female** As female Colombian Torrent Duck, but much brighter underneath, with rich orange-chestnut instead of pale rusty-orange from lower cheeks to undertail-coverts. **Juvenile** As Colombian Torrent Duck, but a little darker grey on upperparts. **Confusion risks** See Colombian Torrent Duck.

DISTRIBUTION AND STATUS Resident in Andes of central Ecuador south to central-southern Peru. There is a gap in distribution between this subspecies and Colombian Torrent Duck to north. Habitat as that of Colombian Torrent Duck. Population unknown, but estimated in low thousands and probably stable. Faces most of same threats as Colombian Torrent Duck.

BLUE DUCK

Hymenolaimus malacorhynchos
Polytypic. Two subspecies recognized here (the population on North Island has sometimes been regarded as a separate race, but as often not, though recent authorities have confirmed the validity of two subspecies): (1) South Island Blue Duck *H. m. malacorhynchos*, resident in west of South Island, New Zealand; (2) North Island Blue Duck *H. m. hymenolaimus*, resident central North Island, New Zealand.

South Island Blue Duck

Hymenolaimus malacorhynchos malacorhynchos
L 50-57 cm (20-22 in), WS 65-80 cm (26-31 in)
Uniform grey-blue colouring of this mountain-stream duck of South Island, New Zealand, precludes confusion with other wildfowl.

IDENTIFICATION Male breeding and non-breeding Virtually whole plumage is slaty-grey with a bluish sheen. Head a little darker and crown brown-grey, though brownish tinge often slight or even absent. Breast paler grey, heavily mottled with reddish-brown elongated blotches, which often arranged, at least in centre of breast, into ill-defined streaks running down onto upper belly, mottling petering out onto anterior flanks; undertail-coverts dull chestnut. Smudgy black mottling on mantle and scapulars. Upperwings same uniform blue-grey colour, but inner secondaries have black edges and outer six secondaries have very narrow white tips; underwings uniform paler grey, with white tips to secondaries showing. Bill pale pinkish-white with black nail, and black pendent lobes of skin on each side of tip; nostrils blackish. Legs and feet light brown with darker brown patches. Call a strong whistle, *whio* (giving it its Maori name). **Female** As male, but with mottling on breast less extensive and rarely reaching flanks or belly. Wings, tail and bare parts as male. Has a low, rasping quack. **Juvenile** As adults, but lacks bluish sheen; mottling on breast absent at first and then brown, lacking reddish colour, and more limited in extent than on female. Upperwing-coverts with brown tinge. Bill very pale flesh-grey, with black nail, skin lobes and stripe down centre of upper mandible almost to tip. Adult plumage acquired during first year, but some dark markings on upper mandible remain into second year. **Confusion risks** Uniform blue-grey plumage unlike any other wildfowl, within or outside restricted range and preferred habitat of mountain streams. On the water or in flight, lacks any distinctive markings, apart from spotting on breast.

DISTRIBUTION AND STATUS Resident in western mountainous regions of South Island, New Zealand, where very local and dispersed in small, isolated populations through range; thought to be most numerous in south, *eg* Southland and Otago. Confined to fast-flowing streams of clear water in mountains. Population very small; recent estimate, of 2,000-4,000, included North Island Blue Duck, too. Has declined for many decades and formerly more widespread, even down to sea-level, but has been driven out of lower, more suitable, reaches by development, such as damming for hydro-power, and pollution of vital clear water by *eg* agricultural run-off on neighbouring land. Introduced mammalian predators a serious problem. Captive-breeding programmes suffer from low productivity.

North Island Blue Duck

Hymenolaimus malacorhynchos hymenolaimus
L 50-57 cm (20-22 in), WS 65-80 cm (22-31 in)
Uniform grey-blue colouring of this mountain-stream duck of North Island, New Zealand, precludes confusion with other wildfowl.
IDENTIFICATION Male and female breeding and non-breeding, juvenile As South Island Blue Duck, but darker on back and scapulars.
Confusion risks Uniform blue-grey plumage unlike any other wildfowl, within or outside restricted range and preferred habitat of mountain streams. On the water or in flight, lacks any distinctive markings, apart from spotting on breast.

DISTRIBUTION AND STATUS Resident in very restricted areas of mountainous regions of central and eastern North Island, New Zealand. Habitat as for South Island Blue Duck. Formerly more widespread, even down to sea-level. Population very small, and undoubtedly much scarcer than South Island Blue Duck; only recent estimate, of 2,000-4,000, includes both subspecies. Threats as for South Island Blue Duck.

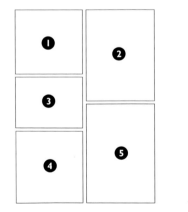

1 *South Island Blue Duck (adult)*
2 **South Island Blue Duck** (pair, from re-introduced stock, New Zealand
3 *South Island Blue Duck (18 day old chick)*
4 **North Island Blue Duck** (adult, Manganui a te ao River, New Zealand)
5 **North Island Blue Duck** (pair, Manganui a te ao River, New Zealand)

DABBLING DUCKS

SALVADORI'S DUCK

Anas waigiuensis L 38-43 cm (15-17 in), WS 56-71 cm (22-28 in)

Monotypic. Small, dark-headed, long-tailed duck of fast-flowing rivers and streams, with no confusion species within or outside range.
IDENTIFICATION Male breeding and non-breeding Some individual variation in overall tone, especially darker birds, showing little or no barring on almost black underparts. Typical bird described here. Head and neck uniform grey-black. Breast and all underparts, including undertail-coverts, white to buff, variably spotted black on breast and anterior flanks, spots increasing in size rearwards on flanks and merging into bold black barring; centre of belly, vent and undertail-coverts lightly spotted or none. Entire upperparts blackish with slight green gloss, feathers of back and scapulars with whitish tips forming obvious barring, continuing onto rump and uppertail-coverts. Tail dark brown, narrowly barred whitish, and with long, pointed central feathers. In flight, primaries and their coverts blackish-brown, with very small white tips to the innermost primaries, secondaries black, glossed purplish, broadly tipped white and bordered in front with white, and median and lesser coverts dark grey-brown with whitish edges; underwings pale brown, almost whitish, with darker grey flight feathers and mottled brown on coverts; white trailing edge formed by tips of secondaries. Bill bright yellow, often spotted black, though becomes duller outside breeding season. Legs and feet yellowish-brown with darker brown or black blotching, mainly on webs. Red eye. Has soft whistling call. **Female** As male, but a little smaller and with greyer, black-spotted bill and brown eye. Only call a harsh two-note quack or even croak. **Juvenile** As adults, but generally duller and lacking iridescence on upperparts and secondaries. Bill dark grey to olive-brown, and legs pinkish-grey with some black on tarsus.
Confusion risks Slim, long-tailed shape, with tail usually cocked up, together with uniform dark head and spotted and barred plumage are a unique combination among wildfowl, even if not very restricted in both range and habitat. Upperwing pattern, especially green speculum bounded fore and aft by white bars, reveals relationship with dabbling ducks, though has previously been placed in different genus.
DISTRIBUTION AND STATUS Resident in uplands and mountains of Irian Jaya (Indonesia) and Papua New Guinea. Favours fast-flowing rivers and streams, from about 500 m to at least 4000 m. Population estimated at 5,000 and thought to be declining. Many threats come from hunting by indigenous tribes, now equipped with guns, pollution of the required clear water through extensive deforestation and, perhaps, the introduction of insectivorous fish, such as trout, which may reduce available food. Extremely difficult to study or count in remote and rugged terrain though nature of habitat likely to be best safeguard for the future of the species.

BLACK DUCK

Anas sparsa
Polytypic. Two subspecies recognized here (third subspecies, *A. s. maclatchyi* of Gabon and Cameroon, not widely accepted): (1) Abyssinian Black Duck *A. s. leucostigma*, resident central and eastern Africa; (2) African Black Duck *A. s. sparsa*, resident southern and south-west Africa.

Abyssinian Black Duck

Anas sparsa leucostigma L 48-58 cm (19-23 in), WS 84-95 cm (33-37 in)
Large, heavily built dabbling duck, very dark all over with bold white scalloping on scapulars and flanks. Only possible confusion with African Yellowbill (see below).
IDENTIFICATION Male breeding and non-breeding Overall body plumage dark brownish-black. Head greyer-brown, with very slightly darker crown and lighter cheeks and throat (produced by very narrow buff edgings to feathers) really apparent only in fresh plumage. Sometimes has whitish neck patches, which may meet to form smudgy collar. Underparts slightly more olive-brown than upperparts; a few rear flank feathers barred buff (variable, and may extend to feathers on vent). Scapulars and tertials have broad buff bars, while uppertail-coverts and tail have narrower buff barring. In flight, upperwing dark brown on primaries, while secondaries form bluish iridescent speculum, bordered behind and in front by black and white bars; underwing-coverts much paler brown with white tips, contrasting with darker flight feathers; white tips to secondaries form whitish trailing edge. Bill pinkish-grey with black nail and black patch on upper mandible, sometimes extending over most of bill, though pinkish at base. Legs and feet yellow-orange with blackish blotching. Call a whistling *peep*. **Female** As male, but slightly smaller size apparent when in a pair. Some tendency to be a little blacker than male, but individual variation occurs. Loud quacking call. **Juvenile** Not so dark brown as adults, with whitish belly with diffuse brown barring; barring on upperparts reduced or even absent at first. Speculum lacking iridescence. Bill grey. Becomes as adult by end of first year.
Confusion risks No other dabbling duck in Africa is as dark brown or with so few pale markings. Yellow-billed Duck is fairly dark overall, but with pale feather edgings over most of body, as well as bright yellow sides to bill and, in flight, greener speculum with much narrower white border in front and paler underwings. May intergrade with African Black Duck, but no details.
DISTRIBUTION AND STATUS Resident over much of eastern and central Africa from Sudan and Ethiopia south to Mozambique, Zambia and Namibia, where probable zone of intergradation with African Black Duck to south; also in Gabon, Cameroon and Nigeria, but uncertain whether geographically separated. Inhabits rivers and fast-flowing streams mainly in wooded areas, but also appears on large standing waters in more open country. Population estimated at 10,000-25,000, but perhaps only c 1,000 in West Africa. No major threats, but some local declines as result of damming of rivers and deforestation.

African Black Duck

Anas sparsa sparsa L 48-58 cm (19-23 in), WS 84-95 cm (33-37 in)
Large, heavily built dabbling duck, very dark all over with bold white scalloping on scapulars and flanks. Only possible confusion with African Yellowbill (see below).
IDENTIFICATION Male and female breeding and non-breeding As Abyssinian Black Duck, except barring on upperparts and flanks white or whitish, thus appearing bolder and more conspicuous; speculum greenish-blue instead of blue. Bill slate grey, lacking any pink, though with similar black nail and black patch on upper mandible. **Juvenile** As Abyssinian Black Duck.
Confusion risks See Abyssinian Black Duck, above. Speculum colour not so blue, and therefore not quite so distinct from that of Yellow-billed Duck.
DISTRIBUTION AND STATUS Resident in southern Africa from south Mozambique, Zambia and Namibia to the Cape; probable zone of intergradation with Abyssinian Black Duck to north. Habitat as that of Abyssinian Black Duck. Population estimated at several tens of thousands.

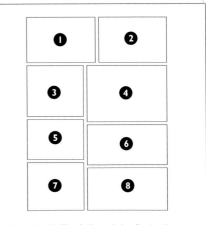

1 **Salvadori's Duck** (pair, Lake Omha, Papua New Guinea)
2 **Salvadori's Duck** (adult, Papua New Guinea)
3 **Salvadori's Duck** (adult, Papua New Guinea)
4 *Abyssinian Black Duck* (adult)
5 *Abyssinian Black Duck* (adult)
6 **African Black Duck** (adult, South Africa)
7 *African Black Duck* (adult)
8 *African Black Duck* (adult)

85

DABBLING DUCKS

MADAGASCAR TEAL

Anas bernieri L 38-40 cm (15-16 in), WS 58-64 cm (23-25 in)

Monotypic. Small all-brown dabbling duck restricted to Madagascar, where no similar wildfowl.

IDENTIFICATION Male breeding and non-breeding Warm brown on head and neck, very finely streaked and freckled darker brown. Darker, duller brown on crown, nape and hindneck, producing slight capped appearance, and very slightly paler on chin and upper throat. Underparts richer warm brown than head and neck; entire underparts have darker brown feather centres and wide buff tips creating overall spotted appearance, spots larger and darker on flanks, smaller and more diffuse on lower breast and belly, and continuing onto vent and undertail-coverts. Upperparts also rich warm brown, with narrow buff edgings and less pronounced dark centres to feathers than underparts; tail dark brown. Flight feathers dark grey-brown to blackish, secondaries with slight green iridescence and white tips, bordered in front by broad white bar on greater coverts, with median and lesser coverts grey-brown; underwing mainly dark brown, but central area showing whitish from pale median coverts. Bill reddish, with black nail and nostrils. Legs and feet pinky-red. **Female** Apparently as male, but bill, legs and feet more brown-red. **Juvenile** No information, though presumably as dull female. **Confusion risks** There is no other small, all-brown dabbling duck within range. White-bordered dark speculum obvious in flight.

DISTRIBUTION AND STATUS Resident in Madagascar, where restricted to a few localities close to the west coast. Found only on saline lakes and neighbouring marshes and rice-fields. Most recent counts (1993) suggest a maximum population of 500, but probably fewer. Formerly more numerous and widespread, but decline has been long-term, associated with gross changes to habitat and island fauna and flora. Lack of any controls on shooting in Madagascar, coupled with increase in conversion of wetlands to rice-growing, major threats. Captive-breeding programme begun in 1993.

GREY TEAL

Anas gibberifrons

Polytypic. Three subspecies extant, plus one extinct: (1) Australian Grey Teal *A. g. gracilis*, occurs Irian Jaya, Papua New Guinea, Australia and New Zealand; (2) East Indian Grey Teal *A. g. gibberifrons*, resident central and southern Indonesia; (3) Andaman Grey Teal *A. g. albogularis*, confined to Andaman Islands; (4) Rennell Island Grey Teal *A. g. remissa*, formerly found on Rennell Island in Solomons, but extinct (last seen 1959).

Australian Grey Teal

Anas gibberifrons gracilis L 39-47 cm (15-19 in), WS 60-67 cm (24-26 in)

Small teal, with possibility of confusion with Chestnut Teal and Brown Teal in southern parts of range.

IDENTIFICATION Male breeding and non-breeding Head brown, finely freckled pale buff, darker, almost blackish, on crown, nape and hindneck, where elongated nape feathers produce small erectile crest or mane, and much paler, almost whitish, on cheeks, throat and foreneck. Breast, flanks, belly, vent and undertail-coverts dark grey-brown, strongly patterned by pale buff feather margins, with markings smallest on chest and larger and more pronounced on flanks; belly and vent rather duller grey-brown than rest of underparts. Mantle dark-grey brown, scapulars and tertials somewhat paler and greyer, all with buff margins; back, rump, uppertail-coverts and tail darker brown, with smaller margins. Speculum on upperwing iridescent green and black, with green towards base of wing, bordered in front by broad white band on tips of greater coverts, and to rear by thin white band on tips of secondaries, with primaries and upperwing-coverts grey-brown; underwing dark brown, with contrasting white axillaries and median coverts. Bill grey. Legs and feet grey-black. Iris red. Has variety of calls, including clear whistle, typical teal-type *prip*, and a chittering call. **Female** Very similar to male, but a few minor differences which most obvious between birds of a pair. Slightly smaller and slightly paler. Head lacks nape mane and thus smaller. Iris generally less bright red. Bill, legs and feet as male. Has typical dabbling-duck decrescendo call of high-pitched and rapid quacking notes. **Juvenile** As female, but paler still, especially on head and neck, and with reduced green on speculum. Becomes as adult during first year. **Confusion risks** Both sexes very similar to female Chestnut Teal, and large overlap in ranges in southern Australia, but latter much scarcer or only a vagrant further north. Grey Teal is slightly smaller and paler than Chestnut Teal, and has overall grey tone to brown of plumage rather than warm brown tone of Chestnut Teal, which also more heavily mottled on underparts (note that Grey Teal's plumage can be affected by reddish iron-staining); Chestnut Teal has much less difference in colour between darker crown, nape and hindneck and paler cheeks, throat and foreneck; in flight, very little difference between wing patterns. In New Zealand, Grey Teal can be confused with Brown Teal, which has similar wing pattern, but Brown very much darker, especially on head, which overall dark brown.

DISTRIBUTION AND STATUS Resident, dispersive and nomadic over much of Australia, though commonest in south-west and south-east and east, including Tasmania; seasonal movements, influenced by rains, take birds northwards, sometimes in large numbers, to other parts of Australia, where breeds sporadically. Also found in Irian Jaya and Papua New Guinea, and neighbouring small islands including the Moluccas, and on New Caledonia. May overlap in range with East Indian Grey Teal (see below). Spread to New Zealand c 100 years ago, and now widespread, aided by very large influx in 1957 and 1958 occasioned by drought in Australia. Uses great variety of freshwater, brackish and saline wetlands, from inland floods to coastal lagoons and swamps. No reliable estimate of Australian population, though thought to number several hundreds of thousands; New Zealand population estimated at 15,000-20,000. Subject to shooting, but shows considerable ability to adapt to different wetland types and to move long distances if need be.

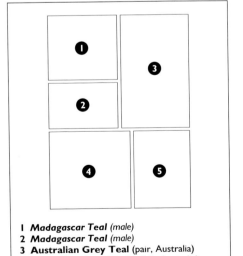

1 **Madagascar Teal** (male)
2 **Madagascar Teal** (male)
3 **Australian Grey Teal** (pair, Australia)
4 **Australian Grey Teal** (adult, Australia)
5 **Australian Grey Teal** (pair, New Zealand)

DABBLING DUCKS

East Indian Grey Teal

Anas gibberifrons gibberifrons L 37-45 cm (15-18 in), WS 60-67 cm (24-26 in)

IDENTIFICATION Male and female breeding and non-breeding, juvenile As Australian Grey Teal, but very slightly smaller and warmer brown in tone, with more contrasting markings on body plumage arising from blackish-brown centres to feathers and more buff margins. Most noticeable difference is presence of pronounced bulge on front of head, producing distinctive high forehead and flattish crown; the bulge is caused by an enlargement of the frontal sinus, though the reason for this is unknown. **Confusion risks** There are no other small grey-brown dabbling ducks within this teal's range, apart from vagrant Chestnut Teal; see above under Australian Grey Teal for separation.

DISTRIBUTION AND STATUS Resident central Indonesia, particularly Sulawesi and southern Sumatra and from Java to Timor. Exact limits of range uncertain and may overlap with Australian Grey Teal. Identification of subspecies on some islands, e.g. Tanimbar and Oer Islands, uncertain. Recently recorded from Borneo. Habitat as Australian Grey Teal, perhaps with more concentration on coastal wetlands; also some use of rice-fields. Population estimated at between 10,000 and 25,000, and perhaps more, and subject to threats from shooting and habitat destruction.

Andaman Grey Teal

Anas gibberifrons albogularis L 37-47 cm (15-19 in), WS 60-67 cm (24-26 in)

Small grey-brown teal, unlike any others within range.

IDENTIFICATION Male and female breeding and non-breeding, juvenile As East Indian Grey Teal, but if anything more rufous-brown in tone and with variable amounts of white on head and throat. This can vary from small, but noticeable, white eye-ring, to white patch around eye, often a small white area on centre of crown, and small to considerable areas of white on face, chin, throat and foreneck. Some males, in particular, can be almost white-headed, but uncertain whether amount of white is, in fact, linked to sex, though certainly juvenile birds have less white in their first year. Bill dark grey, with pinkish areas towards tip. **Confusion risks** No other small grey-brown dabbling ducks, with or without white on the head and neck, occur within the range of this subspecies.

DISTRIBUTION AND STATUS Resident Andaman Islands, and on Great Coco Island to the north, where it inhabits mangrove swamps and tidal creeks. Population estimated at 3,000-4,000 in early 1990s, which regarded by some as much too optimistic, while partial survey in mid-1990s found 400. Formerly reported as much more numerous. Drainage of wetlands and agricultural and commercial development seen as real or potential threats.

Rennell Island Grey Teal

Anas gibberifrons remissa L 35-43 cm (14-17 in), WS 58-63 cm (23-25 in)

Extinct since 1959. First described as separate race, found only on Rennell Island in Solomon Islands group, in 1942, and apparently restricted to a single lagoon. Extinction has been blamed on introduction of cichlid fish *Tilapia* into the lagoon to provide food for islanders. The fish, which are noted for their capacity for prolific breeding and high growth potential, are assumed to have outcompeted the ducks for the available food.

CHESTNUT TEAL

Anas castanea L 35-46 cm (14-18 in), WS 60-66 cm (24-26 in)

Small dabbling duck with distinctive male, but female similar to other species within range.

IDENTIFICATION Male breeding Blackish head and neck highly glossed green. Breast, flanks, belly and vent rich chestnut-brown with blackish spots, latter small or even absent on upper breast, becoming larger and obvious on belly and, especially, flanks, where largest towards rear; white or sometimes whitish sides to vent in front of blackish undertail-coverts. Mantle and scapulars dark brown with narrow reddish-brown to buff edgings; back, rump, uppertail-coverts and tail blackish. Upperwing shows green iridescent speculum on secondaries (though outer feathers black), broadly banded white in front and narrowly behind, otherwise dark brown, darkest on primaries; underwing slightly paler brown, with darker forewing and white axillaries and median coverts. Bill bluish-grey. Legs and feet grey. Iris bright red. Main call a high-pitched whistle. **Male eclipse** Duller than male breeding, with less green gloss on head, chestnut of body duller and browner; whitish patch at sides of vent turns brownish. **Female** Dark brown head, with blackish crown and lighter, buff-brown, throat and foreneck. Body warm brown, but not chestnut as male, with paler feather edgings. Remainder as male breeding, except iris not so bright red. Decrescendo call as Grey Teal, but fewer notes and higher-pitched. **Juvenile** As female, but less well-defined spots. **Confusion risks** For separation from Australian Grey Teal, see that species. Some similarities to extralimital Brown Teals of New Zealand and adjacent islands, but they lack dark flank spots and have white eye-ring, while most also have white collar.

DISTRIBUTION AND STATUS Mainly resident south-west Western Australia and in south-east South Australia, Victoria, Tasmania, New South Wales and extreme south Queensland; some dispersal and wandering in response to rains, with sporadic breeding further north, but not to same extent as Australian Grey Teal. Inhabits coastal lagoons and marshes; less frequent inland on lakes and other shallow wetlands. Population estimate of between 25,000 and 100,000. Probably commonest in

Tasmania and adjacent mainland. Severe decline earlier this century caused by overshooting and drainage of coastal marshes. Still hunted extensively but population probably stable or increasing, aided by local nest box schemes.

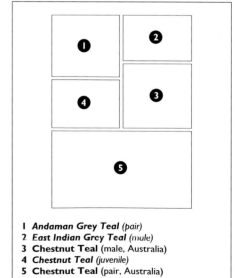

1 *Andaman Grey Teal* (pair)
2 *East Indian Grey Teal* (male)
3 *Chestnut Teal* (male, Australia)
4 *Chestnut Teal* (juvenile)
5 *Chestnut Teal* (pair, Australia)

DABBLING DUCKS

BROWN TEAL

Anas aucklandica
Polytypic. Three subspecies: (1) New Zealand
(Brown) Teal *A. a. chlorotis*, resident in few
localities in North Island and South Island, New
Zealand; (2) Auckland Island (Brown) Teal *A. a.
aucklandica*, confined to islets off Auckland
Island, New Zealand; (3) Campbell Island
(Brown) Teal *A. a. nesiotis*, only on Dent Island,
off Campbell Island, New Zealand.

New Zealand (Brown) Teal

Anas aucklandica chlorotis L 38-48 cm (15-19 in),
WS 55-60 cm (22-24 in)
Rare small dabbling duck of a few localities in
North and South Islands, New Zealand, unlike
any other small wildfowl within range.
IDENTIFICATION **Male breeding** Uniform dark
brown head and neck, relieved only by narrow
but conspicuous white eye-ring and small patch
of green-glossed feathering behind eye. Often,
but not invariably, white or whitish feathers
form narrow collar at base of neck. Breast
chestnut-brown, variably spotted dark brown
and black, becoming paler and browner on
belly and flanks, former lightly spotted, latter
more heavily so, with spots forming distinct
vertical black barring; whitish patch on side of
vent, which otherwise brown, spotted black;
undertail-coverts black. All upperparts,
including uppertail-coverts and tail, dark brown
with lighter brown edgings. Speculum iridescent
green and black, bordered with buff stripe in
front and narrower whitish band behind, while
rest of upperwing dark brown; underwing
brown, with white axillaries and some paler
tips to coverts. Bill blue-grey, with darker
shading on upper mandible. Legs and feet dark
grey. Soft whistling call except in display, when
high-pitched wheezy, whistling *peep* and *pop*
calls. **Male eclipse** Resembles female, but
whitish patch retained at sides of vent. Some
males like this all year, but not certain whether
two colour phases of breeding plumage (bright
and dull), or related to age, or some birds
remain in 'eclipse' plumage most or all of year.
Female As dull male, but lacking green gloss
on head and whitish sides to vent. Underparts
less obviously spotted than male, and flanks
spotted rather than barred; also has brown,
not blackish, undertail-coverts. Wings and bare
parts as male. Low-pitched quacks, including
decrescendo call. **Juvenile** As female, but
breast and flanks more obviously marked.
Confusion risks For separation from
Australian Grey Teal, only small duck at all
similar within range, see that species.
DISTRIBUTION AND STATUS Formerly
widespread and numerous, now found in very
restricted areas of New Zealand: on North
Island, on northern peninsula (Northland) and
on Great Barrier Island and other islands in
Hauraki Bay off east coast of Auckland, and on
Kapiti Island off west coast of Wellington; on
South Island, may survive in Fiordland in south-
west. Small pools and marshes in wooded areas
and sheltered coastal bays and estuaries.

Estimated 1,500-2,000 individuals: 1,000-1,500
Great Barrier Island, under 500 Northland, and
only tiny numbers elsewhere; and declining,
especially in Northland where predator control
much more difficult than on islands. Brought
close to extinction by heavy shooting (until
protected in 1921), destruction of habitat, and
introduced predators, eg ferrets, stoats, cats
and rats. Feral cats caused extinction on
Stewart Island, off South Island, in 1972. Large-
scale captive-breeding programme began in
1960s with releases in many areas but had little
success: eg over 1,000 released Northland
1984-94, but decline continued there.
Programme now scaled down, and targeted at
island release sites where introduced predators
absent or eliminated.

Auckland Island (Brown) Teal

Anas aucklandica aucklandica L 34-44 cm
(13-17 in)
Small, flightless duck of islets off Auckland
Island, New Zealand.
IDENTIFICATION **Male and female breeding
and non-breeding, juvenile** As New Zealand
Teal, but slightly smaller and darker, lacking
chestnut tone to brown of breast, flanks and
belly. Vent patch grey-white. Wings very short,
barely reaching past pale vent patch. Speculum
present, visible on closed wing. Legs brown-
grey. **Confusion risks** Even if flightless state
not apparent, no other small brown dabbling
ducks occur within same range.
DISTRIBUTION AND STATUS Known only from
ten small islets off Auckland Island, 460 km
south of New Zealand; eliminated on Auckland
Island by 1942 following introduction of
mammalian predators and of rabbits, pigs and
cattle, which destroyed the vegetation. Mainly
coastal, foraging along shore, but also inland
along streams. Population estimated at 500-600
in 1986, but now, with better surveys, numbers
2,000 and stable. Introduced rabbits and cattle
are to be eliminated successively from the
islands, with intention of finally re-establishing
this duck on Auckland Island itself.

Campbell Island (Brown) Teal

Anas aucklandica nesiotis L 34-44 cm (13-17 in)
Small, flightless duck confined to single tiny
island off Campbell Island, New Zealand.
IDENTIFICATION **Male and female breeding
and non-breeding, juvenile** As Auckland
Island Teal, but even darker and lacking
discernible markings on underparts. No
speculum. **Confusion risks** Even if flightless
state not apparent, no other small brown
dabblings duck occur within same range.
DISTRIBUTION AND STATUS Confined to Dent
Island, close to Campbell Island, 800 km south
of New Zealand; extinct on Campbell Island
since 1958 following introduction of cats and
rats. Not discovered on Dent until 1975.
Apparently has limited access to precipitous
coast and, in absence of permanent water, uses
marshy areas and tiny streams among the
predominating tussock grass. Population
estimated at 30-100 individuals, and probably

near island's capacity. Captive-breeding
programme established, and releases are being
contemplated on an island close to South
Island, while plans are made to exterminate
alien mammals from the 11,000-ha Campbell
Island.

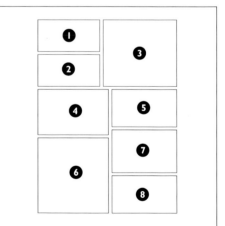

1 **New Zealand (Brown) Teal** (pair, New
Zealand)
2 ***New Zealand (Brown) Teal*** (*female*)
3 **New Zealand (Brown) Teal** (female,
Matangi Island, New Zealand)
4 **New Zealand (Brown) Teal** (eclipse male,
Matangi Island, New Zealand)
5 **New Zealand (Brown) Teal** (female,
Matangi Island, New Zealand)
6 **Auckland Island (Brown) Teal** (female,
Enderby Island, New Zealand)
7 ***Campbell Island (Brown) Teal*** (*male*)
8 ***Campbell Island (Brown) Teal*** (*female*)

DABBLING DUCKS

MALLARD

Anas platyrhynchos
Polytypic. Taxonomy subject of continuing
discussion, in particular on divisions into
species or subspecies. Seven subspecies
recognized here: (1) Mallard *A. p. platyrhynchos*,
widespread in northern hemisphere,
introduced Australia and New Zealand; (2)
Greenland Mallard *A. p. conboschas*, resident
west and south Greenland; (3) Florida Duck *A.
p. fulvigula*, resident southern Florida; (4)
Mottled Duck *A. p. maculosa*, mainly resident
Gulf coasts of USA and Mexico; (5) Mexican
Duck *A. p. diazi*, mainly resident extreme south-
western USA and north and central Mexico; (6)
Hawaiian Duck *A. p. wyvilliana*, resident on
three Hawaiian islands; (7) Laysan Duck (Teal)
A. p. laysanensis, only on Laysan Island, Hawaiian
group.

Mallard

Anas platyrhynchos platyrhynchos L 50-65 cm (20-
26 in), WS 81-98 cm (32-39 in)
Large, very widespread dabbling duck, male
unmistakable, but female similar to, though
larger than, other female dabbling ducks.
IDENTIFICATION Male breeding Iridescent
bottle-green head and neck, sometimes with
purplish sheen, with narrow white collar at
base. Breast rusty-purple; flanks, belly and vent
very finely vermiculated pale grey; undertail-
coverts black. Mantle and scapulars grey-
brown, vermiculated black and white, becoming
blackish on back and black on rump, uppertail-
coverts and central tail feathers, which curled
upwards almost into circle; outer tail feathers
whitish-grey. In flight, conspicuous purplish-blue
speculum on secondaries, with black
subterminal border and white tips, and white
band in front, while outer wing dark grey-
brown, and forewing grey with some buff
edges; tertials pale grey, with chestnut on
coverts; underwing-coverts whitish, flight
feathers grey with white tips to secondaries.
Bill variably olive-green to bright yellow with
black nail, though sometimes with bluish tinge.
Legs and feet orange. Weak, rasping *raeb* call.
Male eclipse As female, but crown and nape
darker, face paler, underparts less densely
spotted. Bill duller in colour. **Female
breeding** Dark brown on crown and
hindneck, paler on cheeks and foreneck, very
finely streaked darker brown. Paler supercilium
above dark eye-stripe, which widens between
eye and bill. Underparts pale, warm brown,
well mottled with spots, streaks and V-shaped
marks, larger and more obvious on flanks,
smaller and fainter on belly. Upperparts darker
brown with buff edgings and darker centres; tail
pale brown with darker markings. Wing as
male, but less colour on speculum and dark
brown, not grey, coverts. Bill brown, with
variable extent of orange behind nail and along
sides; legs and feet orange. Loud quacking calls,
including several together in decrescendo call.
Female non-breeding As female breeding,
but with paler markings on body. **Juvenile** As

female, but darker overall and more heavily
streaked on underparts. Bill dull red-horn.
Purplish-blue of speculum more confined to
inner secondaries. Acquires adult plumage
during first year. **Confusion risks** Male
unmistakable. Female very similar to female
Gadwall (which see for separation), and to both
sexes of Florida and Mottled Ducks and
American Black Duck. Florida and Mottled
Ducks darker overall, with more contrast on
head and more heavily mottled black on body;
bill of male is bright yellow with black nail and
black spot at gape; speculum lacks white border
at front and has very thin white border behind.
American Black Duck similar to very dark
Mallard females, but lacks whitish sides to tail,
which has uniformly dark coverts; speculum
more blue in colour and lacks white border at
front, with rear border only very thin or
absent. For distinctions from Mexican Duck,
see that subspecies (below).
DISTRIBUTION AND STATUS Occurs almost
throughout northern hemisphere, apart from
tundra, mountains and deserts; sedentary in
temperate regions, but northerly populations
migratory, wintering south to northern Mexico,
Mediterranean, Sudan, India and southern
China. Introduced Australia and New Zealand.
On all types of fresh water, as well as estuaries
and coastal lagoons; highly adaptable, even to
lakes in urban parks. Most numerous wildfowl;
post-breeding or wintering estimates/counts of
c 11 million in Palearctic, 17-18 million in
Holarctic, and *c* 1 million in New Zealand.

Greenland Mallard

Anas platyrhynchos conboschas L 55-72 cm (22-
28 in), WS 88-105 cm (35-40 in)
Both sexes unmistakable within restricted
range.
**IDENTIFICATION Male and female breeding
and non-breeding, juvenile** As Mallard,
differing only in slightly larger size, paler
plumage and shorter bill, all adaptations to life
in a colder climate. **Confusion risks** No
identification problems within range except
with vagrant American Black Duck (see under
Mallard, above), when contrasts greater
because of larger size and paler plumage.
DISTRIBUTION AND STATUS Resident west and
south-west coasts of Greenland; some
southward movement of more northerly birds
in winter. Sheltered coastal bays and nearby
fresh waters. Population estimated at a few
tens of thousands and not seriously threatened.

Florida Duck

Anas platyrhynchos fulvigula L 53-58 cm (21-23
in), WS 81-90 cm (32-35 in)
Large dabbling duck restricted to southern
Florida; very similar to Mottled Duck, but no
overlap of range.
**IDENTIFICATION Male breeding and non-
breeding** Dusky brown on crown and nape;
dark eye-stripe, paler grey-buff supercilium and
on rest of head and neck, sometimes appearing
pinkish-buff on cheeks and throat. Whole of
upperparts and underparts warm brown, boldly

marked with black 'V's formed by subterminal
bands on feathers, which edged buff; markings
strongest along flanks and smaller and paler on
belly and towards rear. Tertials dark brown
and only thinly edged paler. Speculum bluish-
green, bordered with warm brown in front and
black to rear, with white tips to secondaries
either very small or absent, and outer wing
dark brown, with coverts similar but with paler
tips; underwing very pale, almost white, with
darker primaries and secondaries, though some
primary coverts pale grey. Bill bright yellow,
with black nail, nostrils and around base, plus
quite obvious spot at very base of upper
mandible. Legs and feet orange. Calls as
Mallard. **Female** As male, but paler and more
streaked on underparts through broader
edgings to feathers. Bill dull orange-yellow with
olive spots, these concentrated in middle of
upper mandible; legs and feet orange. Calls as
Mallard. **Juvenile** As adult, but duller brown,
less well marked on underparts, particularly
flanks, and darker on upperparts, with smaller
pale feather edgings. **Confusion risks** Almost
identical to Mottled Duck (see below), though
slightly longer-necked and less heavily marked,
so appearing a little paler. Ranges of the two
subspecies believed discrete. For separation
from female Mallard, see that subspecies
(above). American Black Duck is much darker,
with less distinct markings, and has a more
purplish-blue speculum with white border
absent at front and reduced or absent at rear.
DISTRIBUTION AND STATUS Confined to
southern Florida as far north as Tampa, where
it occurs in freshwater and coastal marshes.
Recent winter counts have averaged 11,700.

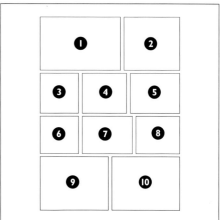

1 **Mallard** (pair, Merseyside, England)
2 **Mallard** (male, Merseyside, England)
3 **Mallard** (pair in flight, Sussex, England)
4 **Mallard** (eclipse male, Lancashire, England)
5 **Mallard** (juvenile, Lancashire, England)
6 *Greenland Mallard* (pair)
7 *Greenland Mallard* (male)
8 **Florida Duck** (Florida, USA)
9 **Florida Duck** (adult male, Florida, USA)
10 **Florida Duck** (pair, Florida, USA)

DABBLING DUCKS

Mottled Duck

Anas platyrhynchos maculosa L 53-58 cm (21-23 in), WS 81-90 cm (32-35 in)
Large dabbling duck resident Gulf coast of USA and Mexico; very similar to Florida Duck, but no overlap of range.

IDENTIFICATION Male and female breeding and non-breeding, juvenile As Florida Duck, but overall darker and more heavily marked, so appearing blacker, especially on head. Slightly shorter-necked. **Confusion risks** Almost identical to Florida Duck (see above). For separation from female Mallard, see that subspecies (above). American Black Duck is even darker, with less distinct markings, and with a more purplish-blue speculum which lacks white border at front and has border reduced or absent at rear.

DISTRIBUTION AND STATUS Mainly resident in extreme south of USA, along Gulf coast from Mississippi delta west and south about 200 km into Mexico as far as central Tamaulipas; some movement southwards to Veracruz district. Occurs in mainly coastal freshwater and brackish marshes. Winter population counts of *c* 175,000, and stable, with no obvious threats.

Mexican Duck

Anas platyrhynchos diazi L 51-56 cm (20-22 in), WS 76-86 cm (30-34 in)
Large dabbling duck of extreme southern USA and Mexico; very similar to Mottled and Florida Ducks, but little or no overlap in ranges.

IDENTIFICATION Male breeding and non-breeding Resembles small female Mallard. Body plumage darker and richer in colour, especially on breast, which rich reddish-brown; feathers on breast and underparts with large dark brown to blackish areas in their centres, with tendency for these to be aligned in broad streaks. Belly, vent and undertail-coverts darker than female Mallard, with ends of tail-coverts almost black. Tail all dark or, on a few individuals, paling to whitish at the edges. Feathers on mantle with U-shaped darker markings internally and pale edgings, while on longer scapulars marks are elongated and V-shaped. Upperwing as Mallard but darker, and speculum vivid green, less blue than Mallard's, and with white bar at front more buff. Bill olive-yellow; no black spot at base of upper mandible as on Florida and Mottled Ducks. Legs and feet deep orange. Calls as Mallard. **Female** As male, but not so rufous overall. Bar in front of speculum tawny-buff. Bill more olive-green, with only traces of orange at base; legs and feet dull orange. Calls as Mallard. **Juvenile** More streaked than adult, and more finely marked on breast than Mallard. **Confusion risks** Doubtfully separable from Mottled and Florida Ducks, but no overlap in range. Distinctions from Mallard as given above, noting especially that tail much darker than Mallard's and speculum greener, less blue. Note that considerable hybridization has taken place with Mallard, particularly in southern USA, though birds of central Mexico thought still to be pure.

DISTRIBUTION AND STATUS Breeds locally in extreme south of USA, in south-east Arizona, southern New Mexico, and south-west Texas and across border into northern Mexico, then locally south through uplands of central Mexico to about Mexico City; northern birds are migratory, wintering south to central Mexico. Occupies variety of inland fresh waters, including marshes, floods, rivers and pools. Population thought to number about *c* 55,000 birds and is declining, including through hybridization with Mallard, with perhaps only 5,000 remaining in USA and those of doubtful provenance. Also subject to heavy shooting pressure in Mexico.

Hawaiian Duck

Anas platyrhynchos wyvilliana L 44-49 cm (17-19 in), WS 70-78 cm (28-31 in)
Small endemic of a few Hawaiian islands. No confusion species.

IDENTIFICATION Male breeding Somewhat variable in overall colouring. Crown and hindneck blackish-brown with varying amounts of green iridescence, though not strongly so and head sometimes merely dark brown with little or no green. Pale buff supercilium above dark eye-stripe, though neither of these is always well defined, with pale eye-ring. Cheeks, throat and neck paler brown. Breast rufous to purplish-brown with small, blackish spots, but can be more heavily marked. Rest of underparts warm brown, marked black and buff, with markings on flanks producing strong scalloping or, often, wavy vertical barring; more spotted on belly, vent and undertail-coverts. Mantle and scapulars with dark centres and broad paler edgings, but tertials paler grey-brown and unmarked; rump and uppertail-coverts blackish. Tail grey, with whitish sides, sometimes brownish, the central feathers being slightly upcurved. Upperwing mainly dark grey-brown, with green speculum bordered in front with whitish-buff and behind with black and then white; underwing whitish, with brown flight feathers. Bill olive-grey, with black nail and darker base and centre to upper mandible. Legs and feet orange. Calls as Mallard, but higher-pitched. **Male eclipse** As female, but bill as male. **Female** Very similar to female Mallard, though much smaller. Breast slightly warmer, reddish-brown, and eye-stripe sometimes less distinct. Bill dusky grey-brown, with fleshy-yellow behind nail and short distance along sides of upper mandible. Legs and feet orange. Calls as Mallard, but higher-pitched. **Juvenile** Duller brown than female, with more diffuse markings on body. **Confusion risks** Only small duck within range. Introduced Mallard much larger, but, if any doubt, latter has blue, not green, speculum. Occasional hybridization with Mallard has been recorded, but see below.

DISTRIBUTION AND STATUS Resident Kauai island in Hawaiian Islands, having been exterminated from all other occupied islands by mongooses and other introduced predators. Reintroduced from captive-bred stock on to islands of Oahu and Hawaii. Breeds on remote ponds, montane bogs and rivers at high altitude. Estimated population (1993) of 2,500, with 2,000 on Kauai, 300 on Oahu and 200 on Hawaii. Extermination programme in train for removal of any hybrids and all introduced Mallards, as well as reduction of introduced mammalian predators.

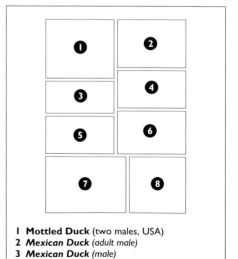

1 **Mottled Duck** (two males, USA)
2 *Mexican Duck* (adult male)
3 *Mexican Duck* (male)
4 *Mexican Duck* (pair)
5 **Hawaiian Duck** (pair, Oahu, Hawaii)
6 *Hawaiian Duck* (male)
7 *Hawaiian Duck* (female)
8 *Hawaiian Duck* (group)

Laysan Duck (Laysan Teal)

Anas platyrhynchos laysanensis L 35-40 cm (14-16 in), WS 65-72 cm (26-30 in)
Small endemic duck restricted to Laysan Island, where no confusion species.

IDENTIFICATION Male breeding and non-breeding Head and neck blackish-brown with very variable white markings. At most reduced, white restricted to wide ring around eye, often with short backward-pointing stripe towards ear; usually more extensive, with broad patch around eye and white flecks or larger marks in front of eye and to rear towards crown and nape; at most extensive, additionally speckled white under chin and down sides of neck. White probably increases with age. Underparts and upperparts dark rufous-brown, heavily marked with darker spots and bars. Tail dark brown, with slight upward curve to central feathers. Green speculum, bordered in front with whitish and behind with black and white, with rest of upperwing grey-brown; underwing-coverts whitish, flight feathers grey-brown. Bill grey-green. Legs and feet orange. Calls softer version of male Mallard's. **Female** As male, but with reduced white on head; although white also seems to increase with age, within paired birds female generally has less white. Underparts browner. Central tail feathers straight. Speculum lacks green gloss, appearing dull brown. Bill brownish-yellow with dull orange on sides and behind tip; legs and feet orange. Calls as female Mallard, but softer. **Juvenile** Close to female, but duller brown overall, with reduced markings. **Confusion risks** No confusion species within very restricted range.

DISTRIBUTION AND STATUS Confined as resident to Laysan Island (Hawaiian Islands), some 1350 km north-west of Honolulu. Utilizes almost whole island (c 370 ha), including brackish central lagoon, but feeds and nests among tall vegetation. Population currently (1995) nearly 200 birds, but fluctuating in recent years between 100 and 500, probably dependent on food supply and water levels. Was reduced almost to extinction by guano-diggers, shooting and, especially, introduction of rabbits, which removed vegetation providing food and safety; perhaps only six or seven birds by 1911, and reasonably reliable report of only single pair in 1930, of which male died, but female reared brood. Rabbits now eradicated and island fully protected, with strictly limited landings. Population has been as high as 700, but island's carrying capacity probably nearer more recent peaks of 500. Further security provided by comparatively large numbers in captivity, where breeds quite freely.

AMERICAN BLACK DUCK

Anas rubripes L 53-61 cm (21-24 in), WS 85-96 cm (33-38 in)
Monotypic. Large, dark dabbling duck, with similarities to dark female Mallard and Mottled Duck, as well as to extralimital Mexican Duck.

IDENTIFICATION Male breeding Head and neck buff-brown with narrow black streaks; eye-stripe, crown and hindneck blackish with very small pale brown feather edges. Breast, belly and flanks blackish-brown with U-shaped buff markings on the feathers, these larger on flanks. Upperparts similar, becoming darker on lower back and rump; tertials with narrow grey fringes; tail-coverts and tail blackish-brown with reduced paler margins. Upperwing dark brown, with speculum iridescent purplish-blue, bordered at front and behind with black, with very narrow (often absent) small white tips to secondaries to rear; underwing white to whitish, with grey flight feathers. Bill olive-yellow to dull orange. Legs and feet reddish-orange. Calls as Mallard. **Male eclipse** As male breeding, but head more heavily streaked, and U-shaped markings absent from underparts. Bill olive-grey; legs and feet duller. **Female** As male, but with stronger streaking and therefore less contrast on head; markings on underparts more V-shaped than U-shaped. Speculum reduced, with more black on outer secondaries. Bill olive-green, with black on culmen and black dots along sides of upper mandible; legs and feet orange-brown. Calls as Mallard. **Juvenile** As adults, but more heavily streaked on underparts. Bill greyish, that of male becoming yellow by end of first winter.
Confusion risks For separation from Mallard and Mottled Duck, see above. Mexican Duck does not overlap in range and has white borders to speculum. Hybridization with Mallard takes place widely, but resulting offspring always less dark and usually show green head on males and whitish sides to tail on females.

DISTRIBUTION AND STATUS Breeds widely over eastern half of North America from Manitoba, Ontario, northern Quebec and Labrador south to south of Great Lakes from Wisconsin to Atlantic coast, where south to North Carolina; winters within southern part of this range and south to Gulf coast, Florida and Bermuda. Vagrants to Pacific coast and east Asia, and to Europe, where hybridization with Mallard has occurred. Has declined steeply in last 50 years; winter censuses in 1952-53 revealed 1.3 million, but only 800,000 by 1959-62 and 277,000 in 1992. Habitat loss one cause of decline, but land-use changes and release of large numbers of Mallards for sport have led to increasing hybridization and exclusion by much more numerous and far more adaptable Mallard. The eventual extinction of the Black Duck as a separate species has been forecast.

MELLER'S DUCK

Anas melleri L 63-68 cm (25-27 in), WS 95-110 cm (37-43 in)
Monotypic. Only large dabbling duck of Madagascar or Mauritius.

IDENTIFICATION Male and female breeding and non-breeding Apparently no difference between the sexes. Head and neck brown, streaked black, with very slightly darker crown and nape and trace of darker eye-stripe. Underparts and upperparts dark brown with reddish-brown feather markings. Upperwing dark brown, with brilliant emerald-green iridescent speculum bordered at front by black subterminal band and narrow reddish tips to greater coverts, and behind by black subterminal band and narrow white tips to secondaries; underwing whitish to pale grey, with darker flight feathers. Bill large and long, olive-green with black nail and, usually, black around base. Legs and feet orange to orange-brown. Calls as Mallard. **Juvenile** More reddish than adults, particularly on underparts.
Confusion risks No other large dabbling ducks resembling Mallard within range.

DISTRIBUTION AND STATUS Resident eastern and central uplands of Madagascar, where, although range considerably reduced, still occurring quite widely. Introduced Mauritius, c 840 km east of Madagascar, before 1800 and still surviving there. Mainly inland fresh waters from sea-level to 2000 m, also on rivers and streams and seen feeding in rice-fields. Population in long-term decline, currently estimated at between 2,000 and 5,000 individuals, and subject to pressure from shooting and habitat destruction. No more than 30 pairs believed to survive on Mauritius, where several hundred pairs thought to exist in 1930s. Small captive-bred stocks exist.

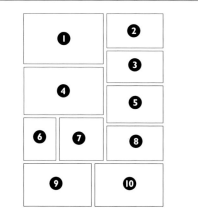

1 **Laysan Duck (Teal)** *(male)*
2 **Laysan Duck (Teal)** *(male)*
3 **Laysan Duck (Teal)** *(juveniles)*
4 **American Black Duck** *(pair, Gatasay NRA, USA)*
5 **American Black Duck** *(male, New York, USA)*
6 **American Black Duck** *(male in flight, New York, USA)*
7 **American Black Duck** *(male, Scilly, England)*
8 **Meller's Duck** *(male)*
9 **Meller's Duck** *(inderterminate age)*
10 **Meller's Duck** *(male)*

DABBLING DUCKS

YELLOW-BILLED DUCK

Anas undulata
Polytypic. Two subspecies: (1) African Yellow-billed Duck *A. u. undulata*, resident southern parts of East Africa, south to South Africa; (2) Abyssinian Yellow-billed Duck *A. u. rueppelli*, resident Sudan to northern East Africa.

African Yellow-billed Duck

Anas undulata undulata L 51-58 cm (20-23 in), WS 81-98 cm (32-39 in)
Only large dabbling duck within range with bright yellow bill.
IDENTIFICATION Male breeding and non-breeding Uniformly dark grey head and neck very finely streaked buff, contrasting with lighter grey-brown breast and entire underparts, where broad pale buff to whitish edgings produce mottled effect, paler on centre of breast, where edgings almost obscure darker feather centres, and darker on flanks, where edgings smaller. Upperparts similar, but with more scalloped effect on mantle and scapulars; tail dark grey-brown with buff edges. Dark olive-brown primaries and blackish secondaries, the latter with green speculum bordered at front and behind by black and, to the outside, white bars; underwing-coverts very pale brown to whitish, contrasting with darker flight feathers. Bill bright lemon-yellow, with black stripe down centre of upper mandible stopping just short of black-nailed tip; narrow black edges to upper mandible. Legs and feet dark brown, often with yellowish or reddish tinge. Has low whistling calls. **Female** As male, but slightly smaller and tending to be lighter in overall appearance, with less contrast between body feathers and their pale edges. Less green and more blackish on speculum. Bill duller yellow. Quacks like rather hoarse Mallard. **Juvenile** As adults, but darker on head and appears more spotted than mottled on underparts.
Confusion risks No other Mallard-sized dabbling duck with bright yellow bill occurs within range. Speckled Teal and Chilean Pintail are both smaller, the former considerably so, the latter slender and with longer pointed tail, and both are also much browner in general tone. For separation from Abyssinian Yellow-billed Duck, see that subspecies (below); no reports of intergrading.
DISTRIBUTION AND STATUS Precise northern boundary unclear, as is extent, or indeed occurrence, of any overlap in range with Abyssinian subspecies. Mainly resident in Africa from southern Kenya and southern Uganda, northern Tanzania, Zaïre and Angola, south to Cape Province, though absent from tropical forest and desert areas; some seasonal movements in response to rains. Uses great variety of large and small freshwater wetlands, including dams and impoundments, which has allowed expansion of range and numbers. Population estimated at 60,000 in South Africa, with a further 50-100,000 in East Africa. No apparent threats.

Abyssinian Yellow-billed Duck

Anas undulata rueppelli L 51-58 cm (20-23 in), WS 81-98 cm (32-39 in)
Only large dabbling duck within range with bright yellow bill.
IDENTIFICATION Male and female breeding and non-breeding, juvenile As African Yellow-billed Duck, but narrower buff edgings to feathers on underparts and upperparts produce significantly darker appearance, with less contrast with already dark head and neck. Speculum blue rather than green, and bill deeper yellow to yellow-orange. **Confusion risks** For separation from other yellow-billed species, see African subspecies, above.
DISTRIBUTION AND STATUS Resident southern Sudan, Ethiopia, northern Kenya and northern Uganda. Occurs in Ethiopia locally to nearly 4000 m, otherwise habitat as for African Yellowbill. Population estimated at several tens of thousands, with no apparent threats.

PHILIPPINE DUCK

Anas luzonica L 48-58 cm (19-23 in), WS 76-85 cm (30-33 in)
Monotypic. Unmistakable large dabbling duck of region, with cinnamon and dark brown head.
IDENTIFICATION Male and female breeding and non-breeding Male larger than female, otherwise apparently identical. Rusty-cinnamon head and foreneck, with blackish-brown eye-stripe, crown, nape and line down back of neck; eye-stripe behind eye stops short of dark line on nape, but occasionally joined to crown at eye. Breast grey with light brown tinge; rest of underparts grey with very slight buff or brown edgings, barely discernible at a distance, when appears evenly grey. Mantle and scapulars grey with very narrow and indistinct buff edgings; back and rump darker grey-brown; tail-coverts and centre of tail dark grey-brown, outer tail feathers broadly edged buff-grey. Speculum on upperwing iridescent green, bordered in front and behind by black bars and, outside them, white bars, with rest of wing grey-brown; underwing-coverts greyish-white, with darker grey-brown flight feathers. Bill blue-grey, nail black. Legs and feet grey-brown. Both sexes call as Mallard. **Juvenile** Duller and paler, and much less cinnamon, on head than adults, and with more obvious buff edgings to feathers of underparts and upperparts. Speculum with less green. **Confusion risks** No other large dabbling duck is grey all over, with cinnamon and dark-striped head.
DISTRIBUTION AND STATUS Restricted to Philippines, where resident: occurs mainly on islands of Luzon, Mindoro, Leyte, Bohol, Olango and Mindanao, and formerly found also on Masbate. Occupies variety of freshwater wetlands, from coastal pools and rivers to mountain lakes. Population estimated to number some tens of thousands, and declining. These ducks are heavily shot for food, but have proved adaptable to changing habitat.

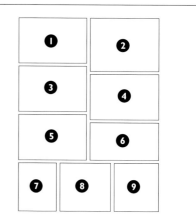

1 **African Yellow-billed Duck** (adult, Kenya)
2 **African Yellow-billed Duck** (adult, South Africa)
3 **African Yellow-billed Duck** (adult, Tanzania)
4 *Abyssinian Yellow-billed Duck*
5 *Abyssinian Yellow-billed Duck*
6 *Philippine Duck* (adult)
7 *Philippine Duck* (adult)
8 *Philippine Duck* (adult)
9 *Philippine Duck* (adult)

DABBLING DUCKS

PACIFIC BLACK DUCK

Anas superciliosa
Polytypic. Three subspecies: (1) New Zealand Black (or Grey) Duck *A. s. superciliosa*, resident New Zealand and some adjoining islands; (2) Australian Black Duck *A. s. rogersi*, resident Australia and eastern Indonesia; (3) Pelew Island Black (or Grey) Duck *A. s. pelewensis*, resident Fiji and several other western Pacific island groups. The taxonomy of this species and Spot-billed Duck *A. poecilorhyncha* (see below) is not agreed by all authorities, some of whom lump them into one species with six subspecies. Recent ringing recoveries have shown movement of Australian Black Ducks to New Zealand, which must cast doubt on the separation of those two races. Formerly, various island populations of Pelew Island Black Duck were separated as subspecies, but nowadays these are lumped together, as here. Clearly, both Pacific Black Duck and Spot-billed Duck are also closely related to Philippine Duck *A. luzonica*.

New Zealand Black (or Grey) Duck

Anas superciliosa superciliosa L 54-61 cm (21-24 in), WS 85-93 cm (33-37 in)
Dark brown, Mallard-sized dabbling duck with strongly marked head, distinguishing it from all other wildfowl.
IDENTIFICATION Male breeding and non-breeding Head with five strongly contrasting stripes: three blackish-brown stripes, one over crown and nape, one through eye, and one from base of bill to below eye; and two pale-buff to whitish, one forming supercilium and the other across cheeks. Chin and throat brighter buff; rest of neck pale brown, paler in front than behind. Breast and underparts mottled dark brown among paler feather fringes, these broadest on flanks. Upperparts dark brown with buff to greyish feather fringes; rump, tail-coverts and tail blackish-brown, the tail with fairly obvious buff edges. Speculum glossy green and black, bordered front and back with black, with narrow buff bar at front and white at rear, while rest of upperwing dark brown; underwing-coverts conspicuously whitish, contrasting with dark brown flight feathers. Bill dark grey, sometimes a little paler towards the tip. Legs and feet yellowish, with pale brown webs. Calls as hoarse Mallard.
Female As male, but slightly smaller and duller, appearing browner on crown, back and rump, and with less contrasting mottling on underparts. **Juvenile** As adults, but slightly paler and more spotted on belly and with less green in speculum. **Confusion risks** No other large dabbling duck of region, or elsewhere, exhibits such a strongly marked head; overall grey body also distinctive. In flight, underwing appears very pale. Hybrids with Mallard usually show clear features of latter species, especially on head.
DISTRIBUTION AND STATUS Resident throughout New Zealand, as well as on larger offshore islands, *eg* Auckland, Campbell,

Chatham and Snares, up to 800 km from main islands. Uses very wide variety of freshwater and brackish wetlands, but outcompeted by introduced Mallard. Although once the most numerous and widespread wildfowl in New Zealand, a major problem exists with introduced Mallard, first established in latter part of 19th century, as hybridization commonplace, with recent DNA studies suggesting that at least half of Black Ducks tested were contaminated with Mallard blood. Indeed, it has been suggested that rather fewer than 20% of Black Ducks are pure, these mainly on remote swamps and on the offshore islands. The whole existence of this subspecies is thus seriously threatened. Total population, including hybrids, up to 1 million, but best estimate for pure-blood Black Ducks only between 80,000 and 150,000, and certainly declining.

Australian Black Duck

Anas superciliosa rogersi L 54-61 cm (21-24 in), WS 85-93 cm (33-37 in)
Dark brown, Mallard-sized dabbling duck with strongly marked head, distinguishing it from all other wildfowl.
IDENTIFICATION Male and female breeding and non-breeding, juvenile Virtually identical to New Zealand Black Duck. Has been suggested that it is smaller, but this has recently been shown not to be the case. Has also been suggested that it is overall paler, but this not so, though it averages a little duller in tone on the body. Face pattern slightly less contrasting, with a little more buff rather than white on supercilium, cheek-stripe, chin and throat, though differences marginal. **Confusion risks** Not likely to be confused with any other wildfowl of range.
DISTRIBUTION AND STATUS Widespread in Australia, except in driest central areas, making dispersive movements in response to rains and drought; also Louisiade Islands and southern Papua New Guinea, and Indonesia from Irian Jaya westwards through Moluccas and Sulawesi to Java and Sumatra. Habitat as for New Zealand Black Duck. Population estimated at up to 1 million. Hybridization with Mallard a problem in, among other areas, south-west Australia.

Pelew Island Black (or Grey) Duck or Lesser Grey Duck

Anas superciliosa pelewensis L 47-56 cm (19-22 in), WS 82-90 cm (32-35 in)
Dark brown, Mallard-sized dabbling duck with strongly marked head, distinguishing it from all other wildfowl.
IDENTIFICATION Male and female breeding and non-breeding, juvenile Virtually identical to New Zealand Black Duck, but smaller and daintier, with broader eye-stripe, darker on neck and with narrower pale feather edges on the body plumage. There is some variation in size and tone across the very scattered range, reflecting some of the formerly separated subspecies mentioned

above. **Confusion risks** Not likely to be confused with any other wildfowl of range.
DISTRIBUTION AND STATUS Resident on large number of islands in Pacific, roughly north-west to south-east: Palau, Caroline Islands (Federal States of Micronesia), northern Papua New Guinea (including Bismarck Archipelago), Solomon, Vanuatu, New Caledonia and Loyalty Islands, Fiji, Western Samoa, Tonga, Cook and Society Islands, and Tubuai Islands (French Polynesia). Habitat as for New Zealand Black Duck, but with more use of brackish and coastal wetlands. Population probably between 10,000 and 25,000, but inadequate information on status on individual islands, on some of which undoubtedly scarce.

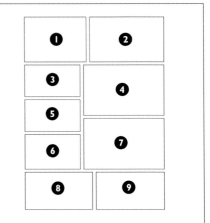

1 **New Zealand Black (or Grey) Duck** (adult, New Zealand)
2 **Australian Black Duck** (adult, Perth, Australia)
3 **Australian Black Duck** (pair, Sydney, Australia)
4 **Australian Black Duck** (adult, Perth, Australia)
5 **Australian Black Duck** (adult, Stansthorpe, Australia)
6 **Australian Black Duck** (adult, Sydney, Australia)
7 **Australian Black Duck** (adult, Perth, Australia)
8 **Pelew Island Black (or Grey) Duck or Lesser Grey Duck** (adult, New Caledonia)
9 **Pelew Island Black (or Grey) Duck or Lesser Grey Duck** (female, Tahiti)

DABBLING DUCKS

SPOT-BILLED DUCK

Anas poecilorhyncha
Polytypic. Three subspecies: (1) Indian Spot-billed Duck *A. p. poecilorhyncha*, resident Indian subcontinent; (2) Burma Spot-billed Duck *A. p. haringtoni*, resident western Assam, Burma and southern China; (3) Chinese Spot-billed Duck *A. p. zonorhyncha*, breeds eastern Russia, Japan, Korea and China, winters within and to south of range. The Chinese subspecies shows similarities to the Pacific Black Duck *A. superciliosa* and fertile hybrids have been produced in captivity, leading some authorities to consider the Spotbills conspecific with that species, though others suggest full specific status for the Chinese race.

Indian Spot-billed Duck

Anas poecilorhyncha poecilorhyncha L 58-63 cm (23-25 in), WS 87-95 cm (34-37 in)
Large, bulky dabbling duck, heavily spotted underneath, with white on tertials and striking black and yellow bill. No confusion species within range.
IDENTIFICATION Male breeding and non-breeding Whitish to pale buff head finely streaked darker, with blackish crown, eye-stripe and line down back of neck. Breast, belly and flanks whitish, spotted and streaked dark grey-brown, with spots enlarging onto and towards rear of flanks; centre of lower belly, vent and undertail-coverts dark grey-brown and unmarked. Mantle and scapulars dark grey-brown with whitish feather edgings; back, rump, uppertail-coverts and tail unmarked blackish-brown. Speculum greenish-purple, with black borders and white outer borders, rest of wing dark grey-brown, except for pure white terminal half of inner tertials (these show on resting bird, as well as very obviously in flight); underwing-coverts and axillaries whitish or white, with darker flight feathers. Bill blackish, with bright yellow tip (up to a quarter of bill length) behind a black nail, and with swollen waxy-red spots at base; these spots brighter and more swollen in spring, but this the only apparent seasonal difference. Legs and feet bright orange-red. Calls similar to those of Mallard. **Female** As male, but slightly smaller and duller, with smaller spots on underparts. Red spots at base of bill smaller and much less prominent. Calls as Mallard. **Juvenile** Duller than adults, darker brown below with less obvious spots. No red spots at base of bill.
Confusion risks Apart from unique bill pattern, the prominent white area on the tertials, very visible in flight and also normally showing on closed wing, distinguishes this duck from all other large dabbling ducks, within or outside its range. Large, bulky body obvious both on the water, and in flight. Take-off appears more laboured and flight less manoeuvrable than eg Mallard. For distinctions from Chinese and Burma Spotbills, see below. Not known whether intergrades with Burma Spotbill occur.
DISTRIBUTION AND STATUS Resident almost throughout Indian subcontinent, including Pakistan, Bangladesh, Sri Lanka and western Assam; some dispersal in response to rains. Unknown whether range overlaps with that of Burma Spotbill. Found mainly on well-vegetated lowland fresh waters, but also on coastal lagoons and marshes. Population estimated at no more than 50,000, despite wide distribution. Some hunting pressure, but not thought to be threatened.

Burma Spot-billed Duck

Anas poecilorhyncha haringtoni L 55-60 cm (22-24 in), WS 83-91 cm (33-36 in)
Large, bulky dabbling duck, heavily spotted below, with distinctive bill pattern.
IDENTIFICATION Male and female breeding and non-breeding, juvenile
Slightly smaller than Indian subspecies, though considerable overlap in measurements, this subspecies shows some characteristics intermediate between those of Indian and Chinese Spotbills, but is closer to Indian, particularly in possession of white tertial patch, green speculum and, usually, presence of red basal spots to bill. **Confusion risks** None within range.
DISTRIBUTION AND STATUS Resident eastern Assam, Burma (Myanmar) and eastwards to Yunnan province of southern China, and south into northern Laos and Vietnam. Habitat as for Indian Spotbill. Population believed to lie in range 25,000-100,000. Not thought to be threatened despite some hunting.

Chinese Spot-billed Duck

Anas poecilorhyncha zonorhyncha L 55-60 cm (22-24 in), WS 83-91 cm (33-36 in)
Large, bulky dabbling duck, heavily spotted underneath, with white on tertials and striking black and yellow bill. No confusion species within range.
IDENTIFICATION Male and female breeding and non-breeding, juvenile Similar to Indian and Burma Spot-billed Ducks and same size as latter, but much browner overall. The supercilium is still whitish, but the face is stronger buff and there is an additional short black stripe running back from base of bill and reaching to not quite level with eye. Breast is warm buff-brown, darkening on flanks and belly, and breast and flanks are less heavily spotted, grading to darker brown towards the rear. Speculum blue, not green, and with very narrow white bars in front and behind; additionally, white on inner tertials reduced to narrow edgings, which hardly show in flight or on closed wing. Bill lacks any red spots at base.
Confusion risks Apart from yellow on bill, this subspecies perhaps closer in appearance to Australian Black Duck, particularly in head pattern, than to the other two Spotbills. Not known whether any intergrading with Burma Spotbill.
DISTRIBUTION AND STATUS Breeds eastern Russia, Mongolia, northern and eastern China, Korea and Japan; resident in south of range and in Japan, but northernmost populations winter from Japan south to southern China. Unknown whether any range overlap with that of Burma Spotbill. Habitat as that of Indian Spotbill. Population estimated to number several hundred thousand, with over 130,000 wintering in Japan in the 1980s. Some hunting pressure around rice-fields.

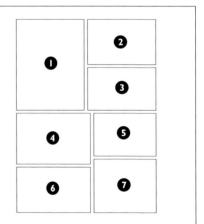

1 **Indian Spot-billed Duck** (female, Bharatpur, India)
2 **Indian Spot-billed Duck** (pair, Keoladeo, India)
3 **Indian Spot-billed Duck** (male, India)
4 **Burma Spot-billed Duck** (adult, Hong Kong)
5 **Chinese Spot-billed Duck** (adult, Mai Po, Hong Kong)
6 **Chinese Spot-billed Duck** (adult, Mai Po, Hong Kong)
7 **Chinese Spot-billed Duck** (adult, Mai Po, Hong Kong)

DABBLING DUCKS

BRONZE-WINGED (or SPECTACLED) DUCK

Anas specularis L 46-54 cm (19-21 in), WS 84-95 cm (33-37 in)
Monotypic. Unmistakable, medium-sized to large dabbling duck with very distinctive pattern on head and neck.
IDENTIFICATION Male breeding and non-breeding Head and upper neck dark brown, with clear white oval patch in front of eye, and second white patch on chin and throat extending up sides of neck to broad point below ears. Lower neck, breast, flanks and belly fawn-brown, lightly mottled darker brown on breast and belly, but with heavier uneven scallop marks on flanks, contrasting with pale feather edgings; centre of belly, vent and undertail-coverts unmarked fawn-brown. Mantle and scapulars dark brown to blackish, with paler feather edgings, and with slight green-purplish sheen, this more apparent on completely dark tertials; back, rump, uppertail-coverts and tail dark brown. Conspicuous brilliant bronze iridescent speculum, variously shot with pinkish-purple, bordered to rear with black and white bands, while rest of upperwing, both coverts and primaries, very dark brown with purplish sheen; underwing dark, except for grey axillaries. Bill blue-grey, with black on culmen and black nail. Legs and feet yellow-orange, with brownish webs. Call, during display, a loud whistling trill. **Female** As male, but slightly smaller and duller, having less sheen on upperparts and upperwings. Gives three-syllable barking call, *pa-ta-perrr*, accented on the last syllable. **Juvenile** Much duller than adults, with facial patch reduced or even absent, and breast and underparts heavily streaked.
Confusion risks No other duck has this distinctive dark brown and white head pattern. The bright bronze speculum is also very obvious, including at rest.
DISTRIBUTION AND STATUS Breeds southern Chile and west-central Argentina south to Tierra del Fuego; winters within and to north and east of breeding range. Nests by fast-flowing rivers in densely wooded country and also uses nearby standing fresh waters. Population estimated at a few tens of thousands and not threatened, despite some shooting in winter.

CRESTED DUCK

Anas specularoides
Polytypic. Two subspecies: (1) Patagonian Crested Duck *A. s. specularoides*, southern Andes of South America, and Falklands; (2) Andean Crested Duck *A. s. alticola*, central Andes of South America.

Patagonian Crested Duck

Anas specularoides specularoides L 51-57 cm (20-22 in), WS 85-95 cm (33-37 in)
Long-bodied, long-tailed, buff-brown duck with slight crest, unlike any other duck within range.
IDENTIFICATION Male breeding and non-
breeding Pale grey-brown head and neck, with shaggy crest from nape down back of neck. Darker eye patch has extension which fades to grey behind eye. Whitish throat and foreneck forming broad incomplete band around base of neck. Breast fulvous-brown, lightly spotted darker; flanks and rest of underparts light grey-brown with darker grey centres to feathers, giving more mottled appearance, with largest markings on flanks; lower belly, vent and undertail-coverts darker grey-brown to blackish. Mantle and scapulars brown, with greyish centres and darker tips; uppertail-coverts a little paler; tail blackish. Speculum bright iridescent bronze (strikingly similar in colour to that of Bronze-winged Duck), with narrow black band and broad white band behind, and primaries and wing-coverts dark grey-brown; underwing with white axillaries, median coverts and trailing edge, remainder dark brown. Bill, legs and feet dark grey. Iris bright orange-red, even ruby-red in breeding birds. Call a two-note buzzy whistle, *shee-ooo.*
Female Slightly smaller than male, with shorter crest and less bright iris. **Juvenile** As female, but lacks crest, has pale brown head, and has much paler underparts, streaked rather than spotted, and becoming whitish, lightly streaked darker, on belly. **Confusion risks** No other pale duck in range. This duck is noticeably long-bodied and long-tailed; crest not particularly conspicuous, but contributes to 'heavy-headed' appearance.
DISTRIBUTION AND STATUS Breeds Andes, from Talca in central Chile and Mendoza in west-central Argentina, south to Tierra del Fuego, and resident on Falkland Islands; some movement north by more southerly breeders, also movement from high altitude to low, with wintering on Chilean and Argentine coasts. Breeds on wide variety of freshwater, brackish and saline wetlands, wintering on lowland fresh waters and coastal wetlands. Not uncommon, particularly on Falklands, and total population estimated as between 10,000 and 25,000 birds, with no obvious threats.

Andean Crested Duck

Anas specularoides alticola L 54-61 cm (21-24 in), WS 90-100 cm (35-39 in)
Long-bodied, long-tailed, buff-brown duck with slight crest, unlike any other duck within range.
IDENTIFICATION Male and female breeding and non-breeding, juvenile As Patagonian Crested Duck, but slightly larger and paler brown, with few or no spots on underparts. Speculum darker and more purplish, lacking bronze or green tinge. Iris orange-yellow, not red. **Confusion risks** No confusion species, as for Patagonian Crested Duck. Ranges of the two subspecies apparently contiguous, but no information on intergrades.
DISTRIBUTION AND STATUS Breeds Andes, from Lake Junin, southern Peru, and western Bolivia south to Talca in central Chile and Mendoza in west-central Argentina; some birds resident, while others move from high altitude to low altitude for the winter. Range appears
to meet that of Patagonian Crested Duck, but no information on overlap, if any. Habitat as for Patagonian Crested Duck. Regarded as relatively abundant, and probably numbering several tens of thousands. No apparent threats.

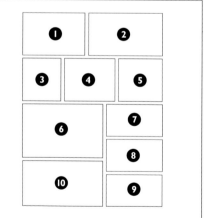

1 **Bronze-winged (or Spectacled) Duck** *(female)*
2 **Bronze-winged (or Spectacled) Duck** *(pair, male foreground)*
3 **Bronze-winged (or Spectacled) Duck** *(female)*
4 **Patagonian Crested Duck** (male, Falklands)
5 **Patagonian Crested Duck** (female, Falklands)
6 **Patagonian Crested Duck** (pair, Falklands)
7 **Patagonian Crested Duck** (pair, Falklands)
8 **Andean Crested Duck** (adult)
9 **Andean Crested Duck** (adult)
10 **Andean Crested Duck** (adult)

DABBLING DUCKS

PINTAIL

Anas acuta
Polytypic. Three subspecies: (1) Northern Pintail *A. a. acuta*, widespread and abundant in northern hemisphere; (2) Kerguelen Pintail *A. a. eatoni*, confined to Kerguelen Island; (3) Crozet Pintail *A. a. drygalskii*, confined to Crozet Islands. Some authorities consider the two remote island subspecies as forming a separate species; treated here as conspecific with Northern Pintail.

Northern Pintail

Anas acuta acuta L 51-66 cm (21-26 in), WS 81-95 cm (32-37 in)
Long and slender dabbling duck, male with distinctive elongated central tail feathers, female slimmer and with plainer head compared with other female dabbling ducks.
IDENTIFICATION Male breeding Chocolate-brown head, throat and hindneck, darker on crown and nape. Most of breast pure white, extending onto lower neck, with broad tapering stripe up sides of upper neck. Sides of lower neck and breast, and flanks, finely vermiculated grey, and belly whitish; vent white, with yellow-buff sides; undertail-coverts black. Entire upperparts vermiculated grey, with elongated and pointed scapulars and tertials purplish-black with broad creamy-white to greyish margins; uppertail-coverts grey-black, edged cream. Tail grey-brown with whitish margins, central feathers black and greatly elongated. Speculum green, with buff stripe in front and black and white bars behind, and rest of upperwing grey-brown; underwing pale grey, with darker leading edge. Bill blue-grey, with black nail, edges and stripe down upper mandible. Legs and feet dark grey. Fluty whistling call, like Common Teal's but deeper.
Male eclipse Close to adult female, but retains male wing, with green speculum, and is greyer on scapulars and darker on tail.
Female breeding Grey-brown head with light darker mottling, especially on crown and nape. Paler on throat, foreneck, breast and underparts, with faint darker mottling, most obvious on breast; flanks darker brown with blackish scallop markings. Mantle and scapulars brown with darker scallop markings; back, rump, tail-coverts and pointed tail brown with cinnamon edgings. Speculum unlike male's, being brown, often with faint greenish gloss, bordered in front (narrowly) and behind with white, while rest of upperwing brown; underwing as male. Bill dark blue-grey with black as male, except only few black dots along edges; legs and feet dark grey. Soft quacking calls. **Female non-breeding** As female breeding, but paler feather edges on head and upperparts, more spotted on underparts.
Juvenile As female, but darker, less buff-edged, upperparts and more spotted, less scalloped, on underparts. Moults into adult plumage through first winter, but wing in first summer. **Confusion risks** No other dabbling duck has male's combination of brown head,

white neck and grey body, even without long tail extension. Female distinguished from other similar female dabbling ducks by slender shape with pointed tail, lack of head markings and noticeably scalloped flanks. Flight silhouette of both sexes distinctive, with long neck and pointed tail; green speculum only on male, brownish on female, both with broad white bands behind.
DISTRIBUTION AND STATUS Widespread breeder throughout northern arctic and temperate zones of Eurasia and North America; mainly migratory, a few wintering within southern limits of breeding range, but most south to western Europe, Mediterranean, Black and Caspian Seas, West and East Africa, Indian subcontinent east to southern China, southern USA, Mexico, Central America south to Panama and West Indies. Breeds in shallow marshes and by well-vegetated fresh waters; also on coastal lagoons and estuaries in winter. Very numerous duck, with over 2 million in European/African wintering areas, up to 2 million in Asia and c 3 million in North America, though in last region subject to large-scale fluctuations, eg c 12 million in 1970s.

Kerguelen Pintail

Anas acuta eatoni L 40-45 cm (16-18 in), WS 61-64 cm (24-25 in)
Only small dabbling duck in its very restricted range.
IDENTIFICATION Male breeding
Predominantly resembles small, short-necked female Northern Pintail. Overall tone darker and more reddish-brown, and scalloping on flanks smaller and less obvious. Central tail feathers elongated, though proportionately less than on Northern Pintail. Speculum green, bordered with white. Although no birds assume full breeding plumage resembling male breeding Northern Pintail, suggestions of such plumage, including traces of dark brown on the head and white on the breast and throat and up the sides of neck, can be seen on perhaps 1% of individuals. **Male eclipse** As female, but still with green speculum. **Female** Closely resembles slightly reddish-brown female Northern Pintail, though, as male, much smaller and shorter-necked. Speculum brown, bordered with white. **Juvenile** As female, but duller. **Confusion risks** No other small duck occurs within this subspecies' range.
DISTRIBUTION AND STATUS Confined to Kerguelen Island (c 3500 km) and its outliers in the southern Indian Ocean; introduced Amsterdam Island (c 1600 km north-east) and neighbouring St Paul Island in 1950s and 1960s, but not seen since 1970. Occupies small lakes, pools, marshes and streams; more on coast during winter. The latest estimate of the population (1993) was between 50,000 and 60,000 and apparently not threatened, despite introduced cats and former quite heavy shooting, though now protected. Early estimates varied between 10,000 and 40,000, demonstrating the difficulty of the task.

Crozet Pintail

Anas acuta drygalskii L 40-45 cm (16-18 in), WS 61-64 cm (24-25 in)
Only small dabbling duck in its very restricted range.
IDENTIFICATION Male and female breeding and non-breeding, juvenile Very similar to Kerguelen Pintail, though slightly paler, more buff on breast, and at least some birds show fine vermiculations on lower hindneck and flanks. **Confusion risks** No other small duck occurs within this subspecies' range.
DISTRIBUTION AND STATUS Confined to the main vegetated islands of the Crozet group, c 1100 km west of Kerguelen in the southern Indian Ocean. The latest population estimates date from 1984, when the total was put at 1,350, with 800 on East Island and stable, 200 on Penguin Island and stable, 200 on Possession Island and declining, and 150 on Cochons Island and declining. Cats and rats are established on both Possession and Cochons Islands, and local extinctions seem likely.

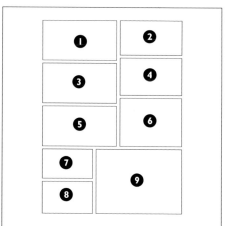

1 **Northern Pintail** (male, Lancashire, England)
2 **Northern Pintail** (pair in flight, Norfolk, England)
3 **Northern Pintail** (juvenile, Lancashire, England)
4 **Northern Pintail** (female, Kent, England)
5 **Kerguelen Pintail** (flight, Mayes, Kerguelen Islands, Indian Ocean)
6 **Kerguelen Pintail** (male, Mayes, Kerguelen Islands, Indian Ocean)
7 **Kerguelen Pintail** (female, Mayes, Kerguelen Islands, Indian Ocean)
8 **Kerguelen Pintail** (juvenile, Mayes, Kerguelen Islands, Indian Ocean)
9 **Crozet Pintail** (male, Crozet Islands, Indian Ocean)

DABBLING DUCKS

YELLOW-BILLED PINTAIL

Anas georgica
Polytypic. Three subspecies, of which one extinct: (1) Chilean Pintail *A. g. spinicauda*, widespread in Andes of South America; (2) South Georgia Pintail (or Teal) *A. g. georgica*, confined to South Georgia, South Atlantic; (3) Niceforo's Pintail *A. g. niceforo*, formerly eastern Andes of central Colombia, extinct since 1952.

Chilean Pintail

Anas georgica spinicauda, L 60-66 cm (24-26 in), WS 70-85 cm (28-33 in)
Large, slender dabbling duck of South America, where only other yellow-billed species is much smaller Speckled Teal.
IDENTIFICATION Male breeding and non-breeding Medium-brown head and neck, with more chestnut crown, marked with fine darker freckles, and paler and almost unmarked on throat and foreneck. Breast and underparts warm buff-brown, spotted and blotched darker all over, with smallest marks on breast, largest on flanks; centre of belly paler and only lightly marked. Upperparts also warm buff-brown with darker markings, mantle and scapulars with pale buff edgings. Long and pointed tail brown. Speculum glossy black with greenish tinge, bordered fore and aft with buff, rest of upperwing grey-brown; underwing quite even grey-brown, with paler trailing edge to secondaries. Bill bright yellow, with bluish colouring behind black nail and black stripe down centre of upper mandible not quite reaching nail. Legs and feet dark grey. Low whistling call. **Female** As male, but paler, almost whitish on less well-marked underparts. Speculum dark glossy brown with buff band reduced in front, broader behind. Bare parts as male. Low quacking calls. **Juvenile** As female, but lacking chestnut on crown and more streaked and less spotted on breast and flanks. **Confusion risks** Only large but slender yellow-billed duck in range. Yellow-billed races of Speckled Teal much smaller and dumpier, with shorter tail and unmarked flanks.
DISTRIBUTION AND STATUS Widespread breeder through Andes, from extreme southern Colombia through Peru, Bolivia, Chile and Argentina to Tierra del Fuego; winters within range, but more southerly birds move north into lowlands of Argentina and Brazil, as well as from highlands to western coasts. Resident on Falkland Islands. Breeds on lakes and marshes, at up to 4600 m in Andes, wintering on lowland fresh waters and sheltered coasts. Population estimated to number several hundred thousands. No apparent threats.

South Georgia Pintail (or Teal)

Anas georgica georgica L 43-50 cm (17-20 in), WS 60-65 cm (24-26 in)
Small island race of dabbling duck, with no other species within restricted range.
IDENTIFICATION Male and female breeding and non-breeding As Chilean Pintail, but smaller and stockier. Overall plumage considerably darker, more red-brown, and heavily spotted, especially on underparts, with belly little differentiated from breast and flanks. Head rounder, with shorter bill slightly upturned. **Juvenile** Little different from adults, but slightly less red-brown. **Confusion risks** No other small dabbling duck within restricted range.
DISTRIBUTION AND STATUS Confined as resident to South Georgia and its outliers, in South Atlantic; occasionally wanders, including south to South Shetlands Islands and to Antarctic Peninsula, where sighting of eight on ice near Faraday Base (65°15'S) in 1979 represents the most southerly record of any wildfowl. Rarely far from coast, where feeds mostly on beaches and among seaweed. Population numbers some thousands, having recovered from severe persecution during period when island used as whaling base. No apparent threats, though brown rats present.

Niceforo's Pintail

Anas georgica niceforo L 43-50 cm (17-20 in), WS 60-65 cm (24-26 in)
Extinct since 1952, having been described as a separate subspecies only ten years earlier. It was darker and more streaked on head and neck than the Chilean Pintail, with a shorter tail and longer bill. Was confined to Andes of eastern central Colombia at 1000-3200 m, and apparently once quite common and widespread. The reasons for its extinction are not fully understood, though excessive shooting may have played a part.

RED-BILLED DUCK (or RED-BILLED PINTAIL)

Anas erythrorhyncha L 43-48 cm (17-19 in), WS 60-65 cm (24-26 in)
Monotypic. Only medium-sized slender dabbling duck with red bill within range.
IDENTIFICATION Male breeding and non-breeding Dark brown crown, down to eye, and nape, with sharp demarcation from whitish-buff cheeks and throat. Neck buff-brown. Breast, flanks and underparts paler buff, liberally spotted dark brown to black, from small speckles on upper breast to large spots and bars on flanks; belly centre paler and almost unmarked. Mantle and scapulars olive-brown with pale edgings; back, rump, uppertail-coverts and tail dark brown to blackish. Speculum buffy-pink, shading to whitish on tips of secondaries, and with black and buff bar in front, with upperwing-coverts and primaries dark brown; underwing dark brown, apart from paler trailing edge to secondaries. Bill bright carmine-red, with brown-black area down upper mandible and black nail. Legs and feet dark grey. Silent except for soft *geee* call during display. **Female** As male, but slightly smaller, with duller bill. **Juvenile** Overall greyer and less buff than adults, and more streaked, less spotted, on underparts. Bill pink with brownish tinge. **Confusion risks** Only other southern African duck with red bill is much smaller and paler Cape Teal, which in any case lacks contrasting dark cap to head. In flight, the pale buffy-pink speculum is unique.
DISTRIBUTION AND STATUS Resident throughout eastern and southern Africa, from southern Sudan and Ethiopia south through East Africa to the Cape, avoiding most arid regions, and in Madagascar; some dispersive movements in response to dry and wet seasons. Uses variety of wetlands, especially shallow, well-vegetated fresh waters. Mainland African population thought to number well over 1 million. Uncommon in Madagascar, with population probably not exceeding 10,000 and declining through excessive shooting and habitat loss. No threats to mainland population.

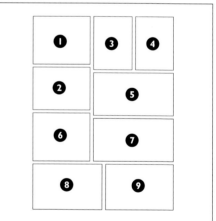

1 **Chilean Pintail** (male)
2 **Chilean Pintail** (male)
3 **Chilean Pintail** (female)
4 **Chilean Pintail** (juvenile)
5 **South Georgia Pintail (or Teal)** (adult, South Georgia)
6 **South Georgia Pintail (or Teal)** (pair, South Georgia)
7 **Red-billed Duck (or Red-billed Pintail)** (adult male, Nakuru, Kenya)
8 **Red-billed Duck (or Red-billed Pintail)** (pair, Ngorongoro, Tanzania)
9 **Red-billed Duck (or Red-billed Pintail)** (male, Ngorongoro, Tanzania)

119

DABBLING DUCKS

WHITE-CHEEKED PINTAIL

Anas bahamensis
Polytypic. Three subspecies: (1) Lesser White-cheeked Pintail *A. b. bahamensis*, resident West Indies and northern South America; (2) Greater White-cheeked Pintail *A. b. rubrirostris*, breeds Argentina, winters more widely central South America; (3) Galapagos Pintail *A. b. galapagensis*, resident Galapagos Islands. Has sometimes been considered conspecific with Red-billed Pintail *A. erythrorhyncha*.

Lesser White-cheeked Pintail

Anas bahamensis bahamensis L 41-48 cm (16-19 in), WS 58-65 cm (23-26 in)
Unmistakable within range.

IDENTIFICATION Male breeding and non-breeding Lightly mottled brown crown, down to eye, nape and hindneck. Strong contrast with pure white cheeks, throat and upper part of foreneck. Lower neck and upper mantle, breast, flanks and belly warm fulvous-brown, extensively spotted black, spots smaller on breast and belly, larger and bolder on flanks. Mantle, scapulars and back dark brown with fulvous edges; rump, tail-coverts and tail reddish-buff, unmarked. Narrow bright iridescent green speculum towards bases of secondaries, edged in front with buff, and behind with narrow black band and then very broad buff band, and primaries and upperwing-coverts dark brown; underwing with white axillaries and pale median coverts, darker lesser coverts, and pale trailing edge to dark brown secondaries. Bill has reddish basal half and bluish outer half, with black nail. Legs and feet dark grey. Soft whistling call. **Female** Very close to male, but slightly smaller and duller, less pure white on face and throat, and with shorter tail. Bill is duller and slightly shorter. Weak quacking calls. **Juvenile** As female, but duller and with less green on speculum.
Confusion risks None. This is the only medium-large dabbling duck in its range showing combination of dark cap over white cheeks, red and blue bill and overall warm brown, dark-spotted body. Wing pattern of narrow green speculum with broad buff band to rear is particularly distinctive in flight as is slender shape and pointed tail. Not known whether any intergrading with Greater White-cheeked Pintail, with which it interbreeds freely in captivity.
DISTRIBUTION AND STATUS Resident Bahamas and widespread almost throughout West Indies from Cuba to Trinidad and Tobago, and extending through northern Venezuela, Guyana, Surinam, French Guiana and extreme northern Brazil. Mainly in mangrove swamps, estuaries and tidal creeks. Population estimated at 75,000 and stable. Has declined on some islands, largely as a result of overhunting by man and predation by introduced mammalian predators.

Greater White-cheeked Pintail

Anas bahamensis rubrirostris L 44-51 cm (17-20 in), WS 60-68 cm (24-27 in)
Unmistakable within range.

IDENTIFICATION Male and female breeding and non-breeding, juvenile As Lesser White-cheeked Pintail, but larger and brighter overall, with more ruddy body plumage and blacker spots. **Confusion risks** The only medium-large dabbling duck in its range which has combination of dark cap over white cheeks, red and blue bill and overall warm brown, dark-spotted body. Wing pattern of narrow green speculum with broad buff band to rear is particularly distinctive in flight together with its slender shape and pointed tail.

DISTRIBUTION AND STATUS Breeding status unclear and in need of investigation. Migratory status also poorly known, with some regular seasonal movements but also post-breeding dispersal. Reported to breed now only in Argentina, but is also regarded as abundant in southern Brazil and as occurring widely in Paraguay, Uruguay and Bolivia; some authorities believe that the subspecies is resident in those countries, but this may be based on old information and its current status there may be only that of a wintering bird, which would be the case if breeding is, indeed, restricted to Argentina. Also occurs widely on Pacific coast of Peru and Ecuador, probably only in winter. Formerly bred in northern Chile, but now apparently rare. Uses variety of wetlands, including fresh water and brackish, occurring at up to 2500 m in Andes. Population estimated at several hundred thousands. Reason for decline in Chile not known. No important threats though hunted extensively for food.

Galapagos Pintail

Anas bahamensis galapagensis L 38-45 cm (15-18 in), WS 55-62 cm (22-24 in)
Unmistakable within range.

IDENTIFICATION Male and female breeding and non-breeding, juvenile As Lesser White-cheeked Pintail, but smaller and duller overall, with whitish cheeks and throat flecked with grey, so that contrast with dark brown crown and nape much less. Bill colour less bright. **Confusion risks** Only medium-sized dabbling duck in range with combination of dark cap over pale cheeks, red and blue bill and overall warm brown, dark-spotted body. Wing pattern of narrow green speculum with broad buff band to rear particularly distinctive in flight.
DISTRIBUTION AND STATUS Confined as resident to Galapagos Islands, where it is the only endemic duck, apparently restricted to nine islands, including Indefatigable, James, Narborough, San Cristobal and Tower. Occupies the limited fresh waters on those islands, as well as sheltered coasts. Population estimated at several thousands in 1970s, but no surveys have been conducted since then. Threatened by introduced mammalian predators, with its extreme tameness

increasing its vulnerability, and by natural events. In June 1968, the collapse of the bottom of the Fernandina Crater Lake on Narborough caused the death of an estimated 2,000 Galapagos Pintails. In view of such threats, an up-to-date survey would seem to be of considerable importance.

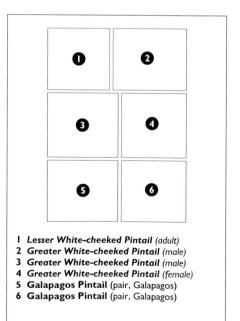

1 **Lesser White-cheeked Pintail** (adult)
2 **Greater White-cheeked Pintail** (male)
3 **Greater White-cheeked Pintail** (male)
4 **Greater White-cheeked Pintail** (female)
5 **Galapagos Pintail** (pair, Galapagos)
6 **Galapagos Pintail** (pair, Galapagos)

DABBLING DUCKS

SILVER (or VERSICOLOR) TEAL

Anas versicolor
Polytypic. Three subspecies: (1) Northern Silver (or Versicolor) Teal *A. v. versicolor*, breeds southern Brazil and Bolivia south to central Argentina and central Chile, winters also further north into Brazil; (2) Southern Silver (or Versicolor) Teal *A. v. fretensis*, breeds southern Chile and southern Argentina south to Tierra del Fuego, with some northward movement in winter, also resident Falkland Islands; (3) Puna Teal *A. v. puna*, resident Andes from central Peru and west Bolivia south to northern Chile and extreme north-west Argentina. It has recently been suggested that the Puna Teal should be regarded as a separate species.

Northern Silver (or Versicolor) Teal

Anas versicolor versicolor L 38-43 cm (15-17 in), WS 58-64 cm (23-25 in)
No confusion species within range for this small, dark-capped dabbling duck with bluish bill.
IDENTIFICATION Male breeding and non-breeding Blackish-brown cap, down to eye, and nape, and thin line down back of neck, sharply demarcated from creamy-white cheeks and throat. Lower neck, breast and anterior flanks buff with small blackish-brown spots, these becoming larger on flanks, where merge into bold, vertical black and white barring over posterior flanks; centre of belly, vent and undertail-coverts finely vermiculated grey. Mantle, scapulars and back blackish-brown with buff edgings; elongated tertials dark brown with very narrow pale edges; rump, uppertail-coverts and tail finely vermiculated grey. Speculum bright iridescent green with narrow white border in front, and narrow black and then white borders behind, while upperwing-coverts slaty grey-blue and primaries and their coverts dark brown; underwing with white centre and dark leading edge, and grey flight feathers. Broad and heavy bill pale blue, with yellow spot behind and below nostrils, black nail and black stripe down centre of upper mandible to tip. Legs and feet dark grey. Almost silent, apart from occasional weak whistle or rattling call. **Female** As male, but slightly smaller and duller overall; barring on flanks less distinct and tertials shorter. Speculum less bright green, as well as less extensive. Bill duller, with little or no yellow at base. Quiet quacking calls. **Juvenile** As adult female, but duller again, with less contrast on head, as crown browner and face tinged pale brown. More streaked than spotted and barred on underparts, and speculum less iridescent green. **Confusion risks** None within range.
DISTRIBUTION AND STATUS Breeds from southern Brazil and Bolivia, south through Paraguay and Uruguay to northern and central Argentina and to central Chile; some northward movement further into Brazil in winter. Wide variety of shallow, well-vegetated fresh waters from sea-level to 3000-4000 m in Andes. No population estimates available, but no declines reported from areas where winter counts take place. No known threats.

Southern Silver (or Versicolor) Teal

Anas versicolor fretensis L 43-48 cm (17-19 in), WS 60-65 cm (24-26 in)
No confusion species within range for this small, dark-capped dabbling duck with bluish bill.
IDENTIFICATION Male and female breeding and non-breeding, juvenile As Northern Silver Teal, but larger. Spotting and barring on underparts dark brown rather than blackish. More extensive yellow on base of brighter blue bill. **Confusion risks** No other small duck in range has combination of dark cap and pale face, with blue bill, and strongly barred flanks. For distinctions from Puna Teal, see below. No intergrades with Northern Silver Teal reported.
DISTRIBUTION AND STATUS Breeds to south of Northern Silver Teal, from southern Chile and southern Argentina south to Tierra del Fuego, with some movement north in winter; resident in Falkland Islands. No information on extent, if any, of overlap with range of Northern Silver Teal. Habitat as that of Northern Silver Teal, but commonest on lowland waters. No population estimates available, but thought to be more numerous in southern Chile and southern Argentina than Northern Silver Teal to the north. Not plentiful in Falklands. No known threats.

Puna Teal

Anas versicolor puna L 48-51 cm (19-20 in), WS 63-70 cm (25-28 in)
Larger version of Silver Teal, with all-blue bill; no confusion species within range.
IDENTIFICATION Male breeding and non-breeding Very similar to Northern and Southern Silver Teals, but larger than the larger Southern subspecies. Crown and hindneck black rather than blackish-brown, and cheeks and throat paler cream so that contrast even more marked. Spots on breast less obvious and barring on flanks much narrower, more or less merging into vermiculations of sides of rump instead of abrupt change. Upperparts greyer, with less clear paler edgings. Upperwings and underwings as Northern Silver Teal. Bill bright hyacinth-blue, brighter than on Northern Silver Teal, and lacking any yellow at base, though similarly with black nail and black stripe down upper mandible. **Female** As male, but browner below and with broader barring on flanks, appearing closer to Northern Silver Teal, but more dark brown and buff than black and white. Bill less bright blue. **Juvenile** Duller version of female, with less green on speculum. **Confusion risks** Isolated in range from Northern Silver Teal.
DISTRIBUTION AND STATUS Resident in Andes of central Peru and western Bolivia south to northern Chile and extreme north-west Argentina. Uses larger lakes and pools in Andes, in the *puna* (arid grass-shrub zone above the upper limits of trees in the Andes). Population numbers several tens of thousands, perhaps as many as 100,000. No recent counts, but 50,000 estimated on Lake Junin, Peru, in late 1970s. No known threats.

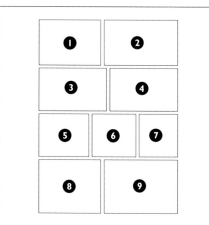

1 **Northern Silver (or Versicolor) Teal** (pair: female right-hand bird)
2 **Southern Silver (or Versicolor) Teal** (female and young, Falklands)
3 **Southern Silver (or Versicolor) Teal** (male, Falklands)
4 **Southern Silver (or Versicolor) Teal** (pair, Falklands)
5 **Puna Teal** (pair, Chile)
6 **Puna Teal** (female)
7 **Puna Teal** (male)
8 **Puna Teal** (male)
9 **Puna Teal** (young, juvenile)

DABBLING DUCKS

HOTTENTOT TEAL

Anas hottentota L 30-36 cm (12-14 in), WS 52-57 cm (20-22 in)

Monotypic. Tiny, dark-capped, brown duck, unmistakable within range.

IDENTIFICATION Male breeding and non-breeding Black crown, down to eye, and nape, sharply demarcated from and contrasting with pale buff cheeks and throat, brighter buff near base of bill, with dusky patch on upper hindneck extending forwards towards ear. Lower neck, breast and underparts buff to tawny-buff, with small dark brown spots on neck and breast, enlarging on anterior upper flanks, but rear flanks unmarked; lower anterior flanks more barred, becoming vermiculated black on buff on lower belly, vent and undertail-coverts. Mantle and scapulars dark brown with pale edgings; back and rump blackish; uppertail-coverts buff, vermiculated black; tail dark brown. Elongated tertials dark brown with greenish gloss. Speculum bright iridescent green with black and white trailing bars, upperwing-coverts and primaries dark brown to blackish with greenish gloss; underwing with white axillaries and median and greater coverts, darker leading edge and flight feathers, and pale trailing edge to secondaries. Bill light grey-blue, with black nail and upper-mandible stripe. Legs and feet dark grey-blue. Male mostly silent. **Female** As male, but duller, with more brown on crown and less contrasting face markings, including less obvious patch on hindneck; underparts less tawny-buff and lacking vermiculations on vent and undertail-coverts. Less gloss to upperwing and duller speculum. Bill less blue. Occasionally quacks on take-off. **Juvenile** As female, but duller. **Confusion risks** Very small duck, and no other species shows contrasting capped head. Green speculum with broad white band behind also very distinctive.

DISTRIBUTION AND STATUS Resident eastern and southern Africa, from south Sudan and Ethiopia south to south-east South Africa and west to Namibia, with isolated population northern Nigeria and Chad; resident Madagascar. On well-vegetated fresh waters of all kinds. West African population only 300 in 1972, but no information since. Several hundred thousands estimated eastern and southern Africa, but fewer than 10,000 Madagascar. No serious threats, even in Madagascar.

GARGANEY

Anas querquedula L 36-41 cm (14-16 in), WS 57-65 cm (22-26 in)

Monotypic. Male strikingly patterned, female very like several other female teals.

IDENTIFICATION Male breeding Blackish crown and upper nape above broad white stripe from in front of eye, tapering down hindneck; black patch on chin. Cheeks, throat and sides of neck reddish-brown, finely streaked whitish. Breast browner with fine, black crescentic markings, sharply demarcated from greyish-vermiculated flanks, darker towards rear; belly

white; ventral region and undertail-coverts whitish with dark brown bars and spots. Mantle brown with black markings; elongated scapulars blackish, strongly striped white, and drooping over closed wing; back, rump, uppertail-coverts and tail blackish. Primaries dark grey, but forewing pale blue-grey, with broad white stripe in front of iridescent dark green speculum, edged very narrowly behind with white; underwing white-centred, with dark leading edge and grey flight feathers. Bill, legs and feet dark grey. Call a distinctive mechanical rattle. **Male eclipse** As female, but retaining wing of male breeding; throat whiter. **Female** Dusky brown crown and eye-stripe, with whitish-buff supercilium and dusky patches on dark-streaked buff cheeks; noticeable pale buff spot at base of bill; whiter on throat. Breast and flanks sepia-brown, with pale pink-buff edgings giving scalloped appearance, particularly on sides of breast and upper flanks; belly and vent white; undertail-coverts whitish, streaked brown. Upperparts blackish-brown with buff edgings; tail sepia with whitish edgings. Forewing grey-brown, speculum with only small amount of green iridescence and bordered narrowly white in front and behind. Quacking calls. **Juvenile** As female, but with spotted and streaked belly. **Confusion risks** Male unmistakable. For separation of female from Green-winged, Blue-winged and Cinnamon Teals, see those species.

DISTRIBUTION AND STATUS Breeds temperate Eurasia from Britain to Pacific coast of Russia; winters sub-Saharan Africa south to Zambia, Indian subcontinent and south-east Asia. Shallow fresh waters; also coastal marshes in winter. Estimated 2 million winter in West Africa and up to 1 million in each of Indian subcontinent and south-east Asia. No significant threats.

BLUE-WINGED TEAL

Anas discors L 37-41 cm (15-16 in), WS 60-64 cm (24-25 in)

Monotypic. Distinctive male, but female very similar to Cinnamon Teal within range.

IDENTIFICATION Male breeding Bold white vertical crescent, very narrowly bordered white, in front of eye. Crown blackish; rest of head and upper neck slate-grey with purplish tinge. Apart from white patch at sides of vent, entire underparts reddish-buff and heavily spotted brownish-black, spots becoming bars on upper flanks. Mantle and scapulars dark brown, latter elongated, pointed and striped black and buff; back, rump, tail-coverts and tail blackish. Bright pale blue forewing separated by white band from iridescent green speculum, which bordered black and with narrow white tips to secondaries, with primaries and their coverts blackish-brown; underwing white-centred, with dark leading edge and grey flight feathers. Bill black. Legs and feet orange-yellow with dusky webs. High-pitched whistling call. **Male eclipse** As female, but with darker crown and streaked head, and retains male wing. **Female** Dark brown crown and eye-stripe, more obvious behind eye, which has pale eye-

ring; whitish-buff oval patch on lores and white chin to upper foreneck, otherwise head and neck buff-brown with darker streaks. Underparts brown, with grey-buff margins giving scalloped appearance, especially on flanks; mottled belly paler. Upperparts darker olive-brown with buff edgings; outer tertials black, with buff streaks and green gloss; tail sepia with pale edges. Upperwing as male, but with paler, less blue forewing, less iridescence on speculum, and white bar narrow and obscure. Bill grey; legs and feet dull yellow-brown. Quacking calls. **Juvenile** As female, but darker above and more heavily marked below (with streaks rather than spots). Legs and feet grey. As adults by mid-winter, but wings retained until first summer. **Confusion risks** Male unmistakable. For separation of female from Cinnamon Teal, see latter. From female Garganey by less clearly marked head, lacking contrast between dark crown and eye-stripe and pale supercilium, and has paler cheeks; belly mottled, not clear white. In flight, pale blue-grey forewing and lack of broad white band behind speculum.

DISTRIBUTION AND STATUS Breeds Canada and USA from southern Alaska to Newfoundland south to prairies; winters southern USA to northern South America. Mainly small and shallow fresh waters; winters on larger fresh waters, coastal marshes and lagoons. Current population c 5 million in spring, rising to c 9 million in autumn. Heavily shot, but not threatened.

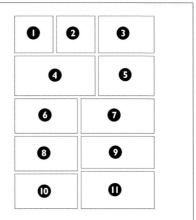

1 **Hottentot Teal** (adult, Lake Nakuru, Kenya)
2 **Hottentot Teal** (juvenile, Ngorongoro, Tanzania)
3 **Hottentot Teal** (group, Lake Nakuru, Kenya)
4 **Garganey** (male, Norfolk, England)
5 **Garganey** (female, Mai-po, Hong Kong)
6 **Garganey** (first year male, Merseyside, England)
7 **Garganey** (flock in flight, Singapore)
8 **Blue-winged Teal** (group, male and female, Florida, USA)
9 **Blue-winged Teal** (males and female in flight, Manitoba, Canada)
10 **Blue-winged Teal** (immature female, Worcestershire, England)
11 **Blue-winged Teal** (pair, Florida, USA)

DABBLING DUCKS

CINNAMON TEAL

Anas cyanoptera
Polytypic. Five subspecies: (1) Northern Cinnamon Teal *A. c. septentrionalium*, breeds western North America, winters south to northern South America; (2) Tropical Cinnamon Teal *A. c. tropica*, resident north-west Colombia; (3) Borrero's Cinnamon Teal *A. c. borreroi*, resident Andes of western Colombia; (4) Andean Cinnamon Teal *A. c. orinomus*, breeds high Andes of Peru, Bolivia and northern Chile, winters there and at lower altitudes; (5) Argentine Cinnamon Teal *A. c. cyanoptera*, breeds southern Peru, Bolivia and southern Brazil south to Tierra del Fuego, resident Falkland Islands.

Northern Cinnamon Teal

Anas cyanoptera septentrionalium L 38-45 cm (15-18 in), WS 58-64 cm (23-25 in)
Unmistakable rufous to chestnut-red male, but female very similar to Blue-winged Teal.
IDENTIFICATION Male breeding Head, neck, breast, sides, flanks and underparts bright rusty-chestnut. Darker brown-black on crown, back, rump and uppertail- and undertail-coverts. Long, black scapulars with prominent buff stripes trail over rear flanks of resting bird. Tail blackish with rusty edges. Wings very similar to those of Blue-winged Teal, with dark brown flight feathers and bright blue forewing separated from green speculum by white band; underwing dark, with whitish central stripe. Bill black. Legs and feet orange-yellow. Iris orange-red. Nasal whistling calls, similar to Blue-winged Teal's. **Male eclipse** Closely resembles female, but overall more chestnut, especially on head and neck, and retaining brighter colours on wing. At close range, bill dark grey, with flesh-coloured areas at gape and along mandible edges. Iris yellow to reddish. **Female** Similar to female Blue-winged Teal, but more rusty, especially on underparts, and more heavily streaked blackish on head and chin, while pale patch at base of bill very small or absent, as is dark eye-stripe. Some birds overall darker than others. Bill dark grey, with pale edges; legs and feet dull yellow; iris dark brown. High-pitched quacking call. **Juvenile** As female, but with more obvious white facial spot, more heavily streaked on underparts and less rufous overall. Chestnut tones of adult appear from October-November. **Confusion risks** Adult male distinctive from other dabbling ducks; see other races for subspecific differences. Female closely resembles female Blue-winged Teal, but is grey-brown rather than rufous and has more obvious head markings, especially the white spot at base of bill and the dark eye-stripe. Juveniles hardest, sometimes impossible to separate from Blue-winged Teal, though following points helpful: less contrast between breast and flanks; bill slightly longer and broader, with very slight flanges along sides near tip.
DISTRIBUTION AND STATUS Breeds western North America south from British Columbia to north-west Mexico; winters south-western states, Mexico, and northern Central America to about Nicaragua, but less often as far south as Colombia in north-west South America. Habitat as for Blue-winged Teal. Estimated population 300,000 at start of breeding season and probably double that at end of season, and thought to be stable.

Tropical Cinnamon Teal

Anas cyanoptera tropica L 35-43 cm (14-17 in), WS 56-62 cm (22-24 in)
Unmistakable rufous to chestnut-red male with black-spotted underparts, but female very similar to Blue-winged Teal.
IDENTIFICATION Male breeding As Northern Cinnamon Teal, but smaller and deeper chestnut-red rather than rusty-chestnut. Lower neck and breast lightly spotted blackish, becoming more heavily spotted on sides of belly and lower flanks, where dark spots surrounded by broad buff feather margins, with finer spots towards rear of flanks. **Male eclipse** As female, but overall brighter chestnut, especially on head and neck, and retaining some spotting on underparts and brighter colours on wing. At close range, bill dark grey, with flesh-coloured areas at gape and along mandible edges. **Female** As female Northern Cinnamon Teal, but more chestnut-red. **Juvenile** Like duller female, with more streaked underparts. **Confusion risks** There may be some slight range overlap with Northern Cinnamon Teal, which occasionally winters in Colombia. Male distinguished from male Northern Cinnamon Teal by spotted underparts; female more chestnut overall than female Northern, but identification difficult, if not impossible.
DISTRIBUTION AND STATUS Resident in lowlands of north-west Colombia, up to c 1000 m, principally in valleys of Cauca and Magdalena; in the Cauca valley, may now be restricted to very small area around Valle. Uses marshes, small pools and lakes. Small population estimated at under 10,000 individuals and declining. Habitat loss and excessive shooting are thought to be putting this subspecies at considerable risk.

Andean Cinnamon Teal

Anas cyanoptera orinomus L 41-48 cm (16-19 in), WS 62-69 cm (24-27 in)
Unmistakable rufous to chestnut-red male, and female more rufous and much less patterned than other female dabbling ducks within range.
IDENTIFICATION Male and female breeding and non-breeding, juvenile As Northern Cinnamon Teal, but substantially larger, with only partial overlap in measurements. Noticeably larger and longer in the bill, too. **Confusion risks** No confusion species within range for either sex.
DISTRIBUTION AND STATUS Breeds up to 3800m in high Andes of Peru, Bolivia and northern Chile, wintering within range and at lower altitudes, including to sea-level on Peruvian and north Chilean coasts. Occupies *puna* zone (comprising the arid grass-shrub zone above the upper limits of trees in the Andes), where it nests beside mountain lakes and pools; winters on lower-altitude marshes and coastal lagoons. Population estimated at some tens of thousands, and particularly numerous on and around Lake Titicaca, with no information on any serious threats.

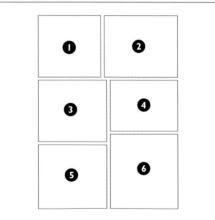

1 **Northern Cinnamon Teal** (female, Florida, USA)
2 **Northern Cinnamon Teal** (male, Florida, USA)
3 *Northern Cinnamon Teal* (eclipse male)
4 *Northern Cinnamon Teal* (female eclipse)
5 **Northern Cinnamon Teal** (four females, one male in flight, California, USA)
6 *Andean Cinnamon Teal* (male)

DABBLING DUCKS

Borrero's Cinnamon Teal

Anas cyanoptera borreroi L 35-43 cm (15-18 in),
WS 56-62 cm (22-24 in)
Unmistakable rufous to chestnut-red male with
black-spotted underparts, but female very
similar to Blue-winged Teal.
IDENTIFICATION Male breeding As Tropical
Cinnamon Teal, but underparts very variably
spotted, with about 50% of individuals showing
no spots. Remainder rarely show more than a
few spots on neck, breast or flanks, but on
belly can range from a few blackish spots to
almost entirely black. **Male eclipse, female,
juvenile** As Tropical Cinnamon Teal.
Confusion risks Difficult to distinguish from
either Northern or Tropical Cinnamon Teal,
but little or no overlap in ranges.
DISTRIBUTION AND STATUS Resident on east
side of Andes in western Colombia, mainly
between 2250 m and 3750 m, where it inhabits
mountain lakes and pools in the high savannahs.
Extremely scarce, and perhaps numbering
fewer than 250 individuals and declining, this
race must be considered on the verge of
extinction. Although apparently numerous as
recently as the 1950s, it suffered heavily from
habitat loss and excessive shooting and was
actually declared extinct in 1974. Very small
numbers were, however, found in the 1980s in
a handful of mountain valleys. There are
obvious practical difficulties in carrying out
survey work in Colombia to find out whether
any still survive and, if they do, in doing
anything to protect this subspecies.

Argentine Cinnamon Teal

Anas cyanoptera cyanoptera L 38-45 cm (15-18
in), WS 58-64 cm (23-25 in)
Unmistakable rufous to chestnut-red male, and
female more rufous and much less patterned
than other female dabbling ducks within range.
IDENTIFICATION Male breeding As Northern
Cinnamon Teal, but deeper chestnut-red,
closer to Tropical Cinnamon Teal, though not
so small as that subspecies. Most, though not
all, birds show small dark brown spots on sides
of breast. Belly with distinct brown tone.
Female, juvenile As Northern Cinnamon
Teal, but more rufous in tone. **Confusion
risks** No confusion species within range, and
no apparent overlap with Andean Cinnamon
Teal except, possibly, in winter in southern
Peru on east side of Andes.
DISTRIBUTION AND STATUS Breeds mainly
lowlands of southern Peru, Bolivia and
southern Brazil south through Chile and
Argentina to Tierra del Fuego, and resident in
Falkland Islands; southernmost breeders move
north in winter, with some individuals
extending further north into Brazil. Breeds on
lowland marshes, lakes and pools, wintering on
similar fresh waters and on coastal lagoons and
marshes. Population believed to number many
tens of thousands; not uncommon in Falklands.
No serious known threats to either mainland
or Falklands population.

RED SHOVELER

Anas platalea L 45-56 cm (18-22 in), WS 66-73
cm (26-29 in)
Monotypic. Sole dabbling duck in South
America having large spatulate bill of shoveler.
**IDENTIFICATION Male breeding and non-
breeding** Head pinkish-buff, lightly and finely
spotted blackish, most heavily on the crown,
where spots larger and producing indistinct
dark 'cap', and most lightly on chin and throat,
which whitish and almost unspotted. Breast,
flanks and underparts variable in colour, from
pale rufous-chestnut to deeper reddish-
chestnut (variation not apparently related to
season or age; there is no separate eclipse
plumage), all quite densely and evenly marked
with round black spots, spots densest and
smallest on breast, becoming slightly larger and
more sparse on flanks, but smaller and still well
spaced on belly and vent; white patch on each
side of ventral region; undertail-coverts black.
Mantle similar to breast; scapulars with broad
central stripes and wide reddish-buff edgings;
tertials slightly elongated, blackish with greenish
gloss and conspicuous white margins; back,
rump and uppertail-coverts blackish. Relatively
long and pointed tail blackish-brown with
whitish outer feathers. Forewing light blue,
greater coverts with broad white margin
forming bar in front of iridescent green
speculum on secondaries, bounded narrowly
behind by black, with primaries and their
coverts blackish; underwing with whitish
axillaries and coverts and darker grey-brown
flight feathers. Long, broad spatulate bill dark
greyish-black. Legs and feet yellow. Iris very
distinctive, pale yellow or whitish. Male has *tuk-
tuk* call, higher-pitched than that of Northern
Shoveler. **Female** Head and neck uniform
greyish-buff, finely streaked black; very slightly
whiter on lores, but otherwise lacking in any
distinguishing marks such as crown- or eye-
stripes. Breast, mantle, flanks and underparts
dull greyish-buff with brown spots, latter
formed by dark feather centres and paler buff
feather margins; spots smallest on breast,
largest on flanks. Lower mantle, scapulars,
upper back and tertials grey-brown with buff
edgings; lower back, rump and uppertail-
coverts darker grey-brown with paler edgings;
pointed tail blackish-brown with lighter outer
feathers. Forewing grey with only tinge of blue,
and only thin whitish bar in front of blackish
secondaries, with limited extent of iridescent
green; underwing as male. Bill brownish-black;
legs and feet yellowish-grey. Female has low
quacking call, but not very vocal. **Juvenile**
Closely resembles female and not always
possible to separate, unless bluer-grey forewing
of male visible. **Confusion risks** No other
shoveler-shaped duck, with huge bill and
relatively short neck, occurs within this species'
South American range. Superficially resembles
Cinnamon Teal if bill cannot be seen, but that
species smaller, generally brighter chestnut and
less evenly spotted, and with shorter, non-
pointed tail.

DISTRIBUTION AND STATUS Apart from a few
small and isolated resident groups in southern
Peru, breeds in central Chile, infrequently
further south, and most of Argentina, south to
Tierra del Fuego; in winter, extends
northwards throughout Argentina and
Uruguay, and into southern Peru, western
Bolivia, Paraguay and southern Brazil. Breeds
on variety of fresh waters, mainly in lowlands,
but at up to 3400 m in Andes, in winter
occupying coastal estuaries, lagoons and
marshes, as well as inland waters. Population
estimated as between 100,000 and 1 million.
No known threats, as although hunted to some
extent, they are generally regarded, as are
most Shovelers, as unpalatable.

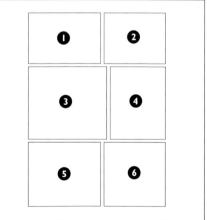

1 **Argentine Cinnamon Teal** (pair, Falklands)
2 *Red Shoveler* (female)
3 **Red Shoveler** (two males, Argentina)
4 *Red Shoveler* (male)
5 **Red Shoveler** (pair, San Clevente, Argentina)
6 *Red Shoveler* (male)

CAPE SHOVELER

Anas smithii L 49-55 cm (19-22 in), WS 68-82 cm (27-32 in)

Monotypic. Sole dabbling duck in southern Africa having large spatulate bill of shoveler.

IDENTIFICATION Male breeding and non-breeding Pale buff head and neck, finely streaked blackish, especially on crown and nape, producing very slight capped appearance, but no other markings on very plain head. Breast, flanks and underparts dark brown, the pale cinnamon-buff edgings to the feathers producing spotted and mottled effect, which at long range really noticeable only on flanks, where marks crescentic and bolder. Mantle dark brown with cinnamon-buff edgings; scapulars and tertials, also back, rump and uppertail-coverts, blackish with purple-blue sheen. Tail blackish-brown with white or buff feather edgings. Forewing pale bluish-grey, with narrow white bar in front of iridescent green speculum, and primaries and their coverts dark brown; underwing whitish, with brown leading edge and grey-brown flight feathers. Large, spatulate bill black. Legs and feet orange-yellow, fading to yellow outside breeding season (but no eclipse plumage). Iris conspicuous bright yellow. Rarely calls, giving an occasional hoarse rasping note. **Female** Duller and paler than male, with less contrast between head and neck and rest of body, where buff feather tips broader but lacking cinnamon colouring. Upperparts lacking purple-blue gloss, more matt dark brownish-black. Upperwing-coverts grey, barely, if at all, bluish, with indistinct white line in front of speculum, which has reduced green iridescence; underwing as male. Bill dark brown; legs and feet yellowish-grey. Low quacking calls. **Juvenile** As female, but more buff on underparts from broader feather edgings. Wings help determine sex during first autumn. Moults into adult plumage during first winter. **Confusion risks** No other shoveler-shaped dabbling duck in southern Africa.

DISTRIBUTION AND STATUS Mainly resident in South Africa, principally Cape Province, Orange Free State and Transvaal, and uncommon further north in Namibia, Botswana, Zimbabwe and just reaching southern Angola; some dispersive movements and even nomadism in response to wet and dry seasons. Large open fresh, brackish and, sometimes, saline waters, also using temporary floods. Population estimate of 25,000-100,000 individuals, with some recent increase in south of range. No apparent threats.

AUSTRALASIAN SHOVELER

Anas rhynchotis

Polytypic. Two subspecies: (1) Australian Shoveler *A. r. rhynchotis*, resident south-east Australia and south-west Western Australia, but wanders quite widely; (2) New Zealand Shoveler *A. r. variegata*, resident North and South Islands, New Zealand. Although two geographically separated subspecies have long been recognized, ringed Australian Shovelers have been recovered in New Zealand and the plumage distinctions are so small in relation to known individual variation as to throw doubt on validity of subspecific division, though still treated as two subspecies here.

Australian Shoveler

Anas rhynchotis rhynchotis L 46-56 cm (18-22 in), WS 72-85 cm (28-33 in)

Sole dabbling duck in Australia having large spatulate bill of shoveler.

IDENTIFICATION Male breeding Head and upper neck slate-grey with variable green-blue iridescence; crown and nape streaked black and so slightly darker. White vertical crescent in front of eye, varying both in length and in definition. Lower neck and breast buff to brown, with black and white mottling and spotting, merging with chestnut of lower breast, flanks and belly, all of which scalloped black, bolder on the flanks; flank markings variable, with scallops sometimes running together to form bars, at other times more spaced and therefore spotted in appearance; large white patch, very lightly vermiculated grey, on sides of ventral region in front of black undertail-coverts. Mantle and scapulars blackish with pale edgings; blackish elongated tertials with white shaft-streaks droop over closed wing; back, rump, uppertail-coverts and tail black, tail with whitish sides. Forewing light blue, with white band in front of iridescent green speculum, and primaries and their coverts dark brown; underwing mainly whitish on coverts with grey-brown flight feathers. Large, spatulate bill black. Legs and feet orange. Bright yellow iris. Quiet *tuk-tuk* call, but not very vocal. **Male eclipse** As female, but more chestnut on flanks and often retaining at least some white on sides of vent, as well as wing and, usually, iris colours. **Female** Buff-brown head and neck, streaked black, darker on crown and with slight eye-stripe, particularly in front of eye. Warm brown underparts heavily mottled dark brown, markings largest on flanks. Upperparts dark brown with pale feather edgings; tail dark brown with pale sides. Upperwing as male, but forewing greyer, less blue, and narrower white band in front of speculum, which blacker with less green iridescence. Bill grey-brown; legs and feet grey-green; iris dark brown. **Juvenile** Resembles female, but underside paler, with smaller, less distinct mottles and spots. **Confusion risks** The only shoveler of Australia. Only other species of region with spatulate bill is smaller Pink-eared Duck, which much paler, with dark face markings and barred underparts, and, in flight, lacks bright colour on upperwing.

DISTRIBUTION AND STATUS Breeds south-east Australia (mainly New South Wales, Victoria and Tasmania) and in south-west of Western Australia; most resident, but may wander quite widely, especially north into Queensland, in response to periods of drought or rains. Occupies well-vegetated lowland lakes, marshes and swamps, as well as temporary floods. Not abundant in either part of range, but probably numbers at least low tens of thousands, perhaps more. Not threatened.

New Zealand Shoveler

Anas rhynchotis variegata L 46-56 cm (18-23 in), WS 72-85 cm (28-33 in)

Sole dabbling duck in New Zealand with shoveler-type large spatulate bill, apart from vagrant Australian Shoveler.

IDENTIFICATION Male breeding As Australian Shoveler, but overall much brighter, with more green gloss on head and, usually, much clearer white crescent; chestnut of flanks richer and deeper in colour. These differences not always apparent because of individual variation in both subspecies. **Male non-breeding, female, juvenile** Little, if at all, different from Australian Shoveler. **Confusion risks** No other resident shoveler in New Zealand; ringed Australian Shovelers have reached New Zealand, but this is probably the only way they can be identified as such.

DISTRIBUTION AND STATUS Resident North and South Islands, New Zealand, avoiding upland areas. Habitat as for Australian Shoveler. Population between 100,000 and 150,000. Quite heavily shot, up to 30,000 annually, but despite this is thought to be increasing in numbers.

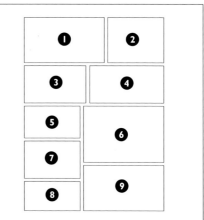

1 **Cape Shoveler** (group, Cape Town, South Africa)
2 **Cape Shoveler** (male)
3 Cape Shoveler (pair)
4 **Australian Shoveler** (male, Australia)
5 **Australian Shoveler** (male, Australia)
6 **Australian Shoveler** (eclipse male, Australia)
7 **Australian Shoveler** (male, immature, lacks facial crescent, Perth, Australia)
8 *Australian Shoveler* (female)
9 **New Zealand Shoveler** (pair, probably of this race)

NORTHERN SHOVELER

Anas clypeata L 43-56 cm (17-22 in), WS 70-85 cm (28-33 in)
Monotypic. Sturdy dabbling duck with short neck and long, spatulate bill, unmistakable within northern-hemisphere range.
IDENTIFICATION Male breeding Head dark iridescent green, except for dark brownish-black crown; appears black at distance. Neck and breast white, with white stripe above chestnut flanks and belly. Pale blue forewing shows on resting or swimming bird, while oval white patch at sides of rump partially obscured by long, drooping, black and white scapulars. Back, rump and tail-coverts black, sides of tail white. In flight, white breast, and pale blue forewing and green speculum with white stripe between, very obvious; underwing whitish with contrasting grey-brown flight feathers. Very large, spatulate bill grey-black. Legs orange-red. Soft *tuk-tuk* call, and whistling rattle from wings in flight. **Male eclipse** Resembles dark female, but more uniformly and redder brown; retains blue forewing and green speculum. Moults back into breeding plumage November-March; intermediate stage in autumn, with whitish facial crescent and pale cheeks. **Female breeding** Overall brown, well marked with pale buff to pink-buff edgings and mottlings. Paler on head, with narrow dark eye-stripe. Pale sides to tail. Wings as male, but forewing grey-blue and speculum duller. Bill dark brown, with yellow-orange at base and sides; legs and feet orange. Quacking decrescendo call.
Female non-breeding Darker, but still paler than eclipse male. **Juvenile** As adult female, but head darker and underparts paler. Adult male plumage gained very slowly, brown spotting remaining on white breast well into spring.
Confusion risks Separated from all other northern-hemisphere wildfowl by heavy-headed appearance, obvious at rest and in flight. Overlap with other shovelers just possible in Africa (Cape Shoveler) and, remotely, Australia (Australian Shoveler). Breeding male always distinguishable; eclipse male can resemble breeding male Australian Shoveler, but has brown, not grey, head. Female from other shovelers by dark eye-stripe, underparts paler than upperparts, pale sides to tail, orange sides to bill and orange legs.
DISTRIBUTION AND STATUS Breeds temperate and sub-arctic zones of North America and Eurasia; winters within milder parts of range, *eg* north-west Europe, but mainly south to south USA, Mexico, Central America (small numbers as far as Panama and Colombia), and around Mediterranean, in sub-Saharan West Africa, East Africa, Indian subcontinent and south-east Asia. On wide variety of shallow fresh waters; also coastal lagoons and estuaries in winter. Widespread and common; *c* 2 million pre-breeding season in North America, and 750,000 wintering Europe, Africa and south-west Asia, and perhaps up to 1 million in south and east Asia. Stable or increasing except southern Asia, where believed declining.

PINK-EARED DUCK

Malacorhynchus membranaceus L 36-45 cm (14-18 in), WS 57-71 cm (22-28 in)
Monotypic. Small duck with huge spatulate bill.
IDENTIFICATION Sexes identical, except that male is slightly larger and has a higher-pitched voice. **Male and female breeding and non-breeding** Forehead, crown, nape and hindneck grey-brown. Oval to triangular dark brown eye patch extends back along sides of crown and down nape sides, with small bright pink spot adjoining rear of eye patch. Whitish between bill and eye patch, whitish eye-ring, and whitish cheeks, throat and foreneck very finely barred grey, to give overall pale grey effect. Lower neck, breast, flanks and belly whitish, strongly barred brownish-black, with narrower barring on breast, becoming bolder and broader on flanks but finer on belly and vent; undertail-coverts buff. Mantle and scapulars finely vermiculated grey and black; rest of upperparts and tertials unmarked dark brown, except for broad white band at base of uppertail-coverts which extends onto sides of body. Tail dark grey, broadly tipped white. Upperwing dark brown, paler on forewing and secondaries, which lack iridescence and are tipped white; underwing whitish, with brown flight feathers. Very long and broad bill grey, made larger in appearance by obvious fleshy flaps near tip, hanging below lower mandible. Legs and feet grey. Repeated chirruping and trilling calls, male's higher-pitched than female's. **Juvenile** As adult, but pink eye patch smaller and paler, sometimes absent altogether. **Confusion risks** Although superficially resembling Australian Shoveler, small size, barred underparts and lack of speculum separate it at all times.
DISTRIBUTION AND STATUS Widespread in Australia, with main breeding areas in south Western Australia, south-eastern South Australia, Victoria and New South Wales; dispersive and nomadic, responding to irregular rains. Mainly shallow fresh, brackish and saline waters. Population thought to number a few hundred thousands, and not threatened.

MARBLED TEAL

Marmaronetta angustirostris L 39-42 (15-17 in), WS 63-67 cm (25-26 in)
Monotypic. Small sandy-coloured duck with no confusion species within range.
IDENTIFICATION Male breeding and non-breeding Sandy grey-brown head, lightly speckled and barred darker brown on forehead, crown and nape, with blunt, shaggy, pendent crest. Ill-defined dark brown patch around eye, becoming diffuse towards nape. Cheeks, throat and neck paler and only lightly streaked brown. Underparts sandy-brown, barred darker brown except on flanks, which a shade darker, with large pale buff spots. Mantle and scapulars dark brown with large, well-spaced pale buff spots; rest of upperparts buff-spotted brown. Pointed tail pale grey-brown, with darker, white-tipped central feathers. Upperwing pale grey-brown,

paler on secondaries, very slightly darker towards bases of primaries; no speculum or bars. Bill blackish, with narrow pale grey line behind dark nail. Nasal *eeep* during display, otherwise silent. **Female** As male, but lacks crest. Bill without pale subterminal line, but with dull olive-green triangular patch at base of upper mandible. Only call a squeaky note in display; does not quack. **Juvenile** As female, but greyer below, with more diffuse spotting on body. **Confusion risks** Unmistakable within range. Total lack of any pattern or speculum on wing distinguishes this from such extralimital species as Crested Duck, Cape Teal, etc.
DISTRIBUTION AND STATUS Fragmented breeding range, with isolated populations southern Spain, north-west Africa, Egypt, Turkey, Israel, Iraq, Iran, Azerbaijan, Turkmenistan, Uzbekistan, Kazakhstan and extreme western China. Spanish and North African birds winter mainly Morocco; some eastern Mediterranean birds winter within or close to breeding areas; further east, main wintering area Iran, Pakistan and India. Well-vegetated shallow freshwater, and brackish pools and marshes. Numbers drastically reduced from former level. Recent increase in numbers wintering Morocco, and west Mediterranean population *c* 2,000; probably only 1,000 in eastern Mediterranean. Main wintering area of Iran holds *c* 25,000, with further 5,000 in Pakistan and India. Total of 33,000, maybe up to 40,000 in good years. Regarded as vulnerable, with shooting and habitat loss continuing threats.

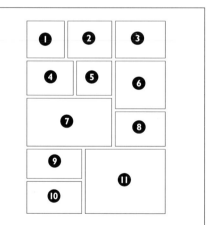

1 **Northern Shoveler** (male, Merseyside, England)
2 **Northern Shoveler** (first year male, Merseyside, England)
3 **Northern Shoveler** (group: three eclipse females and one eclipse male, Merseyside, England)
4 **Northern Shoveler** (female, Merseyside, England)
5 **Northern Shoveler** (female in flight, Norfolk, England)
6 **Pink-eared Duck** (adult, Australia)
7 **Pink-eared Duck** (adults, Australia)
8 **Pink-eared Duck** (flock in flight at dusk, Australia)
9 **Marbled Teal** (adult, Turkey)
10 *Marbled Teal* (male)
11 *Marbled Teal* (juvenile)

DIVING DUCKS

COMMON POCHARD

Aythya ferina L 42-49 cm (17-29 in), WS 72-82 cm (28-32 in)
Monotypic. Relatively distinct diving duck within range, but confusion possible with vagrant species from North America.
IDENTIFICATION Male breeding Uniform glossy chestnut-red head and neck. Breast black, sharply demarcated from greyish-white (actually very finely vermiculated black or dark grey and white) upperparts and underparts, slightly whiter on belly, darker on vent. Rump, tail-coverts and tail blackish. Upperwing pale grey, darker on coverts, outer primaries and their tips, with outer secondaries tipped darker grey, inner tipped white; underwing whitish. Bill pale blue-grey from behind terminal black band to nostrils, then dark grey to base. Legs and feet grey. Iris bright red. Mostly silent. **Male eclipse** As female, but no facial pattern; greyer on body, including darker on breast. Iris orange-yellow. **Female** Medium-brown head and neck, blacker on crown and hindneck, with diffuse and variable whitish markings on throat, chin and cheeks and buff-white line through and around eye. Breast medium brown; rest of underparts pale grey-brown, flanks with browner tinge. Upperparts darker grey-brown, often looking mottled, browner in summer than in winter; rump, tail-coverts and tail dark brown. Wings as male, but upperwing-coverts browner. Bill as male, but dark grey extends beyond nostrils, restricting area of pale blue-grey; legs and feet grey; iris brown to yellow-brown. Low display calls. **Juvenile** As female, but lacking pale eye-stripe and underparts more variably mottled brown. Bill all dark. **Confusion risks** See Canvasback and Redhead.
DISTRIBUTION AND STATUS Breeds temperate and southern Eurasia from Britain east to Mongolia and west China; winters within breeding range and south to sub-Saharan Africa, south-east Europe, south-west Asia, northern Indian subcontinent and south-east Asia. On well-vegetated fresh waters; winters on larger fresh and brackish waters, also estuaries. Winter estimates of 350,000 in western and southern Europe, 1.25 million in south-east Europe, 350,000 in south-west Asia, and some hundreds of thousands in both south and south-east Asia. Has declined in some parts from excessive shooting and habitat loss.

RING-NECKED DUCK

Aythya collaris L 37-46 cm (15-18 in), WS 61-75 cm (24-30 in)
Monotypic. Small black-and-white diving duck with slight crest; vagrants to Europe confusable with Tufted Duck.
IDENTIFICATION Male breeding Head and neck black with greenish gloss. Nape feathers shaggy, forming crest, giving peaked triangular shape to head. Indistinct narrow chestnut collar around base of neck. Breast black, separated from lightly vermiculated grey and white belly and flanks by pure white band running up sides

of breast to back. Mantle, scapulars and tertials blackish with greenish gloss; back, rump and tail-coverts black; tail dark grey-brown. Upperwing dark greyish-brown, greater coverts glossed greenish, secondaries grey with whitish tips to inner ones, brownish to outer ones; underwing whitish. Bill bluish-grey, with broad white band behind equally broad black tip, and narrow white line at base of upper mandible. Legs and feet grey. Iris bright yellow. Mostly silent. **Male eclipse** Like darker brown female, but much blacker on head and breast, lacking pale eye-ring; retains yellow eye, as well as some gloss on upperwing. **Female** Brown head and neck, darker on crown and hindneck and whitish on throat and lores, with whitish narrow stripe through and around eye. Breast and underparts grey-brown, but brown-mottled whitish on belly and undertail-coverts. Upperparts brown with grey feather margins; rump and uppertail-coverts blackish; tail dark grey-brown. Wings as male, but forewing browner and unglossed. Bill as male, but subterminal band narrower and no basal line; legs and feet grey; iris brown. **Juvenile** Browner and more spotted on belly than female. Black quickly appears on breast of male, and close to adult plumage by mid to late winter. **Confusion risks** Male superficially like male Tufted Duck, but head shape different, and latter has hanging crest, whiter flanks without stripe up breast sides, and less patterned bill; eclipse male retains bill pattern, as well as different head shape. Female and juvenile also have patterned bill, which, together with white on face (especially eye-ring and -stripe), distinguishes Ringneck not only from Tufted but also from Redhead and Common Pochard.
DISTRIBUTION AND STATUS Breeds widely northern North America, from central Alaska to northern California, prairie provinces and states, Nova Scotia and north-east USA; winters Pacific coast south from British Columbia and in southern and eastern USA, Mexico, northern Central America and West Indies. Breeds on freshwater marshes and pools, also wintering on larger lakes, coastal lagoons and bays. Population *c* 1 million prior to breeding season.

WHITE-EYED POCHARD (or HARDHEAD)

Aythya australis L 46-49 cm (18-19 in), WS 65-70 cm (26-28 in)
Monotypic; birds from Banks Islands, New Hebrides, have been described as subspecies (Banks Island White-eyed Pochard *A. a. extima*) because of slightly smaller size and supposedly darker brown head and throat, but population now thought to have arisen from relatively recent colonization by White-eyed Pochards from Australia (also variable in plumage) and is not recognized here. Only large pochard within Australian range; some potential for confusion when irrupting to Indonesia and New Zealand.
IDENTIFICATION Male breeding and non-breeding Rich dark brown on head, neck, breast and mantle, extending to flanks, where feathers slightly edged or barred buff to whitish.

Belly variable, from whitish to brownish, often mottled darker; vent often brownish, undertail-coverts white. Upperparts rich dark brown, scapulars edged buff; rump, uppertail-coverts and tail dark brown. Upperwing dark brown, with rufous tinge to forewing and broad white band across secondaries and inner primaries, all of which dark-tipped; underwing whitish. Long, broad bill dark grey, with black nail and pale grey subterminal band. Legs and feet grey. Iris whitish and conspicuous. Soft display calls. **Female** Very like male, but paler brown, sometimes with whitish centre to throat. Wings as male. Bill with subterminal band narrower and whiter than male's; iris dark brown. Soft display calls. **Juvenile** Like paler female with more mottled underparts. **Confusion risks** No confusion species within Australian range. From smaller juvenile New Zealand Scaup by bill pattern and white undertail-coverts.
DISTRIBUTION AND STATUS Breeds south-west Western Australia and from South Australia, to north-east Queensland. Dispersive and nomadic, has reached New Zealand, Auckland Islands, New Caledonia, Papua New Guinea, and Indonesia; may sometimes breed in such areas, but permanently established only on Banks Islands (see above). Large, deep lakes and marshes, coastal lagoons. Population estimated at several hundred thousands. Threatened by habitat loss.

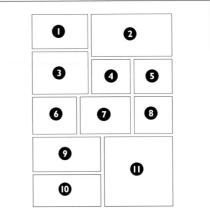

1 **Common Pochard** (female, Lancashire, England)
2 **Common Pochard** (male, Lancashire, England)
3 **Common Pochard** (first year male, Netherlands)
4 **Ring-necked Duck** (pair, Canada)
5 **Ring-necked Duck** (male, Cumbria, England)
6 **Ring-necked Duck** (female, Rio Grande, USA)
7 **Ring-necked Duck** (pair in eclipse)
8 **White-eyed Pochard (or Hardhead)** (male, Lake Manger, Australia)
9 **White-eyed Pochard (or Hardhead)** (male, Lake Manger, Australia)
10 **White-eyed Pochard (or Hardhead)** (female and young, Lake Manger, Australia)
11 **White-eyed Pochard (or Hardhead)** (first year, sex unknown, Perth, Australia)

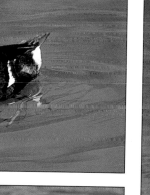

SEA DUCKS

KING EIDER

Somateria spectabilis L 47-63 cm (18-25 in), WS 86-102 cm (34-40 in)
Monotypic. Large-headed seaduck, male unmistakable but female similar to congeners.
IDENTIFICATION Male breeding Prominent orange-red bill and yellow frontal shield, edged black. Crown and bulky nape pale blue-grey, separated from greenish cheeks by narrow black and white lines; throat white with black 'V'; chest suffused pink. Rest of body and tail black, apart from white side patches at base of tail. Two small sickle-shaped points, formed by tertials, raised above back. White patch on wing-coverts contrasts with otherwise black upperwing; more extensive whitish on front half of underwing. Legs and feet dull orange. Cooing *hoo-hoo-hooo* call. **Male eclipse** Uniform dark brownish-black, but retaining white patch on upperwing and, often, some white feathers on breast and back. **Female** Warm rufous-brown, with blackish chevron markings on upperparts and flanks. Head and neck more cinnamon-brown, finely streaked black. Pale buff eye-ring and downcurving rear eye-stripe; pale buff spot at base of bill. Wings dark above, with very thin white stripe along tips of greater secondary coverts; paler below. Bill grey; legs and feet greenish-grey. Low, clucking notes. **Juvenile** Dull grey-brown, males gaining white on breast and rump in late autumn and becoming darker above. Full adult plumage not until third year. **Confusion risks** Adult male from other eiders by white breast and black rear at distance, and head shape and pattern close to. Eclipse male smaller than Common Eider, with shorter bill, slightly bulging forehead and much less white on upperwing. Female and juvenile from Common Eider by: upturned gape line through pale area at base of bill (gape line of Common Eider straight and less visible); bill lobes smaller and feathering less far down bill; less triangular head shape; dark markings on flanks angular rather than barred; short points may be visible on back.
DISTRIBUTION AND STATUS Breeds northern Alaska, northern Canada, coasts of northern Greenland, Svalbard and arctic Russia east to Bering Sea. Nests by tundra marshes and pools; winters in open arctic waters, also along coasts. Population estimated at 1.5 million pairs in Russia and 1-2 million in North America. Vulnerable to pollution of wintering areas.

SPECTACLED EIDER

Somateria fischeri L 52-57 cm (20-22 in), WS 85-93 cm (33-37 in)
Monotypic. Large seaduck of eastern Siberia and Alaska; has noticeably large head with remarkable goggle-like eye patches.
IDENTIFICATION Male breeding Prominent black-rimmed white oval eye patches ('spectacles') on greenish head, shaggy at sides and back. Chin to upper breast, mantle, upperwing-coverts, inner flight feathers and round patch on side of rump white; lower breast to undertail-coverts, tail and main flight feathers dark brown- or grey-black. In flight, upper- and underwings white in front, dark behind. Bill orange. Legs and feet dull yellowish-brown. Weak, cooing *ah-hooo* in courtship.
Male eclipse Overall grey to grey-black, with grey-brown head and darker grey spectacles. White on wing retained only on primary coverts, rest turning grey-brown. **Female** Dull brown, only lightly marked with black. Head paler grey-brown, with large, round eye patches buff, bordered in front with darker brown. Bill grey; legs and feet yellowish-brown. Low calls. **Juvenile** Darker above than female; paler below, heavily barred blackish. Spectacles smaller and less distinct. Male plumage appears from autumn, but not fully adult until third year. **Confusion risks** Unique face pattern of spectacles and bill feathering almost to nostrils distinguishes both sexes and all ages from other eiders. Male, at distance, has black below white upper breast, while other eiders white to waterline; in flight, black on body extends well forward of wings, instead of stopping level with leading edge. Apart from head pattern, visible in flight, female and immatures much as other eiders.
DISTRIBUTION AND STATUS Breeds arctic coasts of Siberia east from *c* 120°E to Bering Sea and on coasts of north-west Alaska; main winter quarters presumed in Bering Sea and Siberian coast. Estimated 400,000 birds in mid-1970s, but major declines in some breeding areas since, though cause uncertain. Vulnerable to marine pollution.

STELLER'S EIDER

Polysticta stelleri L 52-57 cm (20-22 in), WS 85-93 cm (33-37 in)
Monotypic. Small seaduck, highly patterned male unmistakable, female more similar to other eiders but much smaller.
IDENTIFICATION Male breeding White head and neck, with black chin, throat and patch around eye; greenish on lores and forming tufts each side of hindcrown, stemming from black spots. Black collar around neck, narrower at front, joining with black on mantle and extending down centre of upperparts to long and pointed brown tail. Breast, belly and flanks warm chestnut-buff, darker on centre of breast and belly, paler on flanks and becoming white towards wings, with round black spot at sides of breast; vent and undertail-coverts black. Sides of mantle and back white; scapulars and tertials elongated and pointed, black (tinged purplish-blue) with broad white edges, drooping over closed wing. In flight, forewing white, speculum iridescent purplish-blue bordered behind by broad white tips, and primaries blackish; underwing mainly white, with grey flight feathers. Bill, legs and feet blue-grey. Mostly silent, with soft display calls. Wings produce loud whistling noise in flight.
Male eclipse As female, but white upperwing-coverts retained and head and breast with white mottling. **Female** Dark reddish-brown all over. Indistinct pale buffish eye-ring and slightly paler on cheeks. Obscurely mottled black on upperparts. Tertials elongated and sickle-shaped, greyish-blue on outer webs, brown on inner. Speculum as male, but iridescence confined to innermost secondaries, remainder dull brown, and with white bar in front as well as behind, while forewing dark red-brown; underwing as male, but greyer on coverts. Bare parts as male. More vocal than male, with hoarse calls. **Juvenile** As female, but duller brown, without reddish tone, and more clearly marked darker on underparts. Speculum almost lacks blue, and white borders narrow or even absent. Males start to acquire adult plumage in first year, but not fully so before second winter. **Confusion risks** Male totally unmistakable; in flight, lacks black underparts of all other eiders. Female and juvenile much smaller than other eiders, flying faster and more agilely, female with distinctive purplish speculum with white in front and behind.
DISTRIBUTION AND STATUS Breeds eastern coastal Siberia to Bering Sea and coastal Alaska, occasionally further west reaching arctic Norway; winters in northern Norwegian fjords and Baltic Sea, and, especially, Bering Sea and coasts of eastern Siberia and Alaska. Nests by tundra pools and marshes; winters off coasts and in bays. Up to 15,000 winter in Norway and 3,500 in Baltic; numbers wintering Alaska 75,000-100,000; no information from Siberian part of range. Vulnerable to marine pollution.

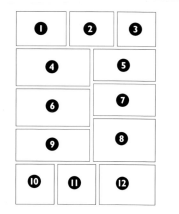

1 **King Eider** (pair, Alaska, USA)
2 **King Eider** (male with male Eider, Ythan Estuary, Scotland)
3 **King Eider** (female, Kolyma, Siberia)
4 **King Eider** (male, Ythan Estuary, Scotland)
5 **King Eider** (eclipse male, Northumberland, England)
6 **Spectacled Eider** (male, Alaska, USA)
7 **Spectacled Eider** (pair, Alaska, USA)
8 **Spectacled Eider** (male, Kolyma, Siberia)
9 **Spectacled Eider** (pair in flight, Kolyma, Siberia)
10 *Steller's Eider* (eclipse male)
11 **Steller's Eider** (males in flight, Siberia)
12 **Steller's Eider** (group in flight, Norway)

151

SEA DUCKS

HARLEQUIN DUCK

Histrionicus histrionicus L 38-45 cm (15-18 in),
WS 63-69 cm (25-27 in)
Monotypic; formerly two subspecies
recognized, one for Atlantic and one for Pacific
parts of distribution, based on slight differences
in overall plumage tone and on bill size, but
always doubtfully valid and no longer accepted.
A small, dainty seaduck, male attractively
patterned, found on fast-flowing water and off
rocky coasts in northern temperate regions of
northern hemisphere.
IDENTIFICATION Male breeding Head, neck,
body and wings dark slaty-blue and black,
richly patterned white and chestnut. Head and
neck with purplish sheen. White cheek patch
extending into thin line above eye, becoming
rufous to rear under black crown; round white
spot behind eye and vertical white stripe along
back of head; further white stripes, bordered
black, around base of neck and down side of
chest. Large chestnut patch on flanks; tiny
white spot each side of rump at base of
pointed black tail. White tertials and black and
white scapulars. Upperwings and underwings
dark slate with purplish speculum; a few white
spots form short, indistinct wing-bar. Bill, legs
and feet blue-grey. Occasional piping whistle
and trill. **Male eclipse** As female, but blacker
body, grey-blue on back, more white on face
and brighter wings. June-July to October.
Female Uniform dull olive- to blackish-brown,
darkest on head, with centre of belly speckled
whitish. Two whitish patches in front of eye,
lower one larger, and clear white circular
patch behind eye. Wings dark above and
below. Bill dark slate-blue; legs and feet
greyish. High-pitched calls, but mostly silent.
Juvenile Resembles female, but upperparts
paler and underparts more spotted. Male
features appear during first winter. **Confusion
risks** In all plumages, very dark at distance,
appearing small with short bill, prominent
forehead, and pointed tail, latter often cocked.
Swims buoyantly. In flight, all-dark wings and
dark body. Female and juvenile may be
confused with Long-tailed Duck, but that
species' facial pattern has whitish streak, not
patch, behind eye, and even dark individuals
are much paler on flanks and belly. Female
White-winged and Surf Scoters have
somewhat similar face pattern, but are
significantly larger.
DISTRIBUTION AND STATUS Breeds Iceland,
west Greenland, eastern fringe of northern
Canada, Alaska to central California, and north
and east Asia, wintering within and to south of
breeding range. Nests beside and feeds in fast-
flowing rivers and streams; winters usually
within 300 m of rocky, exposed coasts.
Estimated populations: western North
America, 100,000-200,000 (1970s estimate of
1 million individuals discounted); eastern
North America, fewer than 1,000; Greenland,
1,000-2,000; Iceland, 6,000-9,000; Asia, up to
100,000.

LONG-TAILED DUCK

Clangula hyemalis L 40-47 cm (16-18 in), WS
73-79 cm (29-31 in)
Monotypic. Small, slim seaduck with noticeably
long tail, especially male, in circumpolar Arctic,
wintering on sea to south.
IDENTIFICATION Exceptionally complex
sequences, in both male and female, of at least
four plumages in course of year; these based on
two moults, as in other wildfowl, but both
moults interrupted and therefore producing
additional plumage types. Some workers have
suggested occurrence of three or even four
moults in a year. Certainly some feathers, *eg*
most scapulars and sides of head and neck are
moulted three times in a year, but the rest of
the head and breast are moulted just twice a
year, while the remainder of the body feathers,
together with wings and tail, are only moulted
once. Perhaps best described as four partial
moults. Birds frequently in moult, and
therefore also showing transitional plumages.
Adult male Elongated central tail feathers
present in all plumages, except during late-
summer moult. Flanks and belly always white
or whitish. In summer (about July to
September), head, neck and chest dark brown,
with white patch around eye; back and
scapulars brownish-black, edged red-brown;
rump and centre of tail black. In winter (about
November to April), head and neck white, with
blackish-brown patch from lower and rear ear-
coverts to side of upper neck; scapulars white;
remainder of plumage as summer. In spring
(around May to June), head becomes dark,
while, in post-breeding period (September to
November), head and neck become whiter and
scapulars shorter. In flight, all-dark wings
contrast with white belly and sides. Bill black,
with broad pink band behind black nail. Legs
and feet blue-grey. Loud, far-carrying, yodelling
call good aid to identification. **Adult female**
Tail pointed, but without extended central
feathers. In summer (about May to August),
brown head, chest and upperparts, with whitish
eye-ring and thin eye-stripe; whitish around
base of neck. White flanks and underparts.
Progressively more white appears on head
through autumn and into winter (from
November), but crown remains blackish-
brown; blackish sides to head and neck similar
to winter male. Wings and tail as male. Bill, legs
and feet dark grey-blue. Low, quacking calls.
Juvenile As female, but duller on upperparts
and variably whitish on head and neck,
becoming whiter through winter, when male
characters also appear. Not adult until second
year. **Confusion risks** For identification, best
to concentrate on size and shape, as well as
most obvious plumage characters while always
bearing in mind the considerable annual
variability in plumage patterns in both male and
female. Only other ducks with long tail are
pintails, none of which has similar head or body
patterns. Females and juveniles similar at times
to Harlequin Duck (which see).
DISTRIBUTION AND STATUS Circumpolar

Arctic, breeding south to *c* 50°N in Labrador;
winters within and to south of breeding range,
around coasts as well as out to sea. Population
minimum 5 million, perhaps as high as 10
million: 2 million winter in north-west Europe,
while North American population up to 3
million; *c* 450,000 in Greenland and Iceland and
may be declining, but other populations
probably stable. Very vulnerable to oil
pollution, fishing nets and shooting.

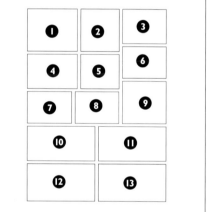

1 **Harlequin Duck** (pair, New Jersey, USA)
2 **Harlequin Duck** (two males, Canada)
3 **Harlequin Duck** (first winter male, New
Jersey, USA)
4 **Harlequin Duck** (two females, first year,
Girvan, Scotland)
5 **Harlequin Duck** (pair, Churchill, Canada)
6 **Harlequin Duck** (male in flight, Churchill,
Canada)
7 **Long-tailed Duck** (male, breeding, Taymyr)
8 **Long-tailed Duck** (pair, breeding, Alaska,
USA)
9 **Long-tailed Duck** (male, summer, Canada)
10 **Long-tailed Duck** (immature first winter,
male and female, Lancashire, England)
11 **Long-tailed Duck** (male moulting late
breeding plumage, Canada)
12 **Long-tailed Duck** (male, winter, Clwyd,
Wales)
13 **Long-tailed Duck** (female, immature,
winter, Merseyside, England)

SEA DUCKS

BLACK SCOTER

Melanitta nigra
Polytypic. Two subspecies: (1) European Black (or Common) Scoter *M. n. nigra*, breeds northern Eurasia, wintering western Europe and north-west Africa; (2) American Black Scoter *M. n. americana*, breeds north-east Siberia and Alaska, and northern Canada, wintering east Asia and north-west and north-east North America. These two subspecies have been suggested for upgrading to full species, but differences relatively small.

European Black (or Common) Scoter

Melanitta nigra nigra L 44-54 cm (17-21 in), WS 79-90 cm (31-35 in)
Large, dumpy, short-necked seaduck of northern Europe and Asia, male all black and female dark brown.
IDENTIFICATION Male breeding and non-breeding All black, more glossy on head, neck and upperparts than underparts. Tail all black and pointed, usually held raised. Upperwings glossy black, but undersides of flight feathers silvery-grey, contrasting with sooty brown-black underwing-coverts; in flight, shows paler rear half of underwing, darker to front. Bill all black, with swollen knob, mainly black, at base of upper mandible; conspicuous yellow-orange patch extends from in front of and around nostrils back to knob, then in thin central line as far as forehead. Legs and feet brown-black. Far-carrying, fluting whistle. Flight low over water, wings making whistling noise. No identifiable eclipse plumage. **Female** Dark sooty brown on crown and hindneck, contrasting with brownish-white cheeks, throat and sides of neck. Rest of upperparts, upperwing and tail dark brown. Lower breast and belly pale brown to whitish, darker flanks barred olive-brown. Underwing as male, with greyish flight feathers contrasting with darker coverts. Bill dark olive-brown to black, lacking knob, with variable, but always small, amounts of yellow on culmen, inside of nostrils and as spots around nostrils. Legs and feet olive-brown. Grating, not fluting, whistles. **Juvenile** As female, but considerably paler on lower head and underparts, which barred whitish. Male becomes blacker in first winter, and small patch of yellow develops around nostrils from January; has small knob and yellow band from nostrils towards forehead by first spring. Not fully adult until second year. **Confusion risks** Male only all-black duck, though white on male Surf and White-winged Scoters can be inconspicuous. Female and immatures differ in head pattern from Surf and White-winged (which see). See American race for subspecific identification.
DISTRIBUTION AND STATUS Breeds Iceland, northern Britain and Ireland, east through Siberia to about Olenek River; winters coasts of north and west Europe south to western Africa, and in north-west Mediterranean. Nests beside small pools and marshy areas, wintering in shallow bays and close to estuaries. Western

European wintering population estimated at 800,000. Major threats from marine pollution.

American Black Scoter

Melanitta nigra americana L 44-54 cm (17-21 in), WS 79-90 cm (31-35 in)
Large, dumpy, short-necked seaduck of northern Pacific region, male all black and female dark brown.
IDENTIFICATION Male breeding and eclipse As European Black Scoter, but bill nearly all yellow-orange, including broad swollen area at base, wider and longer than knob of European subspecies but not so protruding, sloping more gradually to flatter tip of bill. Swollen area sometimes divided by narrow black line. Small area of black at tip of bill and black edges to mandibles. Swollen area reaches to middle of nostrils, which are closer to tip of bill than in European subspecies. **Female, juvenile** No apparent differences from European subspecies. **Confusion risks** For separation from other scoters, see European Black Scoter; from that subspecies, see above.
DISTRIBUTION AND STATUS Breeds from about Lena River, Siberia, east to Bering Sea, and in Alaska and arctic and sub-arctic Canada east (in far smaller numbers) to Newfoundland; winters mainly Pacific coasts of north-east Russia, Japan, Korea and east China, and of North America from Alaska to California; also Great Lakes and Atlantic coast south to South Carolina. Habitat as for European Black Scoter, but also large inland fresh waters in winter. Minimum 500,000 estimated to winter in North America, while 200,000 pairs estimated to breed in Siberia. Marine pollution major threat.

SURF SCOTER

Melanitta perspicillata L 45-56 cm (18-22 in), WS 78-92 cm (31-36 in)
Monotypic. Large, dark seaduck, male with unmistakable pattern, but female dark brown like congeners.
IDENTIFICATION Male breeding All black, except for head, bill and some of underparts. Head has large white patch on forehead, and white, triangular (downward-pointing) patch on nape; nape patch becomes less pure white with wear, black flecking eventually obscuring it altogether. Occasionally, base of foreneck has scattered white feathers, more or less forming ring. Black of chin, throat and centre of belly mottled with browner tips, not very visible at distance. Wings all black. Large, heavy bill with swollen base: pale yellow at tip, bluish-white on sides, and red on culmen above and behind black oval on each side. Legs and feet orange-red, with blackish webs. Iris white. Generally silent. Wings produce humming noise. **Male eclipse** Discernible only by increased wear on feathers, making plumage slightly less black. **Female** Dark brown crown and hindneck, with whitish circular patch on lores, triangular patch on ear-coverts and, sometimes, whitish patch on nape similar to male, but poorly defined. All patches vary in intensity among

individuals, as does rest of plumage, which overall dark brown with some birds darker than others. Wings all black. Large, heavy bill, less swollen at base than male's, dark grey, blacker on sides at base. Legs and feet dull orange. Iris pale brown. Croaks during display. **Juvenile** As female, but lighter brown, especially on face and underparts, where belly whitish. More conspicuous whitish spots on cheeks, sometimes merging, but no pale nape patch. Adult features not fully acquired until second winter. **Confusion risks** Male head pattern unique and, when obscured in late summer and autumn, head profile, with huge, deep bill, differs from other scoters. Female and juvenile have same head profile, with head pattern similar to White-winged Scoter but more contrast between whitish patches and blacker crown (and White-winged never has pale nape patch). In flight, lacks white in wing of White-winged, but harder to separate from Black Scoter unless white on male's head seen, though Black does show slight underwing pattern absent in this species.
DISTRIBUTION AND STATUS Confined as breeder to northern North America from Alaska east through North-west Territories to Hudson Bay, then patchily in Quebec and Labrador; winters Pacific coast from Aleutians south to Baja California, and Atlantic coast from Gulf of St Lawrence to northern Florida, with a few on Great Lakes. Nests small fresh waters in tundra or wooded zone, wintering in estuaries and shallow coastal bays. Breeding population estimated at *c* 750,000 in early 1990s. Major threats from marine pollution.

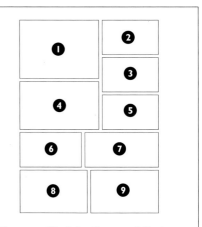

1 **European Black (or Common) Scoter** (first winter female)
2 **European Black (or Common) Scoter** (male)
3 **European Black (or Common) Scoter** (two females, Netherlands)
4 **American Black Scoter** (male, Churchill, Canada)
5 **Surf Scoter** (male, California, USA)
6 **Surf Scoter** (male, California, USA)
7 **Surf Scoter** (female, California, USA)
8 **Surf Scoter** (two adult males and first year male, California, USA)
9 **Surf Scoter** (two males in flight, California, USA)

SEA DUCKS

WHITE-WINGED (OR VELVET) SCOTER

Melanitta fusca
Polytypic. Three subspecies: (1) European White-winged (or Velvet) Scoter *M. f. fusca*, breeds northern Eurasia to Yenisey River, wintering north-west and south-east Europe; (2) Asiatic White-winged Scoter *M. f. stejnegeri*, breeds eastern Siberia to Kamchatka, south to Mongolia, wintering south to Japan and eastern China; (3) American White-winged Scoter *M. f. deglandi*, breeds north-western North America, wintering Pacific and Atlantic coasts. Fourth subspecies (*M. f. dixoni* of Alaska) sometimes listed, but not treated as separate here.

European White-winged (or Velvet) Scoter

Melanitta fusca fusca L 51-58 cm (20-23 in), WS 90-99 cm (35-39 in)
Large, all-black seaduck, male with distinctive white on head and wing, female similar to congeners.
IDENTIFICATION Male breeding All glossy black, except for head and wing. White crescentic spot below and behind eye, which has white iris. Upperwing all black, except for pure white secondaries and tips of greater coverts, which occasionally fringed black (though this almost invisible on flying bird); underwing shows white secondaries and whitish greater coverts, and white tips to axillaries and median coverts, the rest sooty black. Bill has swollen black knob at base, also black on centre of culmen and edges of upper mandible; rest of bill orange-yellow, becoming brighter towards nail, which orange-red to deep pink. Legs and feet orange-red, with black webs. Rarely calls, except for double piping notes in display. **Male eclipse** Having become browner during breeding season through feather wear, eclipse plumage also much duller and browner, with little gloss. **Female** Dark brown head and neck, slightly darker on hindcrown, with buff-white patch on lores and second, whiter patch on ear-coverts, both becoming whiter with wear. Rest of body dark brown, except for faintly whitish-streaked appearance to lower breast and belly, which becomes more mottled with wear. Upperparts similarly show barred appearance towards end of breeding season. Upperwing as male, but coverts dark olive-brown and white tips to greater coverts narrower. Bill blackish-grey, with no basal swelling; legs and feet dull orange-yellow; iris brown. **Juvenile** As female, but duller and greyer overall, and whiter on belly. Same facial patches, but clearer white. Adult features appear during first winter, though not fully acquired until second winter.
Confusion risks Largest of scoters. White in wing, not often showing on resting bird but always obvious in flight, helps separate this species from other two. White eye spot of male difficult to pick out at distance, though mostly yellow bill with black knob at base may still show. For separation of female and juvenile

from Surf Scoter, see that species. Black Scoter female and juvenile have obvious dark-capped, pale-cheeked appearance.
DISTRIBUTION AND STATUS Breeds Scandinavia and across northern Eurasia as far as River Yenisey, with isolated populations further south, including eastern Turkey and neighbouring Georgia; winters on coasts of north-west and western Europe south to northern Spain, and on lakes in central Europe, as well as on Black and Caspian Seas. Nests by pools in boreal forest and tundra, wintering on coasts and a few large fresh waters. Estimated 250,000 winter in north-west Europe, but fewer than 10,000 on Black and Caspian Seas. Threats come mainly from marine pollution, such as oil.

Asiatic White-winged Scoter

Melanitta fusca stejnegeri L 51-58 cm (20-23 in), WS 90-99 cm (35-39 in)
Large, all-black seaduck, male with distinctive white on head and wing, female similar to congeners.
IDENTIFICATION Male breeding and eclipse As European White-winged Scoter, except for slightly larger white spot on face, though this variable, and bill. Knob at base of bill larger and higher, more protuberant. Black at base of bill wider, extending further onto bill, rest of which more orange, less yellow, in colour. Feathering at sides of bill also extends further forwards.
Female, juvenile As European White-winged Scoter. **Confusion risks** For separation from other scoters, see European White-winged Scoter. For separation from other subspecies, see above and under American subspecies. No intergrades known with other subspecies.
DISTRIBUTION AND STATUS Breeds Siberia from Yenisey basin eastwards to Kamchatka and south to Mongolia (ranges of this and European subspecies not known to meet); winters on Pacific coast from Japan to Korea and eastern China. Habitat as that of European subspecies. Population estimated to lie between 50,000 and 100,000. Vulnerable to marine pollution.

American White-winged Scoter

Melanitta fusca deglandi L 51-58 cm (20-23 in), WS 90-99 cm (35-39 in)
Large, all-black seaduck, male with distinctive white on head and wing, female similar to congeners.
IDENTIFICATION Male breeding and eclipse As European White-winged Scoter, except for larger white spot on face (though this variable), more olive-brown than black flanks, and bill pattern. Knob at base of bill larger and higher, more protuberant, though less so than in Asiatic subspecies. Black at base of bill wider, extending further onto bill, rest of which more orange, less yellow, in colour. Feathering at sides and top of bill also extends further forwards. **Female, juvenile** As European White-winged Scoter. **Confusion risks** For separation from other scoters, see European White-winged Scoter. For separation from

other subspecies, see above and also under Asiatic White-winged Scoter. No intergrades known with other subspecies.
DISTRIBUTION AND STATUS Breeds from Alaska across northern Canada to Hudson Bay, and south into Manitoba; winters from Aleutian Islands down Pacific coast of North America to Baja California, and on Atlantic coast from Gulf of St Lawrence to South Carolina, with small numbers on Great Lakes. Habitat as that of European subspecies, with addition of a few large inland fresh waters. Population estimated at c 1 million. Vulnerable to marine pollution.

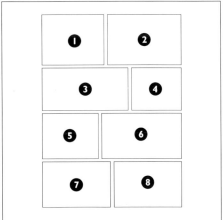

1 **European White-winged (or Velvet) Scoter** (male, Braunensdern, Netherlands)
2 **European White-winged (or Velvet) Scoter** (female, Grunichen, Netherlands)
3 **European White-winged (or Velvet) Scoter** (female, Ujmmiden, Netherlands)
4 **European White-winged (or Velvet) Scoter** (male in flight, Sweden)
5 **European White-winged (or Velvet) Scoter** (immature)
6 **American White-winged Scoter** (male, Massachusetts, USA)
7 **American White-winged Scoter** (male, USA)
8 **American White-winged Scoter** (male immature, USA)

SEA DUCKS

BARROW'S GOLDENEYE

Bucephala islandica L 42-53 cm (17-21 in), WS 67-84 cm (26-33 in)

Monotypic. Medium-sized, large-headed diving duck similar to Common Goldeneye.

IDENTIFICATION Male breeding Head with shaggy crest black, glossed purplish. Large white, crescentic mark between eye and bill. Head has steep, almost bulging, forehead higher than rest of crown. Neck, breast, belly and flanks pure white, except for small black extension from mantle down side of breast in front of closed wing and blackish border to upper flanks; some blackish mottling on thighs and sides of vent. Upperparts, including tail, black; white centres to scapulars, which are round-ended, form line of six or seven white patches above closed wing. Upperwing has black primaries and their coverts, but white secondaries and most of forewing, separated by narrow black band, and with broad black leading edge; underwing grey-brown, with only secondaries white. Short, stout bill black. Legs and feet yellow-orange. Iris bright yellow. Almost silent. Wings whistle in flight. **Male eclipse** As female, but retains male wing, black bill and bright yellow iris. **Female** Smaller than male. Rounded head and upper neck dark chocolate-brown, sometimes with slight purplish gloss, and with shaggy crest; top of head has flattish profile. Narrow white neck collar above dusky grey-brown breast, which forms broad band above whitish belly; flanks, vent and undertail-coverts grey-brown. Upperparts brownish-black, mottled blue-grey, with white tips to scapulars; rump grey, tail blackish. Wings similar to male, but with much less white on upperwing-coverts, forming smaller white patch in front of white secondaries, separated by black band. Bill of two types: western North American birds all yellow with blackish nail; eastern North American and Icelandic birds blackish, with yellow confined to broad band towards tip. Legs and feet yellowish. Iris pale yellow. Soft calls during display. Wings quieter than male's in flight. **Juvenile** As female, but darker above and on wing-coverts. Males show white on face late in first winter. Adult plumage not gained fully until second winter. **Confusion risks** Only confusion species is Common Goldeneye. Head and bill shapes (both sexes) differ: Barrow's has shorter, stubbier bill, nearly vertical forehead, low rounded crown and full mane at rear, giving rounded oval shape; Common longer, more tapering bill, crown with peak in centre and much less shaggy behind, giving broadly triangular profile. Male Common shows less white on head, which glossed green, not purple, but more white on scapulars (pointed, not rounded) and upperwing-coverts (important when seen flying). Female Barrow's has darker head, brown extending further down neck than on Common, and less white on wing, though juvenile females difficult to separate on this.

DISTRIBUTION AND STATUS Four separate breeding populations: western North America from southern Alaska to California and Wyoming, winters mainly adjacent coasts; northern Labrador, winters Gulf of St Lawrence south to Maine; small numbers south-west Greenland, presumably wintering with Labrador birds; resident Iceland. Nests by pools, lakes and rivers, wintering coasts and larger lakes and rivers. Western North American population c 150,000, with c 50,000 wintering north-east North America. Icelandic population probably 1,000-2,000.

COMMON GOLDENEYE

Bucephala clangula

Polytypic. Two subspecies: (1) European (Common) Goldeneye *B. c. clangula*, breeds northern Eurasia, wintering to south; (2) American (Common) Goldeneye *B. c. americana*, breeds northern North America, wintering mainly to south.

European (Common) Goldeneye

Bucephala clangula clangula L 42-50 cm (17-20 in), WS 65-80 cm (26-31 in)

Medium-sized, large-headed diving duck similar to Barrow's Goldeneye, especially female.

IDENTIFICATION Male breeding Black head, glossed green, with white circular to oval patch between eye and bill. Head peaked in centre of crown. Neck and underparts white, mottled brown on thighs and vent sides; narrow black border to upper flanks. Upperparts black; elongated, pointed scapulars white with narrow black margins, forming mainly white patch drooping over closed wing. Tail grey, with black central feathers. Upperwing blackish, with broad white inner area formed by secondaries and median and greater coverts, with black leading edge; underwing grey-brown, with white secondaries. Bill black; legs and feet yellow-orange; iris bright yellow. Whistling calls during display. Wings whistle in flight. **Male eclipse** As female, but wing and bill as male breeding, head a little darker, and trace of face spot often showing. **Female** Smaller than male. Chocolate-brown head above whitish collar. Breast, flanks, vent and undertail-coverts grey to grey-brown; belly whitish. Upperparts darker with paler blue-grey tips (becoming less obvious towards rear); tail grey. Upperwing white on secondaries and greater and median coverts, but divided by narrow black bars on covert tips, with rest of wing blackish-brown; underwing as male. Bill blackish with yellow band behind black nail, rarely almost all yellow, but yellow often absent after breeding season. Legs and feet yellowish; iris very pale yellow. Occasional grunting note. Wings whistle, but less than male's. **Juvenile** As female, but duller, without whitish collar. Males show white spot on face late in first winter. Adult plumage not attained fully until second winter. **Confusion risks** For separation from Barrow's, see that species.

DISTRIBUTION AND STATUS Breeds northern Eurasia from Iceland and northern Britain to Kamchatka; winters temperate parts of range, eg Iceland, north-west Europe, and in northern Mediterranean, Black and Caspian Seas, central-southern Asia, and in east Asia from Kamchatka to east China. Nests at wetlands in wooded and forested areas, wintering on larger fresh waters, coastal lagoons and coasts. Estimated 300,000 winter western Europe, 20,000 Mediterranean/Black Sea, c 10,000 Caspian Sea area, and some tens of thousands eastern Asia.

American (Common) Goldeneye

Bucephala clangula americana L 45-53 cm (18-21 in), WS 68-84 cm (27-33 in)

Medium-sized, large-headed diving duck similar to Barrow's Goldeneye, especially female.

IDENTIFICATION Male and female breeding and non-breeding, juvenile As European Goldeneye, but slightly larger: bill averages 10-11% larger with little overlap, but wing, tarsus and tail less than 5% different with considerable overlap. Also suggested that it has more peaked crown, so even more triangular-shaped head. **Confusion risks** Separable from European subspecies only by bill measurements.

DISTRIBUTION AND STATUS Breeds northern North America from Alaska across Labrador and Newfoundland, extending into extreme north USA around Great Lakes and in north-east; winters Pacific coast from Aleutians to California, in Mississippi Valley, Great Lakes, and Atlantic coast from Gulf of St Lawrence to Gulf coast, occasionally into northern Mexico and West Indies. Habitat as for European Goldeneye. Population at least 1 million.

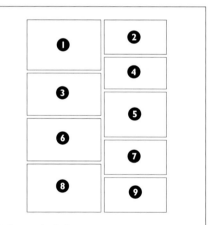

1 Barrow's Goldeneye (male, Reykjavik, Iceland)
2 Barrow's Goldeneye (female, Vancouver, Canada)
3 Barrow's Goldeneye (female with young, Laxardalur, Iceland)
4 Barrow's Goldeneye (male, two first year male Barrow's and first year male American Goldeneye, San Francisco, USA)
5 European (Common) Goldeneye (male, Lancashire, England)
6 European (Common) Goldeneye (male, Merseyside, England)
7 European (Common) Goldeneye (first winter male, Merseyside, England)
8 European (Common) Goldeneye (female, Merseyside, England)
9 American (Common) Goldeneye (male, California, USA)

SAWBILLS

BUFFLEHEAD

Bucephala albeola L 32-39 cm (13-15 in), WS 54-61 cm (21-24 in)
Monotypic. Small, large-headed diving duck; no really confusable species.
IDENTIFICATION Male breeding Head black, glossed bronze, green and purple, with large triangular wedge of white from below eye extending to rear, forming bushy crest. Neck, upper mantle, breast, flanks and belly white, flanks narrowly bordered black above; vent and undertail-coverts pale grey. Lower mantle and back black; rump black with grey sides; tail grey, tipped white. Inner scapulars black, outer white, producing broad white band along closed wing. Upperwing black, with large white patch extending from forewing, apart from leading edge, onto secondaries, while white of scapulars forms stripe each side of back, separated from white on wings by black tertials; underwing greyish, with secondaries white. Bill blue-grey, with darker nail, tip and base. Legs and feet pale pink. Almost totally silent. **Male eclipse** As female, but with large white patch on head; wing as male breeding. **Female** Head smaller than male's, dark brown with long narrow white patch below and behind eye. Neck and all underparts grey-brown, apart from whitish centre to lower breast and belly. Upperparts darker sooty brown, greyer on rump and tail-coverts. Upperwing blackish-brown, with white restricted to inner and middle secondaries and inner greater coverts, separated by dark band; underwing as male, but less white on secondaries. Bill dark bluish-grey; legs and feet pinkish-grey. Occasional guttural call, but mostly silent. **Juvenile** As female, but smaller white patch on head, and duller brown above and greyer below. Adult features gained during first winter, completed by second.
Confusion risks Small size rules out most other black-and-white ducks. Head pattern, and head shape, of male unmistakable. Female and juvenile recall small grebe, also confusable with larger juvenile Long-tailed Duck.
DISTRIBUTION AND STATUS Breeds central Alaska to northern California, and across southern Canada to southern Hudson Bay and Great Lakes; winters southern Alaska south to Mexico and southern part of USA, and up Atlantic coast north to Newfoundland. Nests by freshwater wetlands in forested areas; winters on coasts, brackish lagoons and larger fresh waters. Estimated population just over 1 million. Winter pollution and hunting potential threats.

HOODED MERGANSER

Mergus cucullatus L 42-50 cm (17-20 in), WS 56-66 cm (22-26 in)
Monotypic. Small crested sawbill, both sexes unmistakable.
IDENTIFICATION Male breeding Glossy black head and neck, forehead brownish-black, with large white patch extending from behind eye into long shaggy crest, which outlined in black; crest erectile into nearly 90° black-edged white

fan. Breast and belly white; two black stripes on sides, rear one edging reddish-brown flanks, which finely vermiculated grey and black; vent and undertail-coverts light greyish-brown. Upperparts blackish-brown, shading to greyish-brown rump and sooty-brown tail; scapulars black; elongated and pointed tertials black with white central stripes, drooping over end of closed wing. Upperwing blackish, with paler brown forewing, white stripe across tips of greater coverts and thin white margins to black secondaries; underwing-coverts whitish, with darker grey leading edge and flight feathers. Long, thin bill black. Legs and feet dull yellowish-olive. Iris yellow. Rolling frog-like *crroooo* call during display. **Male eclipse** As female, but head mottled whitish, paler brown flanks, and more white in wing. Yellow iris and black bill retained. **Female** Head and neck dull grey-brown; rufous-tinged crest from behind eye to well beyond head, tipped pale buff. Whitish throat and foreneck; rest of neck, breast and flanks grey-brown; belly whitish. Upperparts dark brown, with paler tips on scapulars and tail-coverts; tail sooty brown. Drooping tertials with white central stripe, elongated and pointed, but shorter than male's. Upperwing as male, but less contrast between forewing and rest. Bill blackish, with yellow base and lower mandible; legs and feet brown-grey; iris brown. A hoarse croak. **Juvenile** As female, but shorter crest and no white on tertials and coverts. Adult plumage completed by second winter. **Confusion risks** Elongated crest of both sexes produces striking head shape, with little possibility for confusion. Looks long-headed in flight, with minimal white in wing.
DISTRIBUTION AND STATUS Breeds two areas of North America: south-eastern Alaska south to Oregon and Montana, and central-southern Canada and adjacent USA east to Nova Scotia and south down Mississippi Valley; winters Pacific coast from Alaska to California, and Atlantic and Gulf coasts south into Mexico. Nests beside fresh waters in wooded areas, wintering on larger lakes, brackish lagoons and estuaries. Estimated population *c* 100,000. Destruction of forests and pollution of streams are threats on breeding grounds; persecution on fish-farms and by anglers significant problem.

SMEW

Mergus albellus L 38-44 cm (15-17 in), WS 55-64 cm (22-25 in)
Monotypic. Smallest sawbill, both sexes with distinctive plumages.
IDENTIFICATION Male breeding White head with loose shaggy crest having narrow black stripe on sides, enlarged when crest erected; black patch from base of bill to behind eye. Breast and belly white, with two thin black lines each side of chest forming inverted 'V' descending from black upper mantle. Flanks vermiculated grey and white; vent and undertail-coverts greyish. Upperparts black, becoming greyer on rump, uppertail-coverts

and tail; scapulars white. Upperwing blackish, with broad white panel on median coverts, and narrow white bars formed by tips of greater coverts and secondaries; underwing-coverts whitish, with darker grey leading edge and flight feathers. Bill blackish. Legs and feet grey. Iris red-brown, but pale grey in older birds. Soft rattling call. **Male eclipse** As female, but darker above and more white on wing. **Female** Smaller than male. Chestnut head and hindneck, blackish on lores (brownish in summer), with contrasting white chin, throat, lower cheeks and foreneck; very slight crest on nape. Breast, flanks and ventral region grey; belly white. Upperparts darker grey, scapulars slightly lighter; rump, tail-coverts and tail more silvery-grey. Wings as male, but slightly smaller white patch on upper median coverts. Iris reddish-brown, never pale grey. Rattling call. **Juvenile** As female, greyer on belly and broader white tips on greater coverts and secondaries. Adult features appear in first winter. **Confusion risks** Little risk of confusion with other wildfowl, though winter Black Guillemot *Cepphus grylle* surprisingly similar to male.
DISTRIBUTION AND STATUS Breeds taiga zone of northern Eurasia, from Scandinavia to Pacific coast of Siberia; winters western and south-eastern Europe, Black and Caspian Seas and into central Asia, as well as China and Japan. Breeds by small fresh waters and winters on large lakes, coastal lagoons and estuaries. Wintering populations: 15,000 in north-west Europe; 65,000 in Mediterranean/Black Seas; 30,000 in south-west Asia; and some tens of thousands in eastern Asia. Vulnerable to pollution on wintering grounds.

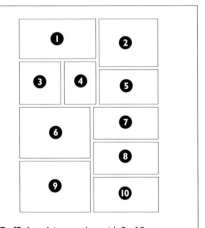

1 **Bufflehead** (two males, with Surf Scoters, California, USA)
2 **Bufflehead** (female, Bosque del Apache, USA)
3 *Bufflehead* (eclipse male)
4 **Bufflehead** (male in flight, California, USA)
5 *Hooded Merganser* (eclipse male)
6 **Hooded Merganser** (male, USA)
7 *Hooded Merganser* (two females, moulting)
8 *Smew* (eclipse male)
9 **Smew** (male and female, Netherlands)
10 **Smew** (female, Merseyside, England)

SAWBILLS

BRAZILIAN MERGANSER

Mergus octosetaceus L 49-56 cm (18-22 in), WS 62-69 (24-27 in)
Monotypic. Slender sawbill, unlike any other wildfowl of region.

IDENTIFICATION Male breeding and non-breeding Head and neck black with strong dark bottle-green iridescence and very long spiky crest, which may be reduced by wear. Lower neck, breast and flanks grey, vermiculated with whitish; belly, vent and undertail-coverts brown, barred whitish. Upperparts dark greenish-brown. Upperwing blackish, apart from white secondaries and greater coverts, divided by black bar; underwing grey. Long, thin bill black. Legs and feet rosy-pink. Loud *queek* uttered in flight. **Female** As male, but smaller and with shorter bill. Crest shorter, and often heavily worn and reduced in both length and number of feathers. **Juvenile** No reported differences from female. **Confusion risks** Looks like no other wildfowl in South America.

DISTRIBUTION AND STATUS Resident in small area of southern Brazil, together with adjacent parts of eastern Paraguay and north-eastern Argentina. Lives on fast-flowing streams and rivers in tropical forests. Very scarce and threatened. First described from skins in 1817; not seen alive after 1922 and feared extinct; rediscovered in 1948, but extremely rare. Recent surveys have failed to find any in Paraguay and may now be extinct there; known breeding groups in Brazil and Argentina becoming isolated through forest clearance. Tentative estimate that population no more than 250 individuals, and perhaps much lower. Habitat destruction and illegal hunting continuing serious problems.

RED-BREASTED MERGANSER

Mergus serrator L 52-58 cm (20-23 in), WS 70-86 cm (28-34 in)
Monotypic; birds breeding Greenland have been separated as subspecies, but not recognized here. Medium-large sawbill with shaggy crest, both sexes, and especially female, with similarities to Scaly-sided Merganser and larger Goosander.

IDENTIFICATION Male breeding Head and upper neck black with strong green gloss; long, shaggy and somewhat double-pointed crest. Broad white collar around centre of neck. Lower neck and breast cinnamon-brown with black streaks; black of mantle extends down to sides of breast and contains several small white patches; belly, lower flanks, centre of vent and undertail-coverts white; upper flanks and sides of vent vermiculated grey and white. Mantle and back black; outer scapulars white; rump and uppertail-coverts vermiculated grey and white. Tail dark brown. Upperwing blackish on outer half, with white inner half divided by black bars across tips of greater and median coverts, and blackish leading edge; underwing whitish, with grey primaries. Bill long and

slender, slightly hooked, carmine with black nail and culmen. Legs and feet red. Iris red. Vocal only during display, including cat-like mewing. **Male eclipse** As female, but retaining extensive white on wing and red iris, and with less white on chin. **Female** Rufous-brown head and neck, with shorter crest than male's, darker around eyes, and gradually merging with whitish lores and throat and foreneck, and greyish on lower neck. Face paler orange after breeding season. Underparts greyish-brown on sides of breast and flanks, grading into whitish centre of breast and belly. Upperparts dark grey-brown, with lighter vermiculations; rump and tail dark grey. Upperwing with white secondaries and greater coverts separated by black bar, and rest of forewing and outer wing blackish; underwing as male. Bill dull red, with brown culmen; legs and feet dull red; iris reddish-brown. Harsh calls during display. **Juvenile** As female, but less whitish, more grey-brown, on breast and belly. Moults towards adult during late winter, completing by second. **Confusion risks** Very similar to Scaly-sided Merganser, but nostrils of latter about midway along bill (close to base on Red-breasted Merganser). Male Scaly-sided has longer crest, white breast and bold black scallops on flanks; female and juvenile also have longer crest and greyer neck and upperparts, but difficult to distinguish in flight. Larger, bulkier Goosander has shaggy, hanging, not spiky, crest, and male has very conspicuous all-white or creamy neck and underparts; female and immature Goosander have more clear-cut separation of reddish-brown head and whitish throat and neck; in flight, no dividing black bar between white of secondaries and greater coverts.

DISTRIBUTION AND STATUS Breeds northern and low-arctic Eurasia and North America, wintering south mainly on coasts of north-west Europe, Mediterranean, Black and Caspian Seas, Iran and Japan, Korea and China; also resident southern Greenland. Nests by lakes and rivers; winters on coasts, at sea and in shallow bays and estuaries. Populations of c 250,000 in North America, 100,000 wintering north-west Europe, 50,000 Mediterranean/Black Sea region, a few thousand south-west Asia, and several tens of thousands eastern Asia, and similar numbers in Greenland. Subject to persecution by fish-farmers and anglers.

SCALY-SIDED MERGANSER

Mergus squamatus L 52-58 cm (20-23 in), WS 70-86 cm (28-34 in)
Monotypic. Medium-large sawbill with long, spiky crest, both sexes, and especially female, with similarities to Red-breasted Merganser and larger Goosander.

IDENTIFICATION Male breeding All-black head and neck, glossed green, with long wispy crest, drooping to touch mantle. Underparts mostly white or creamy-white, tinged salmon-pink; flanks, vent, lower back, rump and uppertail-coverts white, with black edgings

forming bold scallops. Upperparts mainly black, tending to grey on rump and tail; scapulars with broad white edgings. Wings similar to Red-breasted Merganser, but with more extensive white on lesser coverts. Bill dull red, with black nail (pale on some birds) and dark along culmen. Legs and feet orange. Voice resembles that of Red-breasted Merganser. **Male eclipse** As female, but retaining wing and some scalloping on flanks. **Female** Warm brown head and neck with long wispy crest, and good demarcation from whitish throat and white lower neck. Underparts mainly white, but flanks, vent, lower back, rump and uppertail-coverts scalloped as male, but less prominently, and scallops largely absent on flanks in post-breeding period. Mantle and upper back grey. Wings similar to Red-breasted Merganser. Bare parts as male. Voice as Red-breasted Merganser. **Juvenile** As female, probably moulting to adult during first year. **Confusion risks** See above and Red-breasted Merganser for differences from that species. From Goosander by long wispy crest and smaller size, and by scaly appearance on flanks and rear.

DISTRIBUTION AND STATUS Breeds south-eastern Russia, north-eastern China (Manchuria) and North Korea; some resident, others move south to central China in winter. Breeds on rivers in forests; winters on coasts and large inland fresh waters. Total population estimated at 4,000 birds, with majority breeding in Russia, where logging and mining have destroyed some important riverine habitat.

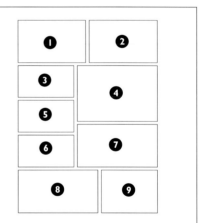

1 **Brazilian Merganser** (adult, sex uncertain, Brazil)
2 **Brazilian Merganser** (pair with young, Brazil)
3 **Red-breasted Merganser** (female, Merseyside, England)
4 **Red-breasted Merganser** (two males, Merseyside, England)
5 **Red-breasted Merganser** (pair, Merseyside, England)
6 **Red-breasted Merganser** (pair in flight, Sweden)
7 **Scaly-sided Merganser** (male, Kisogawa River, Japan)
8 **Scaly-sided Merganser** (female, Biwako Lake, Japan)
9 **Scaly-sided Merganser** (group in flight, Ussuriland, Russia)

SAWBILLS

GOOSANDER or COMMON MERGANSER

Mergus merganser
Polytypic. Three subspecies: (1) (Eurasian) Goosander *M. m. merganser*, breeds northern Eurasia, winters western Europe, Mediterranean and east to China; (2) Asiatic Goosander *M. m. comatus*, breeds central Asia, wintering within and just to south of range; (3) Common Merganser or American Goosander *M. m. americanus*, breeds southern Canada and northern USA, wintering within and to south of range.

(Eurasian) Goosander

Mergus merganser merganser L 58-66 cm (23-26 in), WS 82-97 cm (32-38 in)
Largest sawbill, both sexes showing some similarities to smaller Red-breasted and Scaly-sided Mergansers.
IDENTIFICATION Male breeding Large, rounded head with bushy mane down nape and upper neck black, with strong green gloss. Lower neck, breast, flanks and belly creamy-white, with variable salmon-pink tint; grey on rear of flanks and sides of vent; undertail-coverts white. Mantle and inner scapulars black, outer scapulars white; tertials white, edged black; lower back, rump, uppertail-coverts and tail grey. Outer half of upperwing blackish, inner half white, with innermost lesser and median coverts grey; underwing greyish on outer half, whitish inside. Long, slightly hooked bill red, with black nail and on culmen. Legs and feet deep red. Twanging call during display. **Male eclipse** As female, but retains whiter wing and is darker on mantle and whiter on flanks. **Female** Smaller than male. Red-brown head and neck, with hanging mane at nape, looser than male's, becoming shorter post-breeding, when also pale line from base of bill to eye; otherwise, slightly darker on forehead and lores. Red-brown well demarcated from white of chin and throat and from grey of lower neck, which extends onto sides of breast and flanks; centre of breast, belly, vent and undertail-coverts creamy-white. Upperparts grey with darker shaft-streaks. Upperwing dark grey on outer half, paler grey on forewing, and white on greater coverts and secondaries (sometimes with ill-defined grey bar between them); underwing as male. Bare parts as male; bill not quite so bright. Harsh calls during display. **Juvenile** As female, with more obvious white stripe from bill to eye; duller all over, throat whitish. Adult plumage begins to appear in first winter, often well advanced by spring, but not complete until second. **Confusion risks** For separation from Red-breasted Merganser and Scaly-sided Merganser, see those species. For separation from other subspecies, see below.
DISTRIBUTION AND STATUS Breeds Eurasia, throughout taiga zone and patchily south through temperate zone, from Britain and Scandinavia east to Pacific coast of Russia, north-eastern China and Japan, and including isolated breeding groups in central and south-eastern Europe and south-central Asia; winters within temperate breeding range in north-west Europe, as well as on northern shores of Mediterranean, Black and Caspian Seas, across Central Asia and in eastern China, Korea and southern Japan. Breeds on variety of fresh waters among trees, wintering on larger fresh and brackish waters. Wintering populations of 150,000 in north-west Europe, 10,000 in Mediterranean/Black Sea region, fewer than 10,000 in south-west Asia, and several tens of thousands in eastern Asia. Persecuted at fish-farms and by anglers.

Asiatic Goosander

Mergus merganser comatus L 61-72 cm (24-28 in), WS 85-100 cm (33-39 in)
Largest sawbill, both sexes showing some similarities to smaller Red-breasted and Scaly-sided Mergansers.
IDENTIFICATION Male and female breeding and non-breeding, juvenile As Eurasian Goosander, but slightly larger, with shorter, more slender bill. Wing length *c* 5% longer and bill *c* 8% shorter, but with overlap in measurements, especially in wing length. Legs also reported as shorter, but no measurements available. Reported slight plumage differences for male include more black on upper back and whitish freckling on paler grey lower back and rump, while female has paler head. Some of these differences could be purely seasonal, and do not take into account seasonal variation in Eurasian Goosander. **Confusion risks** Distinguished from other two subspecies by measurements only, plus geographical location. No intergrades reported with Eurasian Goosander, though ranges said to overlap.
DISTRIBUTION AND STATUS Breeds in mountainous regions of Uzbekistan and north-east Afghanistan eastwards through Ladakh and Tibet to Sichuan (China) and Mongolia; some resident, while others undertake southward dispersal in winter, mostly to lower ground, including in northern India and Burma. Probably some overlap with Eurasian Goosander, but extent not known. Habitat similar to Goosander but not so dependent on trees. Population estimate of between 2,500 and 10,000.

Common Merganser or American Goosander

Mergus merganser americanus L 58-66 cm (23-26 in), WS 82-97 cm (32-38 in)
Largest sawbill, both sexes showing some similarities to smaller Red-breasted and Scaly-sided Mergansers.
IDENTIFICATION Male breeding and eclipse As Eurasian Goosander, but bill more deeply based and wing length slightly smaller, though not significantly so, with great overlap. Main difference is presence of black bar separating white secondaries from white greater coverts on upperwing. **Female, juvenile** Doubtfully separable in the field. **Both sexes and all ages** Bill has distinctly smaller hook at tip.

Confusion risks Distinctions from other two subspecies as above, plus geographical location.
DISTRIBUTION AND STATUS Breeds right across forested zone of North America, throughout southern half of Canada and northern USA from Alaska to Newfoundland, and south to California and New England; winters within southern part of this range south through temperate USA to southern California, Gulf coast and Florida. Habitat as that of Eurasian Goosander. Appears to be increasing quite quickly, with estimates of 165,000 in mid-1970s and 640,000 in mid-1990s. Some persecution.

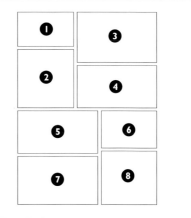

1 **(Eurasian) Goosander** (male, Norfolk, England)
2 **(Eurasian) Goosander** (female, Norfolk, England)
3 **(Eurasian) Goosander** (male flapping, Den Holland, Netherlands)
4 **(Eurasian) Goosander** (two males plus female, Finland)
5 **Common Merganser or American Goosander** (group immatures, Yellowstone, USA)
6 **Common Merganser or American Goosander** (female, New York, USA)
7 **Common Merganser or American Goosander** (male, Florida, USA)
8 **Common Merganser or American Goosander** (male, Florida, USA)

STIFFTAILS

BLACK-HEADED DUCK

Heteronetta atricapilla L 35-40 cm (14-16 in), WS 53-58 cm (21-23 in)
Monotypic. Both sexes of this stifftail distinctive compared with other two stifftails of range.
IDENTIFICATION Male breeding and non-breeding Glossy black head and neck, with variable whitish throat patch. Lower neck and all underparts, including undertail-coverts, warm reddish-brown, vermiculated black, apart from poorly defined silvery-whitish centre to belly, mottled with brown. Entire upperparts, including scapulars, blackish-brown with reddish vermiculations. Tail dark brown. Upperwing dark brown, except for reddish speckles on coverts and whitish tips to greater coverts and secondaries; underwing grey. Bill grey-blue, with black nail and tip and blackish on nostrils and culmen; develops bright rose-red base during breeding season. Legs and feet grey. Soft whistling call. **Female** Brown head, with darker crown and nape and thin dark stripe through eye, with faint pale buff supercilium; cheeks and throat buff, speckled dark brown. Underparts as male, but dull buff-brown rather than warm brown. Upperparts dark blackish-brown. Wings as male, but without reddish speckling on coverts. Bill dark grey, with yellowish base in breeding season; legs and feet grey. Mostly silent, or low clucking in display. **Juvenile** Difficult to separate from female, but more rufous above, more yellowish and less mottled below. **Confusion risks** Other stifftails within South American range are Masked Duck, Argentine Blue-billed Duck and two subspecies of Ruddy Duck. Males of all of these have chestnut or chestnut and black body and bright blue bill. Females of first two have striped head. Female Peruvian Ruddy Duck has darker head but is very different in shape, with large head, heavy bill and short neck, as well as darker on upperparts and whiter on underwing.
DISTRIBUTION AND STATUS Mainly resident in northern and central Argentina, central Chile and Paraguay, dispersing to some extent in winter north to Uruguay, eastern Bolivia and southern Brazil. Uses wide variety of well-vegetated permanent fresh waters. Population uncertain, but probably some hundreds of thousands. Some hunting pressure.

MASKED DUCK

Oxyura dominica L 30-35 cm (12-14 in), WS 52-62 (20-24 in)
Monotypic. South and Central American stifftail mainly inhabiting subtropics, male distinctive but female similar to congeners.
IDENTIFICATION Male breeding Head, except nape and lower sides, black, forming 'mask' of name. Sides of head, upperparts, upper breast and flanks rusty-cinnamon, with black centres to feathers. Underparts dark brown, mottled with white, especially on belly. Blackish upperwings with conspicuous white patch on outer secondaries and some greater and median coverts; underwing blackish, with white axillaries. Bill bright blue, black on tip and nail. Legs and feet dark grey. **Male eclipse** Very like breeding female, but with more white on wing and less contrasting stripes on face. Acquired in autumn and retained until following spring. **Female breeding** Dark brown crown and whitish cheeks and throat, with two dark brown stripes, one through eye and one from base of bill across lower cheeks. Upperparts dark brown, tipped buff. Breast and underparts paler brown, mottled darker, especially on flanks, becoming whitish on belly. Tail and wings dark brown, with white upperwing patch as male, but less extensive on median coverts. Bill, legs and feet grey-brown. **Female non-breeding** Similar to female breeding, but slightly darker above, paler below. Lasts all winter. **Juvenile** Very similar to female, sometimes more mottled on underparts. **Confusion risks** Although white upperwing patch of both sexes unique among stifftails, shows only in flight, which can be infrequent. Male's black tip to blue bill and black 'mask' distinctive. Female and juvenile only stifftails to have two dark facial stripes.
DISTRIBUTION AND STATUS Resident in South American lowlands north from northern Argentina and north-west Peru to Colombia, parts of Central America and West Indies, very locally in Mexico and, rarely, in extreme southern Texas, where, however, present all year. Uses densely vegetated freshwater marshes and swamps. Widespread, but nowhere common, though secretive habits make true assessment impossible. Rough estimate of *c* 10,000 individuals.

WHITE-HEADED DUCK

Oxyura leucocephala L 43-48 cm (17-19 in), WS 62-70 cm (24-28 in)
Monotypic. Apart from introduced Ruddy Duck in Britain and western Europe, only stiff-tailed duck of Eurasia; large-headed and dumpy; sexes different.
IDENTIFICATION Male breeding Large head white, with black crown, size emphasized by large bright blue bill with swollen base. Black neck grades to chestnut upper breast; upperparts and flanks chestnut to greyish-chestnut, finely marked blackish. Uppertail-coverts chestnut. Lower breast and belly paler, with faint brown barring, becoming whitish to rear, where undertail-coverts white. Upperwings and tail brown; underwings pale grey, but white on axillaries and inner coverts. Legs and feet grey-brown. Mechanical rattling noise during courtship. **Male eclipse (winter)** Less chestnut, more grey-brown, than breeding. Cap dark brown, and extending down to eye and onto nape; bill grey. Acquired August-September, kept through winter to April. **Female breeding** Dark chestnut-brown head and neck with whitish cheeks and chin; broad dark band across cheeks almost to brown nape. Upperparts and underparts reddish-brown with blackish barring. Wings and tail as male. Bill blue-grey, swollen at base; legs and feet dark grey. Normally silent. **Female non-breeding** Loses chestnut tinge; cheeks whiter, emphasizing dark stripe. Period as male. **Juvenile** As non-breeding female, but whiter on head and even more obvious cheek-stripe. White head of adult male not attained until second year. **Confusion risks** Breeding male less rufous than smaller North American Ruddy Duck, with much whiter head and larger blue bill. Female more similar to Ruddy Duck, but larger, with larger head and swollen bill, whiter cheeks with more obvious dark stripe; dark of crown also ends closer to gape, giving downward curve not seen on Ruddy Duck. Note that hybrids between the two occur in Spain.
DISTRIBUTION AND STATUS Fragmented breeding range, from southern Spain, Tunisia and Turkey east through Kazakhstan to extreme north-east China; western populations mainly sedentary, eastern move south and west to winter from Turkey to Pakistan. Occupies large, shallow fresh and brackish waters. Total population *c* 19,000 and declining, with *c* 1,000 in west Mediterranean, including 500 in Spain, where recent active conservation saved species from extinction but now threatened by invading Ruddy Ducks. Turkey and Kazakhstan headquarters of eastern population, with 11,000 recorded on one lake in Turkey. Such concentration of a majority of entire world population, together with habitat loss, hybridization problems and hunting pressure, poses very serious threats to this vulnerable species.

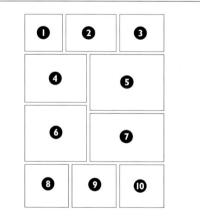

1 **Black-headed Duck** (male)
2 **Black-headed Duck** (female)
3 **Black-headed Duck** (male)
4 **Masked Duck** (female, Venezuela)
5 **Masked Duck** (male, Venezuela)
6 **Masked Duck** (pair, male displaying, Venezuela)
7 **White-headed Duck** (eclipse male, Mallorca)
8 **White-headed Duck** (male, Spain)
9 **White-headed Duck** (female, Spain)
10 **White-headed Duck** (first year female, Utrecht, Holland)

167

RUDDY DUCK

Oxyura jamaicensis
Polytypic. Three subspecies: (1) North American Ruddy Duck *O. j. jamaicensis*, breeds mainly north-western North America, with outliers in Mexico and West Indies, wintering south to Mexico and Guatemala, also introduced, mainly resident, Britain; (2) Colombian Ruddy Duck *O. j. andina*, resident central Colombian Andes; (3) Peruvian Ruddy Duck *O. j. ferruginea*, breeds from southern Colombia to southern Chile and Argentina, southernmost breeders moving north in winter.

North American Ruddy Duck

Oxyura jamaicensis jamaicensis L 35-43 cm (14-17 in), WS 53-62 cm (21-24 in)
Small, dumpy, North American stiff-tailed duck with short neck; rich chestnut-bodied male with blue bill distinct from congeners, brown female more similar.

IDENTIFICATION Male breeding Conspicuous head and bill, with sharp contrast between glossy black crown and nape and white cheeks and chin, plus large bright blue bill. Lower neck, upper breast, flanks and upperparts glossy reddish-chestnut; lower breast, belly and undertail-coverts white or lightly mottled brown; rump and relatively long tail dark brown, with chestnut gloss on uppertail-coverts. Upperwings dark brown; underwings grey, paler on coverts. Legs and feet blue-grey. Short-winged and long-tailed in flight. Mechanical rattling noise during chest-beating 'bubbling' display. **Male eclipse (winter)** Chestnut areas become dark grey-brown; duller crown, and black speckles on white cheeks. Bill dull grey. Acquired August, kept throughout winter to March-April. **Female breeding** Dark brown cap to just below eyes; buff cheeks with darker stripe from bill to nape, poorly defined to rear. Upperparts dark reddish-brown. Breast and flanks dull brown, barred buff, becoming paler and then white on belly and undertail-coverts. Wings and tail as male. Bill, legs and feet grey. Also produces (different) rattling. **Female non-breeding** As breeding, but loses reddish tinge to upperparts and cheek-stripe less obvious. August to March-April. **Juvenile** Closely resembles non-breeding female, but duller and paler, with stronger markings on underparts. As breeding adult by late spring. **Confusion risks** Outside range of other stifftails, unmistakable shape as well as colouring. Confusion possible with White-headed Duck (which see). See other races for separation.

DISTRIBUTION AND STATUS Breeds from north of Canadian prairies, south through Great Plains to south-western USA, also central Mexico and West Indies; winters southern North America south to Guatemala. Introduced Britain, whence wanders to continental Europe. Nests on pools and marshes; winters on larger lakes, coastal marshes and lagoons. North American

population *c* 650,000; some local declines following drainage. British population up to 4,000. Cull proposed following arrival of birds in southern Spain, where hybridizing with threatened White-headed Duck. Threats to North American population include drainage and pollution.

Colombian Ruddy Duck

Oxyura jamaicensis andina L 35-43 cm (14-17 in), WS 53-62 cm (21-24 in)
Small, dumpy stiff-tailed duck with short neck; rich chestnut-bodied male with blue bill and black-and-white head distinct from congeners, brown female more similar.

IDENTIFICATION Male breeding and non-breeding As North American Ruddy Duck but for variably patterned head and face, with black always forming cap over forehead, crown and nape, but cheeks varying from white with some greyish or black spots and lines to almost all black, speckled white. Perhaps most common is black crown descending to further below eye than in North American subspecies, with two black lines spreading out from below eye across white cheeks, one towards base of bill, the other slanting back, one or both then splitting into further short branches. Bill reported to be slightly straighter than in North American subspecies. **Female, juvenile** Claimed that lighter areas rather darker compared with North American Ruddy Duck, but otherwise apparently identical. **Confusion risks** For separation from North American subspecies, see above. For separation from Peruvian subspecies, see below.

DISTRIBUTION AND STATUS Confined to eastern and central Andes of Colombia and Ecuador, where uncommon. Resident on high-altitude lakes between 2500 m and 4000 m. Population probably between 2,500 and 10,000 and thought to be declining, mainly through habitat loss.

Peruvian Ruddy Duck

Oxyura jamaicensis ferruginea L 42-48 cm (17-19 in), WS 57-68 cm (22-27 in)
Small, dumpy stiff-tailed duck with short neck; rich chestnut-bodied male with blue bill and black head distinct from congeners, brown female more similar.

IDENTIFICATION Male breeding and non-breeding As North American Ruddy Duck, but slightly larger and with head all black; only white or whitish area on chin of some individuals. Body colour overall deeper chestnut, and whitish belly mottled pale brown. **Male eclipse** As female. **Female** As North American subspecies, but darker, with much less obvious face pattern because of darker cheeks. **Juvenile** As North American subspecies, but darker. **Confusion risks** Separation from other subspecies as above. Male more similar to Argentine Blue-billed Duck, but latter is smaller, with proportionately longer tail, and straighter, narrower bill, and black of head extends down hindneck onto mantle, compared with chestnut

lower neck of Peruvian Ruddy Duck. Female Argentine Blue-billed Duck has more obvious face pattern, as well as smaller bill.

DISTRIBUTION AND STATUS Breeds from southern Colombia down full length of Andes through Peru, eastern Bolivia, Chile and Argentina to Tierra del Fuego; southern breeders move north in winter, also moving out into lowlands of southern Argentina and Chile. Breeds mainly on high-altitude lakes, at up to 4500 m, but also in lowlands of Peru, almost down to sea-level; makes use of lowland fresh and brackish waters in winter. Population thought to amount to a few tens of thousands.

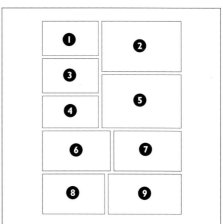

1 **North American Ruddy Duck** (male displaying, Canada)
2 **North American Ruddy Duck** (male, West Midlands, England)
3 **North American Ruddy Duck** (eclipse male, New York, USA)
4 **North American Ruddy Duck** (female, Merseyside, England)
5 **North American Ruddy Duck** (immature, West Midlands, England)
6 **North American Ruddy Duck** (female, West Midlands, England)
7 ***Columbian Ruddy Duck*** (*male*)
8 ***Columbian Ruddy Duck*** (*male, non-breeding*)
9 ***Peruvian Ruddy Duck*** (*male, Chile*)

STIFFTAILS

MACCOA DUCK

Oxyura maccoa L 46-51 cm (18-20 in), WS 65-72 cm (26-28 in)

Monotypic. Only stifftail within African range. **IDENTIFICATION Male breeding** Black head and upper neck. Lower neck and most underparts chestnut, becoming paler chestnut on flanks and silvery grey-brown on centre of belly, vent and undertail-coverts. Mantle chestnut; lower back and rump brown with grey mottling; uppertail-coverts chestnut. Tail narrow and pointed, blackish. Upperwings grey-brown with slight lighter brown freckling; underwings grey-white. Bill bright blue, with whitish nail. Legs and feet grey. Trumpeting call, also frog-like croak. **Male eclipse** Closer to female, but darker-crowned. Bill duller and greyer, with darker nail. **Female** Dark brown crown and nape down to eye, with dark brown stripe from base of bill across cheeks separated from crown by whitish stripe. Lower cheeks, throat and neck buffish. Underparts grey-brown with darker mottling and faint paler barring, especially on flanks; centre of belly whitish through to undertail-coverts. Upperparts dark grey-brown with whitish-buff vermiculation and speckling. Pointed tail blackish. Wings as male. Bill dark grey, with white nail and tip. Mostly silent. **Juvenile** As female, but more uniform on body, lacking markings above, and more brown than grey below. **Confusion risks** No confusable species within range.

DISTRIBUTION AND STATUS Mainly resident in two separate areas: eastern Africa from Sudan and Ethiopia to Tanzania and west to eastern Zaïre, and southern Africa from Zimbabwe to Cape Province, South Africa; some dispersal in response to seasonal rains. Occupies shallow fresh waters, and also found on brackish and saline lakes in winter. Estimate for total population of between 31,000 and 55,000. Subject to local declines.

ARGENTINE BLUE-BILLED DUCK

Oxyura vittata L 36-46 cm (14-18 in), WS 53-63 cm (21-25 in)

Monotypic. Blue-billed, dark-headed stifftail of southern South America, similar to slightly larger Peruvian Ruddy Duck.

IDENTIFICATION Male breeding Black head and neck, black extending down hindneck and just reaching mantle. Underparts and upperparts deep chestnut-red, grading to silvery-grey on belly, vent and undertail-coverts (sometimes some rusty coloration to coverts). Tail blackish. Upperwing blackish with scattered rusty feather tips, but insufficient to show in field; underwing dark grey-brown, slightly lighter towards body. Bill bright blue. Legs and feet dark grey. Drumming noise in display, beating breast with bill. **Male eclipse** Almost identical to female, but a few chestnut feathers may remain on body. Bill becomes dark grey. **Female** Greyish-black crown down to eye and nape, and stripe from gape to nape, above which a pale buff-white stripe below eye.

Cheeks, chin, throat and upper foreneck also buff-white. Underparts mid brown, coarsely marked buff, forming bars, particularly on flanks; paler on belly, vent and undertail-coverts. Wings and tail as male. Bill, legs and feet dark grey. Slight noise made in display, otherwise silent. **Juvenile** As female, but paler above, browner and less barred below. Tail shorter. **Confusion risks** See Peruvian Ruddy Duck, only confusion species within range.

DISTRIBUTION AND STATUS Breeds from Tierra del Fuego north through lowland Chile and Argentina to Uruguay and south-east Brazil; some northward movement by more southerly breeders, reaching Paraguay and south-central Brazil. On shallow, well-vegetated fresh waters, extending to larger lakes and lagoons in winter. Population estimated at several tens of thousands. Destruction of aquatic vegetation a threat on some wetlands.

AUSTRALIAN BLUE-BILLED DUCK

Oxyura australis L 35-44 cm (14-17 in), WS 53-62 cm (21-24 in)

Monotypic. Blue-billed, dark-headed stifftail of Australia, completely distinctive within range. **IDENTIFICATION Male breeding** Black head and neck, lightly flecked chestnut when fresh. Upperparts and underparts dark chestnut, richest on breast and fore flanks, grading into silvery-grey to brown centre to belly, vent and undertail-coverts, with darker mottling. Tail blackish. Upperwing dark brown, with chestnut flecking on coverts; underwing grey. Bill cobalt-blue with black nail. Legs and feet grey. Mechanical sounds in display. **Male eclipse** As female, but with darker head and neck and chestnut tone to breast and flanks. Bill dark grey. **Female** Dark brown head and neck with darker freckling, becoming paler on chin, throat and lower cheeks. Upperparts and underparts dark brown, finely barred buff, grading to paler brown on centre of belly, vent and undertail-coverts. Wings and tail browner than male. Bill, legs and feet dark grey. Makes noises in display. **Juvenile** As female, but paler and less obviously barred. Tail shorter. Bill grey-green. **Confusion risks** Only stifftail in Australia.

DISTRIBUTION AND STATUS Breeds extreme south-west of Western Australia and in southern parts of South Australia and Victoria, extending inland in New South Wales and, occasionally, to Tasmania and north to south-east Queensland; considerable wandering after breeding and in response to droughts and rains. Breeds on shallow, well-vegetated fresh waters, using larger permanent waters outside breeding season. Population estimated at up to 25,000. Threatened by drainage of wetlands and deaths from drowning in gill nets.

MUSK DUCK

Biziura lobata

Male L 61-73 cm (24-29 in), WS 84-90 cm (33-35 in); female L 47-60 cm (19-24 in), WS 68-81 cm (27-32 in)

Monotypic. Remarkable blackish-brown diving duck, male substantially larger than female; no confusion species within range.

IDENTIFICATION Male breeding and non-breeding Almost entirely blackish-brown with fine paler barring and speckling, apart from head, which nearly black on crown and nape, and slightly more obviously freckled buff on cheeks and neck; centre of belly whitish-buff, barred and freckled blackish-brown. Tail and wings, both above and below, black. Bill, legs and feet blackish-grey. Large blackish-grey pendulous lobe under bill, reaching to water, inflated (through blood pressure, *not* air) during display, reaching approximate size of golf ball. Whistling display call. **Female** Considerably smaller than male (less than half average weight); identical in plumage and bare parts, but with only rudimentary lobe. **Juvenile** As female, but with yellowish on front half of lower mandible. Takes some years to attain full size, lobe of males increasing in size at same time. **Confusion risks** None within range.

DISTRIBUTION AND STATUS Breeds south-west Western Australia and from southern South Australia and Tasmania to south Queensland; outside breeding season moves in response to wet and dry periods. Breeds on shallow fresh waters, also estuaries and coastal waters, outside breeding season. Population believed to number some tens of thousands. Not seriously threatened.

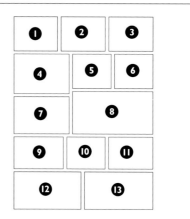

1 **Maccoa Duck** (male, South Africa)
2 **Maccoa Duck** (eclipse male, South Africa)
3 *Argentine Blue-billed Duck* (*male*)
4 *Argentine Blue-billed Duck* (*male, moulting*)
5 **Argentine Blue-billed Duck** (female, Argentina)
6 **Australian Blue-billed Duck** (male, Perth, Australia)
7 **Australian Blue-billed Duck** (female, Perth, Australia)
8 **Australian Blue-billed Duck** (male, Perth, Australia)
9 **Australian Blue-billed Duck** (pair beginning moult, Perth, Australia)
10 **Musk Duck** (female, Perth, Australia)
11 **Musk Duck** (male, Perth, Australia)
12 **Musk Duck** (male, Perth, Australia)
13 **Musk Duck** (immature male, Perth, Australia)

BIBLIOGRAPHY

Cramp, S., and Simmons, K.E.L. (Eds.) *The Birds of the Western Palearctic*, Vol. 1. Oxford University Press, Oxford, 1977.

Hoyo, Josep del, Elliott, Andrew, and Sargatal, Jordi. (Eds.) *Handbook of the Birds of the World*, Vol. 1. Lynx Editions, Barcelona, 1992.

Johnsgard, Paul, A. *Handbook of Waterfowl Behavior*. Cornell University Press, Ithaca, New York. 1965.

Johnsgard, Paul, A. *Ducks, Geese and Swans of the World*. University of Nebraska Press, Lincoln and London. 1978.

Madge, Steve, and Burn, Hilary. *Wildfowl. An identification guide to the ducks, geese and swans of the world*. Christopher Helm, London, 1988.

Ogilvie, M.A. *Wild Geese*. T. & A.D. Poyser, Berkhamstead, 1978.

Ogilvie, M.A. *Ducks of Britain and Europe*. T. & A.D. Poyser, Berkhamstead, 1975.

Palmer, R.S. (ED.) *Handbook of North American Birds*, Vols. 2 & 3. Yale University Press, New Haven & London, 1976.

Todd, Frank S. *Natural History of the Waterfowl*. Ibis Publishing Company, Vista, California. 1996.

PHOTOGRAPHIC ACKNOWLEDGEMENTS

Numbers in bold type in these acknowledgements refer to the page number and those in parentheses refer to the actual picture number.

The following abbreviations have been used:

BBC NHU: BBC Natural History Unit
FLPA: Frank Lane Picture Agency
NF: Nature Focus
NHPA: Natural History Photographic Agency
NP: Nature Photographers
WR: Windrush Photos
WWT: Wildfowl and Wetlands Trust

Theo Bakker 37(1), 49(9)
Wolf Bartmann 163(1), 163(2)
Peter Basterfield/WR 171(13)
Alan Beaumont 73(2), 115(10)
Bruce Beehler/NHPA 85(1)
Julian Bhalerao 115(2)
Joe Blossom/WWT 21(9), 23(4), 33(10), 35(1), 43(5), 45(2), 47(1), 47(3), 73(1), 103(8), 149(8)
D. Boersma 67(7), 67(8)
Leo J.R. Boon 17(9), 37(7), 43(5), 43(6), 43(7), 43(9), 69(1), 71(8), 77(5), 133(9), 139(3), 143(5), 153(9), 155(9)
Roy Broad 69(7)
Kevin Carlson 21(1), 121(1)
Graeme Chapman/NF 131(4), 131(9)
Chew Yen Fook 37(9), 71(2), 79(1)
Robin Chittenden 33(6), 59(1), 165(1), 165(3), 167(4), 167(5)
Bill Coster/WR 57(9), 59(8), 87(7), 117(2), 125(9), 133(5), 135(5), 141(5)
Gerald Cubitt 101(3), 101(6), 111(1), 135(8), 143(8)
J. Davies/WR 53(10), 57(5), 67(3), 111(5), 115(4)
Trevor Davies 79(10), 129(5)
Wendy Dickson 115(6)
Paul Doherty/WR 29(3), 37(6), 103(3), 143(4)
R. Drummond/NF 131(5)
Tom Ennis/WR 19(5), 45(1), 135(4) 141(4), 167(7)
Göran Ekström/WR 49(4), 77(8), 89(6), 91(1), 91(6), 107(6), 157(4), 163(6)
Ian Fisher/WR 79(2)
John Gardner/WR 127(5), 155(7)
T. and P. Gardner/NF 65(2), 73(10), 73(5), 97(3), 97(5), 99(5), 133(7)
Michael Gore/NP 69(2), 135(9)
Tony Hamblin/FLPA 73(1)
H. Hautala/FLPA 29(8)
Andrew Henley/NF 139(8)
Brenda Holcombe/WR 119(5)
Brayton Holt 17(10), 23(5), 33(5), 51(1), 51(2), 51(5), 53(9), 67(4), 73(11), 79(6), 85(6), 111(3), 111(6), 123(2), 129(3), 153(7)
E. and D. Hosking/FLPA 15(3), 15(7), 17(1), 17(12), 23(1), 25(8), 25(10), 25(11), 27(2), 27(3), 27(10), 41(3), 45(5), 51(6), 51(7), 53(8), 57(4), 59(4), 59(5), 61(2), 61(3), 61(8), 65(1), 65(6), 75(1), 75(9), 81(3), 87(10), 87(12), 101(1), 109(2), 113(3), 129(1), 131(1), 133(8), 135(6), 143(9), 165(5), 167(1), 171(1), 171(2), 171(5)

Tony Howard/NF 171(7)
B. R. Hughes/WR 109(1)
Mark Hulme/WWT 51(8)
Frederic Jiguet 117(5), 117(6), 117(7), 117(8)
Paul Johnsgard 81(4), 81(5), 81(6), 85(2)
R. Kampf 81(1), 169(9)
Kevin Karlson 17(3), 21(5), 21(6), 27(9), 27(11), 33(11), 33(12), 39(2), 39(5), 39(7), 39(11), 49(7), 49(8), 49(10), 49(11), 93(1), 93(2), 105(1), 107(5), 127(1), 127(2), 137(4), 137(7), 137(8), 137(11), 145(7), 149(2), 151(1), 151(6), 151(7), 153(8), 161(6), 167(6)
Hannu Kettenen 151(12)
Paul Knight/NP 75(7)
Lasse Laine 57(3)
Frank W. Lane/FLPA 105(2), 135(10)
Mike Lane 17(5), 17(6), 17(7), 37(11), 43(2), 69(5), 69(6), 75(4), 93(3), 139(4), 147(4), 147(6), 147(7), 147(8), 153(2), 153(5), 153(11), 167(8), 167(9), 169(1), 169(2), 169(5), 169(6)
Olivier Langrand 141(7)
Gordon Langsbury/WR 27(5)
Jonathan Leach/WWT 19(1)
L. Lee Rue/FLPA 79(8), 79(9)
Ian Lewis 79(7), 95(1), 149(3), 163(9)
Eric Lindgren 85(3)
T. Lislevand 55(1)
Tim Loseby 41(1), 71(7), 75(3), 77(10)
S. Maslowski/FLPA 149(7)
George McCarthy/WR 49(2), 91(4)
Arthur Morris/WR 17(2), 21(7), 21(8), 39(1), 39(3), 39(4), 39(6), 43(8), 49(6), 77(2), 77(4), 87(9), 93(4), 103(9), 103(10), 107(4), 125(8), 137(9), 139(6), 145(4), 145(5), 145(8), 145(9), 153(6), 155(4), 155(5), 157(7), 159(2), 159(9), 161(2), 161(4), 165(6), 169(3)
Stein Nilsen 59(3), 95(6), 109(3), 119(8), 125(2)
M.A. Ogilvie 39(9), 39(10)
Janos Olah 29(7)
Johan Oll Hllmarsson 159(1), 159(4)
Lynn Pedler/NF 133(6)
René Pop 27(1), 35(3), 41(7), 41(8) 41(9), 53(7), 55(6), 55(8), 55(9), 55(10), 57(6), 57(7), 67(6), 87(11), 95(4), 95(5), 105(5), 113(2), 115(7), 135(3), 147(1), 147(2), 155(3), 155(8), 157(1), 157(3), 159(3), 161(1), 161(9), 165(2), 167(10)
Peter W. Post 113(1)
Peter Reese/BBC NHU 97(4), 101(7)
George Reszeter 145(10), 145(11)
Chris Schenk/WR 33(7)
Paul Sterry/NP 69(8), 121(6)
Morten Strange 19(2), 61(4), 61(5), 61(6), 125(7)
Alan Tate 17(11), 53(2), 53(3), 53(4), 53(5), 53(6), 55(4), 55(5), 55(7), 57(1), 57(2), 65(4), 65(5), 65(7), 79(5), 81(1), 83(4), 83(5), 87(5), 101(3), 101(5), 111(8), 111(9), 113(4), 113(6), 119(6), 123(5), 141(1), 155(6)
E.K. Thompson/NP 63(4)
Roger Tidman 17(4), 49(1), 53(11), 59(7), 63(3), 83(1), 87(1), 151(3), 151(8), 151(9), 155(1), 155(2)
Roger Tidman/NP 151(11)
David Tipling/WR 25(2), 29(4), 29(5), 31(3), 31(5), 33(8), 35(2), 35(4), 37(10), 41(2),

49(3), 49(5), 49(3), 57(8), 59(6), 63(5), 73(6), 75(2), 75(8), 91(3), 117(4), 119(9), 125(3), 125(11), 145(6), 165(4)
Ray Tipper 17(8), 89(1), 89(2), 113(5), 113(7), 125(1), 125(5), 135(1), 135(2)
Frank S. Todd 31(1), 31(2), 31(7), 31(8), 67(1), 67(2), 69(9), 71(9), 73(3), 73(4), 79(11), 79(12), 83(2), 83(3), 85(4), 85(5), 97(1), 97(2), 99(1), 99(2), 101(8), 103(6), 103(7), 105(3), 105(4), 105(6), 105(7), 105(8), 107(8), 107(10), 109(4), 109(5), 115(8), 115(9), 121(5), 123(1), 123(9), 127(6), 135(7), 149(1), 149(4), 149(5), 149(6), 149(9), 149(10), 157(6), 157(8), 165(7), 165(8), 169(7), 169(8), 171(8), 171(9)
David Tomlinson/WR 15(1), 15(2), 15(8), 15(9), 19(4), 25(5), 25(9), 61(7), 65(3), 95(2), 95(3), 95(7), 107(9), 111(7), 143(7)
Arnoud B. van den Berg 153(1), 153(3)
Arnoud B. van den Berg/WR 31(4), 157(2)
Koen van Dijken 39(12), 39(13)
Christophe Verheyden 117(9)
Gregory Wane/NF 99(7)
Tony Wharton 67(5), 115(5)
Dick Whitford/NF 139(9), 139(10)
Roger Wilmshurst/FLPA 63(6)
Martin Withers 19(3), 19(6), 19(7)
Eric Woods 25(6), 25(7), 37(8), 61(9), 79(3), 79(4), 111(2), 131(7), 139(11), 171(10), 171(11), 171(12)
Eric Woods/WR 69(3), 69(4), 71(4), 71(5), 71(6), 111(4), 119(7), 171(6)
Norio Yamagata 163(7), 163(8)
Steve Young All cover pictures, 15(4), 15(5), 15(6), 21(2), 21(3), 21(4), 21(10), 23(2), 23(3), 23(6), 23(7), 25(1), 25(3), 25(4), 27(4), 27(6), 27(7), 27(8), 29(1), 29(2), 29(6), 31(6), 33(1), 33(2), 33(3), 33(4), 33(9), 35(5), 37(2), 37(3), 37(4), 37(5), 39(8), 39(14), 41(4), 41(5), 41(6), 43(1), 43(3), 43(4), 45(3), 45(4), 47(2), 47(4), 47(5), 47(6), 47(7), 47(8), 51(4), 51(9), 51(10), 53(1), 55(2), 55(3), 59(2), 59(9), 61(1), 63(1), 63(2), 63(7), 71(1), 71(3), 73(7), 73(8), 73(9), 75(6), 77(1), 77(3), 77(7), 77(9), 85(7), 85(8), 87(2), 87(3), 87(4), 87(6), 87(8), 87(13), 89(3), 89(4), 89(5), 89(7), 89(8), 91(2), 91(5), 91(7), 91(8), 91(9), 93(5), 93(6), 95(8), 101(2), 103(1), 103(2), 103(4), 103(5), 107(1), 107(2), 107(3), 107(7), 109(6), 109(7), 109(8), 109(9), 115(1), 115(3), 117(1), 117(3), 119(1), 119(2), 119(3), 119(4), 121(2), 121(3), 121(4), 123(6), 123(7), 123(8), 125(4), 125(6), 125(10), 127(3), 127(4), 129(2), 129(4), 129(6), 131(2), 131(3), 131(6), 131(8), 133(1), 133(2), 133(3), 133(4), 133(10), 133(11), 137(1), 137(2), 137(3), 137(5), 137(6), 137(10), 139(1), 139(2), 139(5), 139(7), 141(2), 141(2), 141(6), 143(1), 143(2), 143(3), 143(6), 143(10), 145(1), 145(2), 145(3), 147(3), 147(5), 147(9), 151(2), 151(4), 151(5), 151(10), 153(4), 153(10), 153(12), 153(13), 159(5), 159(6), 159(7), 159(8), 161(3), 161(5), 161(7), 161(8), 161(10), 163(3), 163(4), 163(5), 167(2), 167(3), 169(4), 171(3), 171(4)

INDEX